SCOTTISH RAILWAYS

Scottish Railway Heraldry: coats of arms of the LMS and LNER
together with their constituent companies

SCOTTISH RAILWAYS

O S NOCK
B.Sc. M.I.C.E. M.I.Mech.E. M.I.Loco.E.

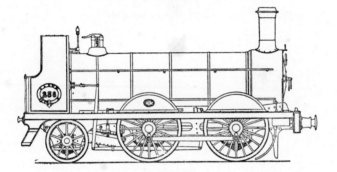

THOMAS NELSON AND SONS LTD
LONDON EDINBURGH PARIS MELBOURNE JOHANNESBURG
TORONTO AND NEW YORK

THOMAS NELSON AND SONS LTD
Parkside Works Edinburgh 9
36 Park Street London W1
312 Flinders Street Melbourne C1

302–304 Barclays Bank Building
Commissioner and Kruis Streets
Johannesburg

THOMAS NELSON AND SONS (CANADA) LTD
91–93 Wellington Street West   Toronto 1

THOMAS NELSON AND SONS
18 East 41st Street New York 17, N.Y.

SOCIÉTÉ FRANÇAISE D'ÉDITIONS NELSON
97 rue Monge Paris 5

————

First published 1950
Revised edition 1961

PREFACE

THERE is a strong though somewhat indefinable fascination about Scottish Railways, a fascination that has grown since the early pioneering days, and which neither grouping nor nationalisation has done anything to reduce. Nationalisation has certainly brought railways into the news, though little enough has been said or written to emphasise the great part railways have played in Scottish life during the past 100 years, or of the great heritage Scotland owns in her railways. In this book I have attempted to tell something of the history of the five Scottish companies existing until the end of 1922; how the lines fared in the 'grouped' period from 1923 to 1948; and something of the new organisation, which has set up a single, wholly Scottish Region north of the border.

Yet the attraction Scottish railways exert upon so many students of transportation is largely stimulated by the Scottish environment. Killiecrankie, Glenfinnan or Kyle of Lochalsh would invest any locomotive with an aura of romance, and so in writing of Scottish railways I have tried to give some impression of the passing scene. As an engineer myself, I have perhaps dwelt unduly upon engineering matters; but again that may not be altogether inappropriate in a country that gave birth to James Watt, Nasmyth and the Stevensons famed for lighthouse building, as well as to such great railway personalities as Alexander Allan, Dugald Drummond, Sir George Gibb and William Whitelaw.

Of the many friends who have helped in the preparation of this book I would like to mention particularly the late Comyn Macgregor of Paisley, of the Caledonian and LMS Railways; Mr David L. Smith of Ayr and Mr Edward Little. I am indebted to the Stephenson Locomotive Society for loan of the blocks from which the line drawings of locomotives were made, and to my friends A. F. Cook, F. C. Hambleton, Kenneth H. Leech and L. Ward, who between them made the drawings. It is a pleasure also to acknowledge the assistance given me by the North British Locomotive Company Ltd., and by Robert Stephenson and Hawthorns Ltd., concerning the construction of certain Scottish locomotives. I have consulted Sir Malcolm Barclay-Harvey's book, *The History of the Great North of Scotland Railway* and Mr Hamilton Ellis's *Highland Engines and their Work*, while among works of reference I have consulted the files of *The Engineer*, *Engineering*, *The Railway Gazette* and the *Railway Magazine*.

My thanks are due to Messrs B. T. Batsford Ltd. for permission to quote the passage on the Galloway line from George Scott-Moncrieff's book, *The Lowlands of Scotland*, and to Messrs A. and C. Black for permission to quote from the opening passage in A. R. Hope-Moncrieff's book, *Bonnie Scotland*.

But above all I am indebted to the Railway Executive for their most generous help and co-operation during the two years that this book has been in the making. The memory of many days and nights spent ' on location ' —as the film people would say—with Scots railwaymen of all grades remains one of the happiest recollections of a very pleasant task.

O S Nock

November 1949

PREFACE TO THE SECOND EDITION

Eleven years have passed since this book was first written, and it would be difficult to imagine a similar period in which more or greater changes have taken place on the railways of Scotland. In the intervening time the Modernisation Plan was launched, and it is now fully into its stride. The line from Glasgow to Helensburgh and Balloch is electrified; many new diesel locomotives and trains are running, and the great new marshalling yards at Thornton, Perth, Millerhill and Carlisle are either completed, or the work is well under way.

Opportunity has been taken, therefore, to revise completely those sections of the book dealing with modern equipment and operating, and in this respect I am much indebted to the Scottish Region of British Railways, and its leading officers for much valuable help. As a professional engineer I have been fortunate enough to be associated with much of the new work already completed, and in course of construction, and in this, as on those occasions where I have been a privileged observer, it has always been a great pleasure to meet and work with Scottish railwaymen of all grades.

In addition to those friends who helped with the first edition I should like to mention particularly Mr W. Robertson of Glasgow, who has put at my disposal some details of remarkable present-day running by the Duchess class Pacifics on the West Coast route.

O S Nock

Sion Hill, Bath
  November 1960

CONTENTS

COLOUR PLATES

BLACK AND WHITE PLATES

LINE ILLUSTRATIONS

ACKNOWLEDGMENTS

THE plate of the Neilson 4–2–2 engine No 123 is from a Dufaycolor photograph by Kenneth H Leech. The plates of the Highland, LNER and LMS trains in motion, the steamer *Waverley* and the coats of arms are from water-colour paintings by the author. The plates of the stationary locomotives are water-colour paintings by V Welch. The black and white plate of Macduff Station is from a photograph by Iain R Smith. In the remaining illustrations the publishers are indebted to the Scottish Region, British Railways.

CHAPTER ONE

HISTORICAL PREAMBLE

The old companies—grouping and regrouping

I

THE *Flying Scotsman* pulled out of Newcastle. It was late spring, and the train had not then embarked upon its regular summer performance of running non-stop from London to Edinburgh. But winter and summer alike the *Flying Scotsman* is an unchanging symbol of speed, and on this occasion the train had scarcely cleared the Newcastle platforms and snaked its way through the Manors before a man in the opposite corner remarked to his companion : ' Well, another hour should see us over the Border.' The pundits will say at once that he was well out in his estimate ; true, in passing the Manors a full 70 miles of open road lay between the *Flying Scotsman* and the Border signpost on the cliffs by Lamberton Toll, but his remark was typical of that quickening of the senses that comes as the first objective of a long journey draws nearer. Never is that feeling stronger, to me at any rate, than in travelling to Scotland ; and even those who have browsed over their news-papers in the morning, and dozed after lunch, will revive at the tinkle of tea-cups and at that first enchanting glimpse of the North Sea at Alnmouth.

Quite apart from any natural inclination one may have to travel to Edinburgh by the *Flying Scotsman* in preference to all other trains—with the added interest, if it be high summer, of sampling the world's longest non-stop run—the East Coast Route leads over the historic course of the very first railway to cross the Border. Many of the earliest railways were local concerns, and bore purely local names ; and like the English Stockton and Darlington, the Liverpool and Manchester and the Leicester and Swannington, Scotland had the Garnkirk and

I

Glasgow, the Edinburgh and Dalkeith and the Glasgow, Paisley and Greenock—to name just a few. But when it came to crossing the Border the whole conception was on a wider scale. Rival English factions had eyes for the Scottish traffic, and the railways projected were intended to become links in the line of through communication between London and the Scottish cities. In anticipation of the future extent and importance of their railway the promoters of the line from Edinburgh to Berwick chose the fine name of North British Railway. It may have been a little grandiose for a concern proposing to build a main line only 57½ miles long with a 4½ miles long single-tracked branch to Haddington ; that was in 1844. But from this beginning the North British grew and prospered, and it was still the North British at the close of 1922 when by the Railways Act of the previous year it became merged into the eastern group, the London and North Eastern Railway of pre-nationalisation days.

2

At the time of the grouping in January 1923 only five of the large British companies were carrying their original names, and three of those five were Scottish. The second of the Scottish companies was no less finely named the Caledonian, and its Act received the Royal Assent almost exactly a year after that of the North British. But for the moment we are concerned with the East Coast Route, and by this time the *Flying Scotsman* has been racing over the most northerly English metals, frequently reaching 80 mph where the track comes down to the coast opposite the holy island of Lindisfarne. A lonely stretch here, with the sea breaking on the dunes ; but far ahead there is now a first glimpse of Scotland, the dim line of the blue Border hills running out to the country of St Abbs. There are several ways of entering Scotland by rail and many well-trodden routes by road ; Solway Moss has a fascination of its own ; the motorist reaching the summit of Carter Bar may well rest awhile and drink in the grandeur of the Border landscape before he dips down into

Teviotdale. But for me, after many years of travelling into Scotland, no route, either road or rail, can compare with that of the *Flying Scotsman* : the astonishing beauty of Berwick revealed suddenly as the train comes over the cliffs at Scremerston ; the final majestic sweep of the Tweed ; the three great bridges, each a masterpiece of its day—and as the train slows down and enters upon the loftiest of the three, Robert Stephenson's Royal Border Bridge, the passenger by the *Flying Scotsman*, surveying this fair scene and watching his motoring friends below crossing the Royal Tweed Bridge with their eyes more intent on the traffic lights at the north end than on the scenery, has, as J. J. Bell once aptly expressed it, ' the advantage of the eagle over the sparrow.'

The London and North Eastern Railway erected two attractive signposts at the actual point where the railway crosses the Border some 2½ miles north of Berwick. Though not quite such a ' no man's land ' as Solway Moss, it is a lonely spot high on the cliffs and beneath the slopes of Lamberton Moor. From this quietly impressive entry into Scotland the railway soon turns inland to cut across the hinterland of the St Abbs country, and then mounts to the summit, 385 feet above sea-level, near Grants-house station, and in a fold of Penmanshiel Moor. From a short tunnel the most severe incline between London and Edinburgh brings the train swiftly down to the sea again at Cockburnspath, and a broad panorama opens out across the Firth of Forth. The most dramatic glimpse is reserved for the driver and fireman— that first sight of the Bass Rock, standing just off the shore well beyond Dunbar. There are several such thrilling first glimpses on the railways of Great Britain that can be seen only from the engine. There is one of Lincoln Cathedral seen when approaching from Sleaford and an equally beautiful one of Salisbury from the western approach ; and each successive time I am privileged to travel in the engine cab I look out for the Bass Rock more eagerly than ever, for the great rock never looks the same twice running, and there is always some combination of brilliant colour or intense light and shade to add a rare charm to the wide sea-scape. So we ride on over historic ground : Dunbar, Prestonpans, to the point where Edinburgh can already be seen far ahead, lying smokily beneath the heights of Arthur's Seat and the Salisbury Crags.

3

But while Edinburgh was the immediate goal of the English railway companies that invested in the North British, and spurred them to an early completion of the work, Glasgow was the principal objective of the Grand Junction, the greatest line of the day. And this English interest in railways on the western side of Scotland provoked a rivalry that did not finally subside until some 90 years later. In Glasgow there was already a strong and wholly Scottish project, the Glasgow, Paisley, Kilmarnock and Ayr Railway, with definite ideas for an extension southwards through Nithsdale to Dumfries and Carlisle. When the Grand Junction interest developed to the extent of sending Joseph Locke to survey possible routes north of Carlisle, that great engineer somewhat naturally reported in favour of a line through Nithsdale, as this offered easier gradients and less difficulty in construction. That was in 1836. But while the Grand Junction promoters and Locke himself were concerned mainly with a through route that would eventually link Glasgow with the great English centres of population and industry lying in their own territory, certain able and far-sighted Scotsmen, in supporting the idea of a through route, saw that the scheme could be turned to far greater local advantage if the proposed railway were taken up Annandale and through the Lowther Hills to upper Clydesdale.

So there began a period of argument, meetings, surveys and even a Royal Commission. J. J. Hope Johnstone, M.P. for Dumfriesshire, and Charles Stewart, factor of the Annandale estates, pointed out with some cogency that whereas a route through Nithsdale would serve only Glasgow, the Annandale scheme would, farther north, tap the rising industrial regions of Lanarkshire and make possible a convenient branch to Edinburgh. Then, while debate on this proposed trunk route was in progress, the Glasgow, Paisley, Kilmarnock and Ayr Railway was

Caledonian Railway: 4–6–0 express locomotive No 50 *Sir James Thompson* designed by John F McIntosh and built 1903 at St Rollox Works

incorporated in 1837, to the embarrassment of Hope Johnstone and the Annandale party. With a line authorised as far as Kilmarnock, it seemed so obvious a development to build the new line from the south by the route of easiest grading to meet it via Nithsdale. Indeed the only active support forthcoming for the enterprise originally sponsored by the Grand Junction was that of the energetic Annandale Committee, and that support was not to the liking of Joseph Locke. But Glasgow interests wanted a railway to the south, and at a meeting of certain influential citizens early in 1837 matters reached the stage of a resolution recommending that two engineers should arbitrate and decide on the most suitable route. The Annandale promoters readily agreed, but the outcome of these new surveys was a deadlock. Messrs Grainger and Miller of Edinburgh were engineers to the Glasgow, Paisley, Kilmarnock and Ayr, and John Miller of that firm, who was employed by the Glasgow party, naturally reported in favour of the Nithsdale route, as this would connect with the line he was already building to Kilmarnock. The Annandale Committee selected Joseph Locke to make the new inquiry on their behalf, and although he, as an engineer, had originally inclined to the Nithsdale route for purely Glasgow traffic as it would be easier to construct and to operate, he now reported in favour of the Annandale scheme in appreciation of the altogether broader conception of Hope Johnstone and his friends, and the fact that the Annandale-Clydesdale route would be some 21 miles shorter.

To try and resolve the deadlock both parties laid their proposals before the Royal Commission then investigating the question of railway communication between London and Scotland and between London and Ireland. In their recommendations issued in March 1841 the Commissioners favoured the Annandale route, on the assumption that traffic into Scotland could only support one railway to serve both Edinburgh and Glasgow. But approval of the route having been obtained, great difficulty was experienced in raising the requisite capital. For a time it was hoped that Government aid would be forthcoming ; when it was not, the whole project sponsored by the Grand Junction hung fire—the

Lancaster and Carlisle link as well as the Annandale-Clydesdale scheme. It was not until two years later that matters had advanced sufficiently for a Bill to be presented to Parliament, and even then it had to be withdrawn. In the meantime the promoters of the East Coast route were getting very busy in Edinburgh. The North British Railway Company had been formed, and when in the session of 1845 the West Coast people were at last ready to promote their Bill the line from Edinburgh to Berwick was not merely authorised but under construction. Early in 1844 the Annandale-Clydesdale scheme adopted the name of 'The Caledonian Railway,' and when the Bill was eventually presented the Nithsdale party redoubled the vigour of their opposition. They contended that the main point in favour of the Annandale scheme cited by the Royal Commission, viz provision of ready access to Edinburgh, had been cut from under their feet by the construction of the North British Railway. The Edinburgh and Glasgow Railway, which was already associated with the North British, joined the opposition, but in spite of a very long and costly Parliamentary battle the Caledonian obtained its Act on 31 July 1845.

The outcome of the nine-year struggle was a triumph for Hope Johnstone, and although the origin of the line was due to English prospecting, it was almost wholly due to Scottish enterprise and persistence that the scheme eventually took shape in the grand manner that it did. With the foundation well and truly laid the Caledonian Railway came to be as much a national institution as the North British. But like many another pioneer Hope Johnstone moved rather too quickly for his times. From the outset the Caledonian Railway was in rather a curious position so far as Glasgow was concerned. Some local lines had already been constructed in the district, and it was over the tracks of two such railways that access to Glasgow was first obtained. Junction was made with the Wishaw and Coltness at a point called Garriongill, near the present Law Junction station, and the last stage lay over the Glasgow, Garnkirk and Coatbridge Railway—the Garnkirk and Glasgow of 1826, which had been renamed on completion of its extension in 1845. As a much

North British Railway: Atlantic type express locomotive No 879 *Abbotsford* built 1906 by the North British Locomotive Company to the design of W P Reid

larger and more powerful concern the Caledonian sought to obtain complete control over these smaller railways, while at a very early stage they had arranged to take over the Glasgow, Paisley and Greenock, which had been opened for traffic in 1841.

The position was not lost upon the proprietors of the smaller railways ; they were well placed to strike a hard bargain with the Caledonian. On the other hand Hope Johnstone and his fellow-directors were so anxious to extend and consolidate their own line that the terms for absorption they offered were more generous than the immediate prospects of the Caledonian justified. Traffic did not develop at the phenomenal rate witnessed on some of the English lines ; a cut-throat competition was waged with the Edinburgh and Glasgow Railway, in which both companies reduced their fares stage by stage until the single fare between the two cities was 6d. This of course was ruinous in itself ; but with the generous terms for absorption of the local railways around Glasgow formally agreed the Caledonian found itself facing bankruptcy no more than five years after its Act had received the Royal Assent. On the Stock Exchange the price of the shares crashed, but the situation was largely saved by the intervention of James Baird, the millionaire ironmaster, who it is said walked casually into the Caledonian offices and said to a clerk, ' I'll take a wheen Caledonians '—just as if they were sweeties ! The financial rearrangements that followed were naturally unpalatable to the shareholders, and practically all members of the original board had to resign. In this unfortunate way the further services of Hope Johnstone were lost to the Caledonian.

4

At the same time as the Caledonian was under construction, Locke and his partner J. E. Errington were acting as engineers to the Scottish Central Railway, running from Greenhill to Perth, and the Scottish Midland Junction Railway from Perth to Forfar. The final link in what eventually became the full main line of the Caledonian, was the Aberdeen Railway, to which Sir William

Cubitt was consulting engineer. The construction of these railways was pushed forward with such vigour that by the spring of 1850 there was unbroken rail communication between London and Aberdeen, and by the year 1866 all these sections north of Glasgow had been absorbed by the Caledonian. But there was one curious legacy from the manner in which the Caledonian obtained access to the north. An arrangement was made at the very outset with a local railway—the Monkland and Kirkintilloch —to use a short section of its line north of Coatbridge ; after only 52 chains another purely Caledonian line diverged to the north-east, running down through Cumbernauld Glen to join the Scottish Central at Greenhill. Now the Monkland and Kirkintilloch was eventually absorbed not by the Caledonian, but by the North British, so that even at the grouping in 1923 trains from Carlisle to Aberdeen by the LMS route proceeded ' by your leave,' so to speak, over the metals of a different company, the LNER, for this 52-chain length. The signal boxes at the points of entry and exit are now known as Gartsherrie (LNER) Junction and Garnqueen South Junction.

The railway geography of Glasgow is complicated and its history still more so. Unlike London, and indeed unlike almost every other city of Great Britain, the services and stations did not assume their present form until a relatively late stage in Scottish railway development. The first railway bridge across the Clyde in Glasgow itself, for example, was not constructed till 1870 ; this led eventually into the new terminus of St Enoch, completed in 1876. The Caledonian at first concentrated all its long-distance traffic, including that to England, at Buchanan Street, and what is now the principal approach to Glasgow from the south was then a local connecting-line, the Clydesdale Junction, running from Motherwell to link up with the Greenock line. There were several terminal stations on the south side of the river, all suffering from difficulty of access from the business centre of the city. The Caledonian as early as 1848 obtained an Act to extend its line from South Side station across the river ; one requirement, however, was that the Admiralty should approve the design for the Clyde viaduct, and their requirements proved unexpectedly severe. It is sometimes considered that these difficulties led to the abandoning of the whole scheme; but it seems more probable that the financial difficulties of 1850 were already looming on the horizon. In any case it was not until 1879 that the Caledonian extension northward over the Clyde was completed and the magnificent Central Station opened.

5

The opening of St Enoch station in 1876 coincided with an even more important development at the southern end of the Nithsdale route. In 1850 that line had been completed to Gretna Junction, where it joined the Caledonian, but in the ensuing 25 years it had played the part of a feeder rather than a direct participant in the Anglo-Scottish traffic. The Glasgow and South Western Railway, as the group of lines originating from the old GPK & A became known, was a closely-knit local concern— albeit a very busy one—but it possessed two long and moderately used main lines to the south, the much-discussed Nithsdale route to Carlisle and the old ' Ayrshire and Wigtownshire ' extending over the Galloway moorlands to Stranraer. When in 1876 the Midland Railway completed the Settle and Carlisle line, and so secured a route to the Scottish border, the expansionist activities of Derby were manifest on every hand, and to the annoyance of the West Coast partners the Midland entered into an alliance with the Glasgow and South Western to operate a new express train service between London and Glasgow. It was on these trains that the Midland introduced Pullman cars both for day and for night travel.

Developments following upon the arrival of the Midland at Carlisle were not confined to the Glasgow and South Western Railway. The tracks of the Edinburgh and Hawick line, sponsored in very early days by the North British, had been extended under the name of the Border Union Railway through the Cheviot Hills and down into Liddesdale, and provided what was actually the shortest route from Edinburgh to Carlisle ; and over it the Midland and North British inaugurated in 1876 a third through express train service between London and Edinburgh, from the very outset in strong competition with the West Coast route, via Crewe, Lancaster and the Caledonian line, and to a lesser extent with the East Coast services, in which of course the North British was already a partner. The Midland route had the effect of putting such important English cities as Leicester, Nottingham, Sheffield and Leeds on to a direct line to Scotland, while the connections with the industrial towns of Yorkshire and East Lancashire were scarcely less important.

It was the North British route no doubt that A. R. Hope-Moncrieff had in mind in the vivid opening of his book *Bonnie Scotland* :

' The dawn broadens, the mists roll away to show a northward-bound traveller how his train is speeding between slopes of woodland, green and grey, here patched by bracken or bog, there dotted by wind-blown trees, everywhere cut by watercourses gathering into gentle rivers that can be furious enough in spate, when they hurl a drowned sheep or a broken hurdle through those valleys opening a glimpse of mansions and villages among sheltered woods. Are we still in England, or in what at least as far back as Cromwell's time called itself " Bonnie Scotland " ? It is as hard to be sure as to make out whether that cloudy knoll on the horizon is crowned by a peat-stack or by the stump of a Border peel.

' Either bank of Tweed and Liddel had much the same look. . . .'

Of the four main lines entering Scotland the actual point of entry on this North British route from Carlisle is the least defined of any. Solway Moss is left away to the west, and here-abouts the line of the Border is marked by the ancient ' Scots Dike ' which the railway approaches at Scotch Dyke station. Northwards the water of Liddel marks the frontier, and although the track is rarely more than a stone's throw away it remains on the English side almost to the tip of Cumberland, where the Kershope burn is crossed by Kershopefoot station 21 miles north of Carlisle. Beyond Newcastleton, where the line ascends the western slope of Liddesdale on heavy gradients, is a tract of that wild Border country in which Scott revelled as much as in his beloved Tweedside; and it is indeed in Liddesdale that associations with the Wizard of the North begin to crowd so thickly upon the passing scene. Passing within a short distance of Dryburgh, Melrose, and that treasure-house of a home of his, Abbotsford, this line is well named the 'Waverley Route.' The title is no mere tag of a romantic journalist, but one bequeathed officially by the North British Railway; engines were named after famous characters in the Waverley novels, and the line joined the East Coast route on the outskirts of Edinburgh to enter Scotland's largest station—Waverley.

6

If the North British, and particularly this route through the Border country, is most closely associated with Scott, the Glasgow and South Western could claim the districts immortalised in the poetry of Burns; but not until the very last year of its independent existence did the 'Sou' West' name an engine, and then only after a director. So there was no *Tam o' Shanter*, no *Highland Mary* to vie with the *Redgauntlet,* the *Meg Merrilies,* the *Bailie Nicol Jarvie* or the *Vich Ian Vohr* of the North British. But for all that, the Glasgow and South Western had an individual character as strongly marked as either of its more powerful neighbours. The deadly rivalry between it and the Caledonian recurs again and again in the story of Scottish railways; there was nothing quite like it anywhere else in Britain, an undying vendetta the origins of which could be traced back to the time when the Grand Junction sent Joseph Locke into Scotland and began to cut across the Nithsdale scheme. The 'Sou' West' of earlier days is fortunate in its historian, Mr David L. Smith; but it is above all the indomitable spirit of every man jack on the line that shines out from his writings. With its blue-green engines and crimson lake carriages it was less picturesque to look upon than the Caledonian, though the main line to Carlisle, for all its easier gradients, includes one of the loveliest stretches to be seen from the train anywhere in Britain—the gorge of the Nith between the north end of Drumlanrig Tunnel and Sanquhar.

7

So by the year 1876 the railways in the Lowlands had largely assumed their present form. In the Far North and in the West Highlands the system was still in process of development; these wonderful stretches of line are a heritage in themselves, and they receive more detailed mention later in this book; but at this stage a brief reference is needed so that the main lines of communication may be appreciated. The Highland Railway, which struck north from its junction with the Caledonian $7\frac{1}{4}$ miles north-east of Perth, ran to within 15 miles of John o' Groats; something of its peculiarities can be realised from its operating a main line 279 miles in length—only 20 miles shorter than that of the London and North Western from Euston to Carlisle—but with less than 150 engines, against more than three thousand! While I have no doubt that even in its earliest days there were long periods when the Highland Railway ran with smoothness and punctuality it is rather through its difficulties of operation that this noble railway will always go down to posterity; the immensity of the snow blocks in winter; the stories of the Jones engines pounding their way over Druimuachdar and Dava summits; the tremendously heavy traffic, and the atrocious punctuality of its passenger trains in the grouse-shooting season. Set in such a sublime mountain country every facet of the Highland Railway was, for good or ill, steeped in romance.

But in later chapters of this book I hope to show something of the very important part the Highland line plays in the economic life of the country as a whole, and of the part it played in the winning of two world wars. To the present generation Scapa

Flow is a household word; its strategic position during the Battle of the Atlantic was generally appreciated. But the railway over which personnel and supplies were conveyed thence was, like railways everywhere in Britain, taken wholly for granted. Every effort was made to impress the need for more and more production of war material, but there was never any doubt, so far as the general public was concerned, that the railway would be able to get the stuff delivered once it was made. And so it was. During the first war when the Grand Fleet was based at Scapa, the vast amount of coal needed for fuelling the big ships had to be conveyed to Thurso by rail, most of it from South Wales. New engines were built during the 1914–18 period to supplement the existing Highland stud, and three of these were of David Jones's famous 'Loch' design of 1896, the heaviest that could then be used on the line from Dingwall to the Kyle of Lochalsh, where additional engine-power was sorely needed for the war traffic.

The Highland was a natural ally of the Caledonian, but with the North British matters were not always so friendly. It is true that quite a high proportion of the through traffic from England was received from the North British at Perth; this came largely from the East Coast route, but partly also from the Midland, which at one time ran a special Highland express at 7.10 p.m. from St Pancras, travelling via the Waverley Route from Carlisle to Edinburgh. Trouble with the North British arose primarily over the latter company's association with the Great North of Scotland, a little line with an imposing title, whose aim had been to secure a direct line from Aberdeen to Inverness. The Highland somewhat naturally looked upon Inverness as their very own, and the merest suggestion that any other company might share the traffic was enough to set the heather on fire; consequently the activities of the 'Great North' were always regarded with some suspicion, if not open hostility. In 1883 there had been a proposal to extend the Speyside line of the 'Great North' westwards from Boat of Garten to cut through the Monadhliath Mountains in a more or less direct line to Inverness. This proposal was strongly backed by the North British, but the High-land countered it with a scheme of their own to build a line from Aviemore over the Slochd pass. This latter proposal was duly authorised by Act of Parliament and this route forms the main line for direct Inverness traffic today, eliminating the long detour of the original line through Forres and Nairn.

If the Highland and the North British indulged in a little mild sparring over the proposed Deeside extension, they came into much more direct conflict twenty years later over the very nearly stillborn ' body ' of the Invergarry and Fort Augustus Railway. The opening of the West Highland Railway from Helensburgh to Fort William was followed by the construction of a single track railway from Spean Bridge on the West Highland, following the line of the Great Glen to a terminus at Fort Augustus. The company promoting this scheme was independent of all the larger railways, and when construction was completed funds were exhausted so that the proprietors were without the means to pro-vide themselves with any rolling stock ! The North British worked the West Highland Railway, and the Invergarry and Fort Augustus people naturally looked to them for assistance. But the North British saw the rather ludicrous position of the Fort Augustus railway and tried to drive home a hard bargain; their terms were not accepted. In the meantime the Highland Rail-way, which had viewed the construction of the Fort Augustus line with some concern, began to take an active interest. North British control would mean that a hostile railhead would be established only 28 miles from Inverness, and as the intervening country beside Loch Ness offered no particular obstacles they feared an extension to Inverness itself.

The Invergarry and Fort Augustus directors were aware of the rival interests of the Highland and the North British, and they succeeded in drawing the two companies into a real Parliamentary dog-fight for the right to operate the engine-less and carriage-less railway. The logical choice was of course the North British, with whose interests the new line had physical contact at Spean Bridge; but the Highland won the day. The necessary Act was obtained on 30 June 1903, and the official opening of the line took place only three weeks later—a remarkable achievement, seeing that in the interval the Board of Trade Inspection had to be carried out and the requisite rolling stock transported. One engine was sufficient to handle the traffic, and this, together with carriages and wagons, worked round via Perth and Dunblane to the Callander and Oban line, and finally over the West Highland from Crianlarich to Spean Bridge.

8

And so I come finally to the fifth of the Scottish companies that lost their separate identity at the time of the grouping in 1923—the Great North of Scotland Railway.

'Once upon a time this was a shocking railway. A really very, very shocking railway. Why it was ever allowed to be called a railway at all passed comprehension. As a matter of fact, part of it between Aberdeen and Inverurie was not originally a railway but a canal, and the company thoughtfully scooped in the canal, baled it out, and made their line on the remains. After which some people in the district bethought themselves, when it was too late, that the canal would have been infinitely preferable. . . . The stopping trains could not even be dignified with the title " slow." They set the pace of a glacier, only the glacier would possibly have got there first. . . .'

In such style E. L. Ahrons, the eminent locomotive historian, opened an article in the *Railway Magazine* of January 1922 dealing with the Great North of Scotland Railway. But the transformation that followed the appointment in 1880 of William Moffatt as General Manager was one of the most spectacular things that have ever happened on Scottish railways. From the 4¼ hours taken by the very best train of the day in 1880 to cover the 80 miles from Aberdeen to Elgin, things so improved that in 1896 the early morning express running in connection with the sleeping-car train from London began its northward run from Aberdeen by covering the 41 miles to Huntly in 45 minutes, an average

15

speed of 54 mph. Generally speaking, however, connections were not a strong point with the GN of S. In the old earldoms of Buchan and Mar they held a monopoly and for many years took advantage of it to treat passengers in a decidedly cavalier way. There was the ghost of an excuse in Aberdeen while their terminus was at Waterloo quay, some distance from the terminus of the line from the south; and tales are told of the Great North trains being held until hurrying passengers from the Scottish North Eastern station hove in sight, when the Elgin ' express ' would be dispatched with the utmost celerity.

Waterloo station was on the canal route of which Ahrons wrote so amusingly. The original section of railway, opened in 1854, ran from Kittybrewster to Huntly, and on the southern part the canal was to be kept in use until the contractor was ready to take over and make such changes as were necessary to convert the track to railway use. The purchase of the canal involved some complicated legal procedure; but before this was completed the contractor, anxious to get on with the work, cut the bank of the canal and let the water pour into the River Don. This precipitancy recoiled on him like a boomerang; all the barges in transit at the time were stranded, and he was called upon in no uncertain terms to make good the breach in the bank and refill the canal with water, so that the barges could convey their cargoes to their destinations! The Great North, despite its high-sounding title, was indeed opened and operated in a singularly unpretentious way. The ultimate object was to build a line throughout from Aberdeen to Inverness, but at the northern end the Highland, or rather the older constituents of the Highland, got in first and the Great North got no farther than Elgin.

But once those early years had been survived and their dreadful feuds had been lived down, the Great North became an extremely useful and efficient railway. It came most into the limelight through its operation of the Deeside line and the working of numerous Royal specials while the Court was in residence at Balmoral. The Deeside line was originally an independent company and was opened in 1854 from Aberdeen to Banchory.

It was not until 12 years later that this line was incorporated in the Great North of Scotland system. Apart from this line running westwards from Aberdeen, the GNSR ultimately consisted of a compact group of railways covering the north-eastern corner of Aberdeenshire and the coastal regions of Banff and Moray. It had always been associated with the North British rather than the Caledonian in conveyance of traffic from the south, including the running of through carriages between Elgin and Edinburgh; so when the grouping came in 1923 it was included in the London and North Eastern Railway and the complications between Keith and Elgin resulting from its old feud with the Highland remained. One has the choice of three different routes between Elgin and Huntly, two by routes of the old GN of S and one by Highland as far as Keith.

9

Such were the 'Big Five,' if one may use a popular cliché; but there was one other railway in Scotland, surely one of the most curious joint concerns that has ever existed. This also set out with a title of exceeding grandiloquence: The British and Irish Grand Junction Railway. The North Channel afforded an excellent crossing from Scotland to Ireland, and it was proposed to establish packet stations at Portpatrick and at Donaghadee in County Down. The Glasgow and South Western Railway was constructing a branch line from Dumfries through Dalbeattie and Castle Douglas to Kirkcudbright, and believe it or not, the British and Irish Grand Junction Railway was intended merely to cover the intervening 60¼ miles between Castle Douglas and Portpatrick. But before even the Bill was presented to Parliament a more appropriate title, the Portpatrick Railway, had been adopted. There was an offshoot of this line, called the Wigtownshire Railway, running from Newton Stewart down to Whithorn, and after a somewhat chequered existence these two little railways were taken over in 1885 by a joint committee of the large companies in whose interests it was important to keep the line from Castle Douglas to the North Channel in first-class condition.

The Glasgow and South Western was obviously involved; so was the London and North Western, for on its metals originated a high proportion of the through traffic for Ireland via this route. The Caledonian came in, not only as Scottish partner of the North Western, but as one having definite interests of its own in Galloway, tapped by the important branch line from Lockerbie to Dumfries. The fourth company represented was the Midland, interested from the viewpoint of traffic to and from its own system as well as with a definite eye to business in Ireland itself, which eventually materialised when Derby assumed control of the one-time Belfast and Northern Counties Railway.

In concluding this chapter I take leave to quote from another Moncrieff—George Scott-Moncrieff—in *The Lowlands of Scotland*. ' . . . when the Galloway lairds,' he writes, ' with half-admirable conservatism, refused to allow the stour of the railway to pollute their policies along the seaboard it was driven across the empty moors at a damnably inconvenient distance from the population. The result is a direct and delightful line from Dumfries to Stranraer, with one or two sidelines seaward. When I made return to Galloway during school holidays, coming from the south of England and a countryside surrendering itself to suburban development where the streams were fouled and surveyors prospected for the defilement of the fields, arriving in a region in which I had known the happiest days of my childhood, my excitement while I travelled along that moorland railroad was exquisite. It was then that I felt the sheer joy of the place— Galloway: the clear and fast waters; the grey lochs; the woods growing as woods should, on steep slopes; and then the moorland, infinitely dignified in immunity from " Development " (there were not even pylons then); the place names in white letters on blue tinplate; the Galloway porters with wind-blown moustaches and gusty voices crying those names on the platforms of stations that seemed to have no other contact with civilisation than the iron rails that took us to them and from them. At Loch Skerrow, where only anglers and shepherds disembarked, the track runs so close to the water that the train seems to paddle.

After paddling, the train appears to fly as it sails across the grand viaduct over Big Water of Fleet, which, little water as it is, cuts a deep furrow through the hills, a leisurely viaduct, pale in the sunlight, unsparing in its arches. The railway viaducts of Galloway are worth noting; it is said that in the Great Railway Age one member of the Board responsible for them, and for the restrained station architecture, was a man of taste. . . .'

Nowadays this fascinating route is little known to the long-distance traveller, for its best trains, the expresses running in connection with the Stranraer-Larne packet boats, traverse its length in the middle of the night. There used to be a morning service from Belfast, and a through train from Stranraer to Euston leaving just after noon; but this has not yet been reinstated since the war. The Portpatrick and Wigtownshire is certainly a fascinating line, but truth to tell I cannot think of a single Scottish railway line that could be called dull. Even those running in the most industrialised areas, in Lanark and Stirling, are never far from noble prospects, and they are no less impressive in the magnitude of the industries displayed at the line-side. And now, with the conclusion of this preliminary sketch of the Scottish railways, the stage is set for a more detailed examination of their traffic and engineering.

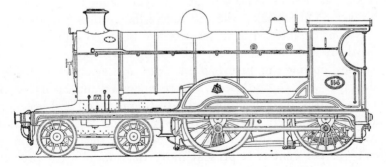

CHAPTER TWO

Railways in Scottish Industry, Commerce and Sport

I

The construction of railways in Scotland, as almost everywhere else, arose partly from the need for quicker transport to foster and expand existing industry and agriculture and partly from speculative building in the hope of attracting business and the establishment of new industries. But then again there is the example of the Highland Railway, a line built more nearly for philanthropic ideals than any other in existence. In the course of time the original purpose of many of the Scottish railways has become obscured, if not actually lost, in a welter of swiftly changing conditions, economic difficulties and a partial shift of the population, so that the part railways are playing in the present life of the community in Scotland might in many cases surprise those who projected them a hundred years ago.

Due to the strongly delineated physical characteristics of the three geographical regions, the Highlands, the Lowland Belt and the Southern Uplands, Scottish industry tends to be grouped into closely-knit zones, though in the case of agriculture there is a greater affinity between the Highlands and the Border country. During the summer and autumn there are important sheep and lamb sales at centres as far separated as Aberdeen, Lairg, Hawick, St Boswells and Lanark; the railway traffic resulting from these sales is considerable, both in interchange between different parts of Scotland and in export to the south. The average weekly dispatches during the first half of 1948 for example exceeded 8,000 cattle and 16,000 sheep. In recent years increasing attention has been paid to the tuberculin testing of milk, and breeders generally have been encouraged to aim at a high proportion of attested cows in their herds. In Scotland the proportion of roughly 30 per cent is at present more than double that prevailing in English herds, and the increasing demand for Scottish stock is providing a steady flow of cattle traffic by rail to the south. There is another interesting item of seasonal traffic from Scotland to England, that of seed potatoes in early spring. It is quite heavy during the short time it lasts and needs particular care to avoid damage by frost. Scottish seed is by far the most valuable of any, and this particular freight has for its kind a value quite out of proportion to its bulk. Much of it originates in the Perth area. An interesting feature of the 1949 season was the dispatch of four trainloads in fully-fitted vehicles from Fraserburgh to Southampton Docks for shipment to South Africa.

Every year the autumn sales bring about a considerable movement of sheep, and the resultant railway traffic is spread over a period of some three months, beginning about the middle of August. But at each centre concerned the concentration of traffic is intense for the few days during which the sales take place. In August 1949, for example, no fewer than 29,650 sheep and lambs were forwarded by rail from Thurso in four days, and eleven special trains were required. This volume of traffic was, however, surpassed by the record of Lairg, on 17 August 1949, where 26,000 Cheviot sheep and lambs were exposed for sale in the one day! Sheep for the south had to be dispatched from the little country station on the single-tracked line southward to Inverness. The regular station staff of three clerks, three porter-signalmen and one porter, in addition of course to the stationmaster, was heavily reinforced for the occasion; an engineers' department dormitory carriage provided sleeping accommodation for the extra staff, and loading of the sheep began at 12 noon on the day of the sale. The work continued until dark, by which time four special trains had been dispatched. The fifth and last followed early the next morning. These five trains among them conveyed a total of two hundred and twenty trucks, and as the loading bank at Lairg has accommodation for only twenty-four trucks at a time some ingenuity had to be exercised in loading and marshalling the excess.

The woollen industry is mainly centred on the Border towns

and in Lanarkshire, Fife, Aberdeen and the Western Isles. Although these locations were originally determined to a large extent by the adjacent sheep-raising areas, the present-day raw materials are largely imported, either from overseas as wool or from the West Riding of England as yarn. In addition to consuming the local wool crop, the specialised tweed industry of the Western Isles draws big supplies of wool and yarn from Scotland and England. Rail transport is largely used for the conveyance both of raw materials and of finished goods, including exports, to Scottish and English consuming areas and to ports.

2

The traffic in livestock is to some extent seasonal, and the conveyance of wool not of sufficient magnitude to require special trains ; with the fisheries of Northern Scotland, however, it is another matter altogether. From Aberdeen sufficient fish is put ashore to require the provision of seven special express trains to the south, day in day out all the year round, while an eighth—the fastest of those using the West Coast route—runs from Perth, conveying fish and meat from the Perth and Inverness districts. It has no stop, except for locomotive purposes, between Carlisle and London, and is booked to average 39 mph over this distance of 299 miles. From Aberdeen itself the early departures are :

12.30 p.m.	EAST COAST, for Edinburgh, Newcastle, York, Peterborough and London (King's Cross)
1.42 p.m.	EAST COAST, for Edinburgh, Newcastle, York, Peterborough and London (King's Cross)
2.10 p.m.	EAST COAST, for Edinburgh, Newcastle and York. This train is continued to London if required
2.15 p.m.	WEST COAST, for Carlisle, Preston, Wigan, Crewe, Wolverhampton and Birmingham

After this procession of fast trains there comes a pause in the fish traffic until the early evening, when three more fast trains are dispatched :

London Midland and Scottish Railway: Glasgow to Birmingham express, with through GWR coach for Plymouth, on the ascent to Beattock Summit. The engine is No 1066, one of the Midland 3-cylinder compound type adopted as standard by the LMS

5.55 p.m.   EAST COAST, for Edinburgh. This train is continued southward if required

6.40 p.m.   WEST COAST, for Carlisle, Carnforth, Lancaster, Preston, Wigan and Manchester

7.45 p.m.   WEST COAST, for Carlisle and Crewe

The departures from Aberdeen are timed generally so that fish will arrive in time for the early markets. The 12.30 and 1.40 p.m. departures are both due in London before 4 a.m. next morning, and the 2.15 p.m. is due in Birmingham at 4.15 a.m. The 6.40 p.m. West Coast train calls at Carnforth, Preston and Wigan, and is designed to catch the early morning markets in Cumberland and Lancashire. Some fast running is made by these trains ; the stock used must necessarily be in first-class condition, for apart from the special fish trains it is a regular practice to attach fish vans to express passenger trains. Perhaps the most remarkable running is made over the East Coast line between Aberdeen and Edinburgh. The 1.42 p.m. up, for example, makes this difficult run of 130½ miles in 3 hr 24 min, with stops at Montrose and Dundee. The overall time from Aberdeen to London is 14 hours. To facilitate the working of the fish trains a total of 275 vans, known as ' Blue Spot vans ' because of their distinguishing mark, have been fitted with roller-bearing axle boxes specially for the fish traffic from Aberdeen and North East Scotland. It will be readily appreciated that to enable four-wheeled vehicles to run safely up to 60 m.p.h. requires the best of maintenance.

Some years ago I was able to witness the work involved in the operation of the then 1.40 p.m. express fish train from that incomparable vantage point, the engine cab. We had a good load of 22 vehicles in all, 11 loaded fish vans through from Peterhead to London and 10 through from Aberdeen, plus the guard's brake van. The maximum permitted with this train is 33, equal to about 410 tons. It is significant that this dead weight is somewhat less than the maximum taken by the same class of engine with passenger trains. The four-wheeled goods vehicles seem to pull heavier ; they tend to nose about while on the run, and in a train of 33 vehicles there would be 66 axles instead of 48 in a train of equivalent weight made up of bogie passenger vehicles. All this increases the haulage effort required from the locomotive. On my trip things were rendered considerably harder by a heavy south-westerly wind that caught the train with something like gale force on the exposed stretches of line. From one cause or another there were many times on the run southward when those 22 vans pulled like 12 or 13 bogie coaches—420 or 430 tons—instead of the actual dead weight of 272 tons.

From Aberdeen our engine was an ex-LNER 2-6-2 of the 'Green Arrow' class, now known as Class 6MT; she was beautifully turned out in the new style—glossy black, with red, grey and white lining, and carrying one of the new five-figure numbers, 60824. Driver Wallace and Fireman Walker of Ferryhill shed, Aberdeen, were in charge. The load was made up and ready to start a little before the booked time, and as the road was clear we were given the right-away at 1.35 p.m. Out on to the cliffs we forged our way, to meet the full force of the wind and to look out over a wild sea covered with white breakers and flying spume. Signals were against us at Muchalls, but then down through Stonehaven in full cry; 62 mph over the viaduct, regulator wide open, cut-off 27 per cent, and we roared into the glen of Carron Water with the gradient steepening to 1 in 92 and the exhaust from the chimney shooting skywards on this sheltered stretch. Sheltered or not, the gradient took its toll and we topped the grade doing no more than 34 mph.

Then down the broad open stretch into the Mearns country, with the strong wind setting up a miniature whirlwind in the engine cab and covering our faces with a fine layer of coal dust. Speed rose to 67 mph as we bowled downhill to the crossing of the North Esk near Marykirk, but then came a slack for permanent way repairs, followed by the regular 15 mph check over Kinnaber Junction. So down the steep final grade into Montrose, where we stopped to attach another 4-wheeled van. The 40¾ miles from Aberdeen had taken 62 minutes, inclusive of two out-of-course slacks—fully up to express passenger standards of running over this difficult route. Continuing in fine style over the hilly road to the south, with 26 mph up the stiff grade to Lunan Bay and 67 mph over the water of Inverkeilor, we were through Arbroath (13¾ miles) in 21¼ minutes, coming down dead slow for the junctions and the curve; and then we entered upon the 16 miles of level along the open exposed coast of Angus—there one could indeed gain some impression of the wind we were fighting, for with the engine blazing away with the regulator almost full open and cut-off set at 20 per cent, working which in calm weather would have taken a 12- or 13-coach passenger train at nearer 70 mph, the most we could do with this 23-van fish train was 56 mph.

But we were keeping good time, and with a slow and careful finish through the Camperdown Tunnel we completed the last 17 miles from Arbroath into Dundee in just 22 minutes. Here engines were changed, and, if anything was needed to emphasise the crack nature of this working, it was to find one of the world-famous Gresley streamlined Pacifics No. 60031, *Golden Plover*, waiting to take us forward to Edinburgh. The driver and fireman, Morgan and Baird of Haymarket shed, Edinburgh, were members of that veritable *corps d'élite* among British enginemen, who work the non-stop expresses between King's Cross and Waverley during the summer months. But there is never any chance of ' streamline ' speed between Dundee and Edinburgh, even with passenger trains; the road is a very synthesis of steep gradients, difficult junctions and sharp curves, and the capacity of this fine engine, still bedecked in the striking garter blue of the LNER, was displayed in uphill work of sterling quality.

At the very start we had a rare battle with the gale in pulling out on to the Tay Bridge; out over the firth in such elemental fury that I had to close the side windows of the cab to keep my breath, I thought instinctively of that tragic night in December 1879 when Bouch's frail viaduct collapsed. It took us just 9 minutes to cover the 2¾ miles to Tay Bridge South Junction, whereas on a calm fine night with the up *Aberdonian* sleeping-car express that same stretch took only 7¾ minutes with one of the slightly *less* powerful A3 Pacifics, *Windsor Lad*. Yet in comparison with our load on the fish train of 284 tons, the load of the *Aberdonian* was 440 tons. Wind or no wind, we came through Fife in good style; we swung through Ladybank Junction at 56 mph and in driving mist and rain pounded our way up the heavy grade to Lochmuir. Today there was no sight of the twin crests of the Lomond Hills, and even at this modest 'summit' we seemed verily in the clouds.

Three heavy slacks followed: 5 mph over the mining subsidence at Thornton; 20 mph through Sinclairtown and 15 mph for permanent way repairs at Burntisland—all these in addition to the regular slacks for the curves at Kinghorn Tunnel and Burntisland station. But then, along the shores of the Forth, and with Edinburgh in sight across the water, we were away in fine style and up the winding ascent at 1 in 100 past Aberdour and through the woods to Dalgetty signal box we were going steadily at 31 to 32 mph. Despite all the out-of-course checks experienced, we had still some five minutes in hand, but when we approached Inverkeithing the road was not clear. We could not have been checked in a worse place, for immediately following is the heaviest grade of the whole route, 2 miles at 1 in 70 leading on to the Forth Bridge.

The driver was taking no chances on this climb, and he set the gear at 40 per cent cut-off; *Golden Plover* responded finely and we entered upon the Forth Bridge at 26 mph. On that ever-majestic passage over the bridge I must not dwell now; on the giant columns, the girders towering above us, of ships far below. Our thoughts were now only of getting ' The Fish ' into Waverley on time. To be late would mean missing our turn in the busy Edinburgh suburban area, delays and a late start on the next stage of the southward run. Soon after leaving the bridge we were running at 58 mph; signals were clear till we neared Haymarket. We were following close behind a local train; but the colour-light signals through the Princes Street Gardens cleared in time and we drew into Waverley at 5.15 p.m.—still 2 minutes early. *Golden Plover* came off the train after a fine run, 105¼ minutes for the 59¼ miles from Dundee in the face of delays that cost at least 12 minutes quite apart from the effect of that wind. A non-streamlined Pacific *Lemberg* came on for the run to Newcastle; meanwhile *Golden Plover* backed down to Haymarket for servicing before going south on the 9.30 p.m. sleeping-car express to London—the *Night Scotsman*.

The intermediate stops of the special fish trains give some idea of the area served by south-bound dispatches from Aberdeen; but in additon to stations specifically mentioned, Bolton, Blackburn, Liverpool, Sheffield, Nottingham and Leicester all take a considerable proportion of the Scottish traffic.

In addition to the regular workings from Aberdeen the seasonal herring fisheries bring a heavy traffic. This comes ashore at Wick, Mallaig, Oban, Kyle of Lochalsh and the Buchan ports, and in the height of the season the traffic is sufficiently heavy to justify the running of special trains to the south. These are arranged to act as feeders to the Aberdeen trains, and thus on the busier sections use time-table paths already allocated to the express fish trains. Connection is made with West Coast services at Law Junction and with East Coast services at Edinburgh. Vans from the West Highland ports are then attached to the regular trains, and if necessary duplicate portions can be run. Apart from seasonal pressure of this kind the fish traffic originating at Kyle of Lochalsh, Mallaig and Oban is usually disposed of by passenger trains, and the big LNER six-wheeled fish vans are familiar objects on most West Highland services.

3

Mention of the West Highland line leads on to the development of the aluminium industry in Scotland. Many travellers will be familiar with the changes wrought in recent years at Loch Treig, where the railway comes down the hillside from the Rough Bounds of Corrour and where the alignment of the track had to be changed owing to the building of the dam and the raising of the water level of the loch. The potential water power of Loch Treig, as also that of Loch Laggan near by, has now been harnessed for the manufacture of aluminium at Fort William. The organisation of this industry provides an interesting example of how good transport can assist in the efficient carrying out of chemical processes. After importation, bauxite, the crude ore, has the white oxide of aluminium extracted. Coal is needed for this first process, and to minimise the cost of transport of the bulky and heavy ore the extraction plant is located at Burntisland, a port lying on the fringe of the Fife coalfield. The reduction of the oxide to pure aluminium is done electrically, and so the alumina in bulk is conveyed across Scotland to Fort William, where the hydro-electric plant fed from the waters of Loch Treig and Loch Laggan was designed specially for aluminium production. The LNER provided special wagons for the conveyance of alumina in bulk from Burntisland to Fort William.

4

But in any consideration of Scottish industry one is drawn sooner or later to the central nucleus of Glasgow, as much the capital of the Highlands—industrially at any rate—as it is, industrially, of the Lowland Belt. The railway traffic resulting from this intense concentration includes a high proportion of short hauls. The Lanarkshire coalfield is relatively near to the heavy industries of Glasgow itself, and of Clydeside. The varied requirements of the shipyards, including an enormous tonnage of steel, are supplied mostly from local sources, so that one finds almost throughout the western portions of the Lowland Belt a frequent service of short-distance goods trains. Loads are not unduly heavy, as in any case destinations of the various consignments within the area are so scattered that it would not be economical to make up really heavy trains. This class of work is reflected in the relatively small size of Scottish goods locomotives. In pre-grouping days, when the London and North Western, the Great Western and the North Eastern had large fleets of eight-coupled engines specially designed for long hauls with 70 to

80-wagon trains, the North British had not a single one, although serving Clydebank and the Fife and Lothian coalfields ; the Caledonian had a modest eight.

Something of the nature of Scottish freight traffic can be gauged from the locomotive stock of the Caledonian in 1922. Of the famous McIntosh 4–6–0 engines by which the Company will always be remembered, 32 were engaged in freight traffic of one sort or another, against a total of 386 of the ordinary six-coupled non-bogie type known as the 0–6–0. The vast majority of these latter were relatively small and old engines ; the latest of them were built in 1909 and weighed only 46 tons without their tenders. This was the type of locomotive that bore the brunt of the enormous freight traffic in and around Glasgow. I must not at this stage digress on the subject of design and construction, but that such small locomotives were adequate, albeit there were plenty of them, is significant of the nature of the business conducted. The bogie six-coupled engines took the long-distance freight trains to and from Carlisle, but were also used on heavy passenger duties where the highest speeds were not required.

In the immediate future the gradual contraction of the Lanarkshire coalfield and the expansion of those in Fife and Lothian will tend to increase coal haulage from short to medium distances. The following approximate percentage utilisation of Scottish coal during 1947 will give some impression of the railway traffic involved:

Household use	15%
Public Utility concerns—gas, electricity etc.	24%
Railway fuel	11%
In manufacture of iron and steel	14%
In general industry	18%
Miscellaneous Scottish uses	9%

This left a balance of 9 per cent shipped out of the country, either in bunkering coal-fired ships or in exports to other countries. At the present time the Scottish steel output is not sufficient to

satisfy all the needs of the Clyde shipyards, and a small proportion is having to be brought in from the Newcastle and
Middlesbrough districts.

A great deal of this freight and mineral traffic passes over a
line that is practically unknown to the ordinary passenger. What
eventually became the main line of the Caledonian from Motherwell into Glasgow Central Station was originally a connecting
line from the main route to the north to the Paisley and Greenock
lines, which were joined at Shields Junction. Nowadays express
passenger trains from the south use this route till they are west
of Rutherglen, but they then swing to the north to cross the
Clyde and enter Glasgow Central. Similarly trains for Paisley
and the coast, starting from either Central or St Enoch, bear
west immediately they are over the river. Through freight
traffic from the Lanarkshire industrial districts passes over the
third side of this roughly defined triangle. There are, however,
in this area so many deviations, connecting lines, branches and
so on, that to speak of a ' triangle ' is very much to over-simplify
the layout. Even the keenest student of railway geography may
be pardoned for becoming confused when travelling hereabouts.

World War I brought a problem in coal haulage that cut
across the closely integrated railway and industrial economy
of Scotland. The stationing of the Grand Fleet at Scapa Flow and
the battle-cruisers under Sir David Beatty in the Firth of Forth
created an exceedingly heavy demand for high-grade steam coal;
the Scottish collieries could not meet the demand, and a very
large tonnage was conveyed from England and Wales. On the
Glasgow and South Western alone, which was rather off the
direct line for naval traffic, 316,210 tons of Welsh coal were
conveyed for Admiralty purposes over and above the ordinary
Scottish coal traffic of the railway. Over the $4\frac{1}{4}$ years of war
this was equal to an average of 200 tons a day. On the Highland, during 1918, no fewer than 3,500 special trains were run
for naval and military supplies, munitions and personnel; and
while by no means all of it was coal, the fact that the tonnage of
freight conveyed over that line in 1918 was 1,323,437 tons against

Cowlairs Incline: splicing the haulage cable. This photograph includes some of the special brake trucks used for controlling trains descending the incline [note *break* for brake]

[*Photo : Westinghouse Brake & Signal Co. Ltd*

Control panel and illuminated track diagram in the new signal box at Cowlairs Junction

In the District Control Office, Polmadie, Glasgow: section controllers at work, with track diagrams before them

The great Caledonian viaduct over the Clyde: an aerial view of the approach to Central Station, Glasgow, showing the original 4-track bridge with the new portion to the left

653,589 tons in 1913—an increase of 102½ per cent—gives some indication of what Scapa Flow meant to the railways of Scotland.

5

Travelling to the Hebrides the summer visitor may be a little surprised at some of the consignments of goods brought by rail to Mallaig, or to Kyle of Lochalsh, and there shipped aboard the steamers bound for Skye and the Outer Isles. Bread, for example, is sent daily from Glasgow bakeries to Portree. But this outward manifestation is actually a very small item. While it is true that about 100 tons of groceries are sent daily from Glasgow to various destinations in the Highlands, these are mostly processed foods, though this amount does include about 3 tons of bread, sent by freight services. The conveyance of bread for the islands by passenger train to Mallaig or Kyle amounts to no more than a daily average of about 10 cwt, destined for Kyle itself, Portree, Harris and Stornoway. The Highlands generally are self-supporting in the primary essentials of life, and these extra items are concerned with the summer-holiday business.

This leads to a more detailed consideration of the tourist industry. At one time this laid a very heavy burden on the Scottish railways in the grouse season. In late Victorian times it was possible for sportsmen or other visitors to engage private saloon carriages for their families and servants; there was no extra charge other than the obligation to take at least eight tickets (four first and four third), or alternatively twelve third-class tickets. These saloons were attached to the ordinary passenger trains, often accompanied by one or more horse-boxes, and from all accounts the shunting from one train to another at stations like Waverley was done with scant regard for the crockery! By the time the East Coast, Midland and West Coast routes had delivered these special 'consignments' at Perth, the Highland had the task of conveying the combined load to the stations nearest to the grouse moors of Inverness-shire, or still farther north. Professor Foxwell in his celebrated work of 1889,

Express Trains English and Foreign, records that the 7.50 a.m. down mail from Perth to Inverness loaded to extraordinary lengths. On 7 August 1888 no less than 25 other vehicles, 13 of which were horse-boxes, were added to the basic make-up— including a Post Office van—of eleven Highland Railway coaches. Marshalled indiscriminately among these horse-boxes were saloons, carriage trucks, through carriages from the south and an East Coast Joint Stock sleeping car! The accumulation of rolling stock, and the difficulties of remarshalling of trains at stations like Edinburgh Waverley and Perth would have set a problem to the most experienced modern operating men; but in those days it would seem that Scotland was, if not without experience, then certainly without the means of extricating its railway services from these perennial tangles. Every autumn the delays to south-bound traffic at Perth were prodigious, while Waverley moved Foxwell to perhaps his greatest heights of vivid description:

' On the platforms of the Waverley Station at Edinburgh may be witnessed every evening in summer a scene of confusion so chaotic that a sober description of it is incredible to those who have not themselves survived it. Trains of caravan length come in portentously late from Perth, so that each is mistaken for its successor; these have to be broken up and remade on insufficient sidings, while bewildered crowds of tourists sway up and down amongst equally bewildered porters on the narrow village plat- form reserved for these most important expresses; the higher officials stand lost in subtle thought, returning now and then to repeated inquiries some masterpiece of reply couched in the cautious conditional, while the hands of the clock with a humour- ous air survey the abandoned sight, till at length, without any obvious reason and with sudden stealth, the shame-stricken driver hurries his packed passengers off into the dark. . . .'

This was before the opening of the Forth Bridge, and, I need hardly add, before the building of the present Waverley Station. At that time North British expresses to and from the Highlands had to travel via Stirling; and at Larbert, the point of junction with the Caledonian main line, the confusion and delay seem to have been second only to those prevailing around Perth. But the quotation from Foxwell throws an interesting light on the changed travelling habits of summer visitors to Scotland as compared with those of the present day. In 1888 the trouble at Waverley occurred ' every evening.' Nowadays pressure is almost entirely concentrated at week-ends. The private motor car has of course replaced the family saloon on the railway, and the travellers by train are nowadays those with a fortnight, three weeks or at the most a month's leave. This change has rendered railway arrangements easier to plan and control, while some of the more notorious stations, amongst which Aberdeen should be included with Perth, Larbert and Waverley, have been completely reconstructed. Inverness, however, remains today an archaic survival of the bad old days of Scottish tourist traffic mishandling. But for the second world war this extraordinary station would no doubt have been rebuilt, and the way in which traffic is nowadays managed in so inconvenient a layout is a great credit to the operating staff.

The present-day arrangements for bringing tourists into Scotland are mostly very good, and the working of some celebrated services will be referred to in a later chapter. But, having brought their visitors to the various centres of holiday traffic, little was done in the past to provide rapid and convenient travel in the most favoured districts. It is certainly true that between the two world wars the ten-shilling run-about weekly season tickets were introduced ; but at a centre like Fort William the infrequency of the train service made the usefulness of these tickets a great deal less attractive than it might have been. Furthermore, riding in ordinary compartment stock on a gloriously fine summer's day was not the most inviting way to set out on an expedition, and the return journey could afford no more than a sad anticlimax. The railway administrations no doubt felt that the traffic prospects did not justify putting on any special services for purely holiday travel over short distances inside Scotland ; and of course much of the period between the wars was a time of consolidation after grouping, and then of intense trade depression when the emphasis was upon economy in operation rather than embarkation on new enterprises.

But there is no doubt that attractive services do, in themselves, create business, and since the first edition of this book was published the beaver-tail observation cars originally designed by Sir Nigel Gresley for the streamlined *Coronation* express have been put on to runs in the West Highlands. They have proved exceedingly popular, especially on that wonderful run from Fort William to Mallaig. One feels, however, that still more could be done in the tourist season to popularise travel in the most favoured holiday districts by running frequent shuttle services with the new diesel railcar sets from, shall we say, Oban, Fort William, Ayr, Pitlochry or Aberdeen. I must not be tempted at this stage to digress upon the attractive routes that might be followed ; but the running of cars of this kind would at least open up to ordinary travellers those fascinating scenic panoramas which are now only seen to the best advantage from the footplate.

On the other hand the Scottish railways did provide, in the years between the wars, some of the finest and cheapest long-distance excursions to be enjoyed anywhere, mostly running on Sundays, from Glasgow and Edinburgh. For 7s 6d or less there were Sunday trips from Glasgow to Beattock, Berwick, Carlisle, Dumfries, Dunbar, Dundee, Fort William, Kirkcudbright, Lockerbie, Montrose, Oban, Portpatrick and Stranraer. Many intermediate stations serving attractive districts were included in the same runs; the trains themselves were composed of modern corridor stock with restaurant cars, and in the height of the season it was advisable to reserve seats in advance. All these trains left Glasgow about 10 a.m., and the longer-distance trips extended to Mallaig and Aberdeen. The Stranraer trip could be extended by steamer to Larne, at a return fare of 11s 6d from Glasgow. Every Sunday a proportion of those making the trips travelled from the south specially for the purpose, and the majority of these excursion trains were timed so as to arrive back in Glasgow in time to connect with the principal night expresses to England. The 'day excursion' on the Scottish railways reached its peak, however, in the special trips run occasionally from Euston to Staffa and Iona, a more recent counterpart of the famous 'Day Trip to Killarney' run by the Great Western and G & SW Railways before World War I. On the Scottish trips, first run in 1936, the departure time from Euston was 7.30 p.m. ; Oban was reached about 9 a.m., with comfortable time to look round before sailing in the MacBrayne steamer. The arrival back in Oban was about 4 p.m., after which the return excursion train left at about 6 p.m. and reached Euston about 9 a.m. The fare was a modest 35s covering rail travel and the long steamer trip.

In serving the day-to-day needs of the population in Scotland, prominence must be given to the heavy short-distance passenger traffic in the Glasgow area. Again the locomotive stock gives a fair impression of the business offered. At the time of the grouping the Caledonian Railway owned about 150 bogie four-coupled passenger engines, of various ages, and they were engaged in express and intermediate traffic all over the system including the bulk of the Anglo-Scottish expresses; at the same time the Company had about the same number of front-coupled tank engines of the 0–4–4 type, by far the greater number of which were employed in the Glasgow area. Even in these days when alternative road services are available in such variety the number of season tickets issued on the Scottish railways in 1959 was 1,224,877, an increase of nearly 40 per cent over the year 1948.

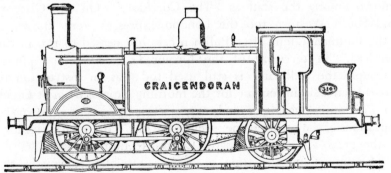

CHAPTER THREE

An Outline of Passenger Train Services

I

THE Anglo-Scottish expresses are well known the world over. Their tradition of service dates from the earliest years of through communication between London and Scotland, and after nearly a century of running the glamour of the mere name *Scotch Express* is as vital today as ever. The purists may tilt at the word ' Scotch,' and nowadays one would hesitate to use it in anything but quotes; but Sir Walter himself used the adjective freely, and *Scotch Express* it always was until the LNER and the LMS began the systematic naming of their crack trains. One recalls some of the famous expresses of 50 years or more ago: the 8 p.m. ' Tourist ' from Euston to Aberdeen and the Highlands; the Midland night Pullmans; and the West Coast Postal which, though not a passenger train, was as famous as any of them. The unofficial names of some trains lingered long after the distinction through which those names were derived had disappeared. There was the West Coast ' Corridor '—the 2 p.m. from Euston to Glasgow, and the corresponding south-bound train; the old sobriquet survived one world war, and even after the LMS had bestowed upon it the title of the *Midday Scot* the train was still known among the staff as ' The Corridor.' On the Glasgow and South Western too the London expresses were known as ' the Pullmans ' long after Pullman cars had ceased to run in the services. In territory of the former G & SWR the phrase ' Couple the Pullman ' is still used today as an instruction to provide an assistant engine for the morning express from St Enoch to London. Subsidiary and extra services became known by variations of the parent name, such as the old ' Forenoon Corridor ' —the 11.30 a.m. from Glasgow Central to Euston.

Grouping and the time of increased publicity brought the

official names. As the Royal Mail route the West Coast introduced the *Royal Scot* and the *Royal Highlander*, which the East Coast countered with the *Highlandman*, the *Aberdonian* and the *Night Scotsman*; and in later years there came the special limited trains the *Queen of Scots* and the streamlined *Coronation* and *Coronation Scot*. And all down the years since June 1862, in fair days or foul, there has run one of the oldest and certainly the most famous of them all, the *Flying Scotsman*. This most historic of trains cannot quite claim to be the oldest named train in the world, for the *Irish Mail* holds that distinction; and it was not until after the grouping that the name was carried on the roof-boards. The train was also referred to on many occasions, both officially and otherwise, as the ' Flying Scotchman.'

At various times since 1927 special travel amenities have been provided on this train, such as a hairdressing saloon, a ladies' retiring-room and a buffet car in addition to the usual restaurant cars, while from the operating viewpoint, the introduction of corridor tenders, so that one engine crew could relieve another *en route* and enable the run from London to Edinburgh to be made non-stop, remained a feature unique to this train until the summer of 1939. After the conclusion of World War II the non-stop run was revived, though by a special express running in advance of the *Flying Scotsman*, and named the *Capitals Limited*. In 1953, the year of the Coronation of Her Majesty Queen Elizabeth, the London–Edinburgh ' non-stop ' was still further accelerated to a time of $6\frac{3}{4}$ hours, and named the *Elizabethan*, while such was the proven competence of the Gresley A4 Pacifics in operating the service that still further accelerations have been found practicable, and in the summer of 1961—probably the last that the ' non-stop ' will be operated by steam locomotives—the overall time was 6 hours 35 minutes, giving an average speed throughout of $59\frac{3}{4}$ mph.

Although the running of the various expresses to and from England does not represent a very high proportion of the total passenger-train mileage run north of the Border, many purely Scottish services, both long-distance and otherwise, are based on

English connections. In the course of time the details of Scottish passenger-train services have changed considerably, though their general character has remained much the same. In referring to them I have thought it best to take the summer 1960 time-tables as a basis, though some of my more detailed observations relate to the period about 1950 when the book was first published.

2

In the dusk of a summer's evening in 1948 I was at Crewe, and saw two great Pacific engines being prepared for the road. Both had a long night's work ahead. The first off the shed, the *Duchess of Abercorn*, was booked for the 10.34 p.m. train, the Inverness ' sleeper,' non-stop from Crewe to Perth[1] ; the second, the *Duchess of Devonshire*, was due for an even heavier train, then 7.30 p.m. from Euston, with sleeping cars for Oban and Forfar, and calling only at Wigan, Carlisle, Larbert and Stirling in the 290-mile run from Crewe to Perth. These two trains, lineal descendants of the celebrated 8 p.m. ' Tourist ' of 1900, still form the nucleus of a series of important Scottish services pene-trating to some of the farthest rail-heads in the west and northern Highlands. But although the line of descent is clear, the operating conditions of today, when the two trains between them may often weigh more than 1,000 tons (not including their 162-ton engines), seem an exceedingly far cry from those of 1896 when the ' Dunalastair ' engines of the Caledonian won such fame in hauling their 120-ton loads non-stop from Carlisle to Stirling. In the heat of an intense competition with the East Coast route the timings were then exceptionally fast, and the 117·8 miles from Carlisle to Stirling had to be covered in 125 minutes. Today the 500-ton 2.38 a.m. from Carlisle is allowed 152 minutes to run the $109\frac{1}{2}$ miles from Carlisle to Larbert.

The ' non-stop ' is purely a Highland train, serving moreover only the stations on the direct line to Inverness running from

[1] There is no stop in the public time-tables, though a stop for operating purposes is made at Motherwell.

London and North Eastern Railway: the former North British Railway paddle-steamer *Waverley* on the Lochgoilhead and Arrochar service. This fine old steamer, built 1899, was sunk in the Dunkirk evacuation

Aviemore via Carrbridge, Tomatin and Moy. The pleasant towns of Grantown-on-Spey, Forres and Nairn are situated on what was originally the main line of the Highland Railway. Admittedly it was a circuitous route, and the claim of those three towns to preferential treatment naturally ranks considerably lower than that of Inverness. At times of lighter traffic, such as the years of depression in the early thirties, one train at each of the old-established departure times from Perth sufficed to serve all the Highland line ; and then Grantown, Forres and Nairn managed to secure more than a few crumbs from the rich man's table. The trains were divided at Aviemore, and one portion ran via Forres. But now, with two sleeping-car trains nightly from London and the noon service from Perth patronised sufficiently to require a second train, the stations on the old line do not fare so well—an arrival of 10.38 a.m. at Forres, against 8.39 a.m. at Inverness, and 4.5 p.m. off the noon departure from Perth against 3.31 p.m. at Inverness.

It is the second of the sleeping-car trains from Euston from which the widest ramifications of service spring, and with it must also be associated the West Coast Postal Special. At Stirling the ' second sleeper ' is preceded by the 4 a.m. mail from Glasgow and followed by the ' Down Special ' as it is known in the Post Office ; with traffic from these trains the 6 a.m. sets off for Oban—English and Scottish mail, a sleeping car and through carriages from London. In the meantime various connections are awaiting the arrival of the main group of trains at Perth. The Dundee train is of importance only from intermediate stations on the West Coast route, as the principal service from London is by the East Coast route. The remnant of the 7.15 p.m. from Euston proceeds to Forfar, but by far the most important of the Perth connections is the down Highland mail. This is the fastest train running at the present time between Perth and Inverness ; it conveys a travelling post office, and takes forward traffic from the 4 a.m. Glasgow mail and the ' Down Special ' from Euston. This train is indeed the primary means of conveyance of mail to all parts of the north and north-west Highlands.

As the journey progresses, so the coming of the train is regarded more and more in a personal light. At Crewe and Carlisle one listened to the loudspeakers and experienced, perhaps, something of that chilling atmosphere of a great station in the small hours. Breakfast on the Highland mail, with the warm-hearted friendliness of the stewards and the majestic scenery passing by the windows, does much to sweep away traces of a night journey ; and when one reaches stations like Achna-shellach, Bonar Bridge or Invershin, proceedings on the platform begin to partake more of a family party. Kyle of Lochalsh can present a still more intimate hurly-burly, with the air vibrant with Gaelic speech, with gulls wheeling round the steamers and the locomotive alike, and cargo of an exceedingly mixed nature going aboard. Most of the passengers watch the proceedings with interest, and perhaps some amusement. They are in the very thick of it all and are to some extent conscious of the factors concerned in the working of the traffic. This scene at Kyle is complementary to the supremely fascinating though rarely glimpsed scene at Crewe, which, 16 hours earlier, marked the preparation of the Pacific for the journey now completed.

The final arrival is the great event of the day in the Hebridean ports, and I have seen the pleasant ritual enacted day after day at Portree, at Lochboisdale and at Tobermory, while no doubt it is much the same at Stornoway in Lewis, where the steamer connecting with the night express from London is due at 7.15 p.m. Some little time before the steamer is due a crowd gathers at the pier-head. Summer visitors will be there too, but the majority are local inhabitants. If the boat has been delayed the crowd will disperse, but not before inquiring the probable time of arrival. At the later hour they will reassemble even if, as I saw once at Lochboisdale, it means turning out after midnight. For the arrival of the boat is of the utmost importance. Imagine the thrill that goes through the waiting throng when it is seen that the new tyres for Angus McTavish's motor-bike have at last arrived—a thrill only exceeded by the sight of the dashing new hat in which old Mrs Nicholson has returned from her stay in Forres.

3

At one time the Highland mail used to convey a portion from the East Coast route ; and during the summer season this portion was heavy enough to form a train of its own—the *Highlandman*. Nowadays the mid-evening departure from King's Cross, the 7.30 p.m. *Aberdonian*, is, with the exception of one important connection at Edinburgh—to be described later—an express for Dundee and Aberdeen pure and simple. It is usually a heavy train, and provides one of the hardest daily tasks set to Scottish locomotives. It leaves Edinburgh at 3.57 a.m., and at that hour few if any of its passengers will be minded to appreciate the grand work done on the footplate in those chill morning hours. But I have several times been privileged to ride in the engine cab, and the crossing of the Forth Bridge, whether in the first light of a summer's dawn or with a February moon shining between banks of snow clouds, makes a wonderfully impressive start to what is always an absorbing journey. The coastal towns of Arbroath, Montrose and Stonehaven are served by this train, but the connections begin in earnest at Aberdeen itself.

The *Aberdonian* is due in at 7.10 a.m., and by 8.30 a.m. three trains are among them weaving their way through the entire ramifications of the old ' Great North ' system. One, a restaurant car express going north, is nearing Insch ; a second, a diesel for Fraserburgh, is just clearing the northern outskirts of Aberdeen ; while there used to be yet another, for Macduff, but this branch is now closed. The third of the group is by this time some 10 miles up the Deeside line, nearing Park. All the principal stations in ' Great North ' territory are served by connections from one or other of these trains. It is like the flow of a river in reverse, with the main stream dividing into a number of tributaries. The 7.48 a.m. restaurant-car express for Inverness divides again at Cairnie Junction, with the main portion taking the inland route via Craigellachie and a second part travelling by the coastal route through Buckie. Both from Aberdeen and from Perth the series of trains running in connection with the sleeping-car expresses from London are the most comprehensive of the day.

The alternative routes of the ' Great North ' between Cairnie Junction and Elgin do indeed present a baffling choice to a traveller who is bent on seeing the best of the country ; for while the inland route through the magnificently wooded Glen Fiddich provides some exceedingly fine river scenery, the coastal route through Portsoy, Buckie and Spey Bay can, on a day of clear visibility, afford a marvellous panorama over the Moray Firth to the distant ranges of Sutherland and Caithness. Between the wars the LNER ran sleeping cars between Lossiemouth and King's Cross, 609 miles—the longest through-carriage service operated from London.

To anyone accustomed to fairly frequent train services in populous districts, the timing of these Highland trains may well appear wrapt in mystery ; little less so is that of the West Highland services, from Glasgow to Fort William and Mallaig, with only two departures daily, at 5.10 a.m. and 3.45 p.m. But these again are based on important connections from the south. The *Aberdonian* conveys a through portion, including a sleeping car, for Fort William, and this is brought across from Edinburgh for attachment to the 5.10 a.m. from Glasgow. In the same way the timing of some of the south-bound Scottish services is arranged to suit the running of night expresses to England. These are booked into King's Cross and Euston well before the rush of suburban and residential trains begins. To do this the principal night express to London has to leave Inverness as early as 5.40 p.m.

In the summer of 1949 a most interesting new service was introduced between Glasgow (Queen St) and Oban, travelling by the West Highland line as far as Crianlarich and transferring there to the former LMS route. The journey included some of the finest scenery on both these famous routes in the West Highlands, and the train was so timed as to provide the means for an excellent round trip to Oban and back, leaving Glasgow at 9.31 a.m and arriving back at 9.56 p.m. This has now been withdrawn.

4

Most of the night trains from the south are timed to arrive in Glasgow or Edinburgh, as the case may be, before breakfast. At Waverley Station the *Night Scotsman* is due at 7.18, preceded by other expresses from King's Cross, while the night train from the Midland route, with traffic from Leicester, Nottingham, Sheffield and Leeds, is due at 7.57 a.m. Often I have found these arrivals very convenient, affording time for breakfast and a pleasant break before one continues the journey farther north. Some of the finest sights in Edinburgh lie within twenty minutes' stroll of Waverley Station, and the bracing promenade of Princes Street or a climb to the Castle ramparts can be a fine refresher after a night in the train. Then, around 10 o'clock, expresses leave for most parts of the north and west. At one time, while at the east end of the station the *Flying Scotsman* was leaving for London, two trains were leaving the west end on parallel tracks—the 10 o'clock for Glasgow, giving connections to resorts on the north shores of the Firth of Clyde, and the 10 o'clock for Aberdeen. These were followed at 10.10 a.m. by an express for Dunfermline and Perth conveying through carriages for Inverness. The times are now changed and the departures are 10 for Glasgow, 10.10 for Aberdeen and 10.18 for Perth.

On the western side of Scotland the magnitude of the industrial concentration centred upon Glasgow naturally brings a large number of long-distance passengers into the city itself, regardless of connections for places beyond, and at Glasgow Central sleeping-car expresses arrive at 6.40 a.m. from Euston, 7.32 a.m. from Birmingham, 7.24 a.m. from Euston and 7.50 a.m. from Liverpool and Manchester. At St Enoch the Midland route 'sleeper' arrives at 8.30 a.m. An interesting connection with all the West Coast trains is the 8.23 a.m. from Central to Gourock, as this feeds the MacBrayne mail steamer to Tarbert, Ardrishaig and the south-west Highlands and islands. During the summer season, when the steamer used to start from Bridge Wharf, Glasgow, instead of from Gourock, several of my friends always made a point of travelling north for their Scottish holidays by the earliest train from Euston, so as to join the famous paddle-steamer *Columba* at Bridge Wharf, leaving at 7.11 a.m. and sailing down the Clyde. Breakfast on the *Columba* was once a favourite choice of epicures. But in recent years most of my journeys to Scotland have been made at times when early arrivals and breakfasts afloat have not been very tempting, and I have been glad of that most comfortable of sleeping-car trains, the *Night Scot*. It leaves Euston at 11.40 p.m., attaches a breakfast car at Carlisle, and reaches Glasgow at the convenient hour of 9.30 a.m., travelling via the old G & SW line from Carlisle.

5

So far as long-distance traffic is concerned, the very fine Central Station in Glasgow deals mainly with the Anglo-Scottish trains. At one time there was very keen competition between the Caledonian and North British for Glasgow–Edinburgh traffic, but nowadays the service provided from Glasgow Central by the former Caledonian route is mostly of an intermediate nature, serving Holytown, Shotts and West Calder *en route*. The old North British line, later LNER, has the advantage of easy grading except, of course, for the very difficult start east-bound from Glasgow up the 1 in 41 of the Cowlairs incline, and a splendid series of restaurant-buffet-car expresses is now provided between the two cities. The great majority of these trains are composed of the new diesel-powered multiple-unit sets of the inter-city type, having compartment accommodation fully equal to long-distance main-line standards. Some of these trains cover the 47·3 miles in 55 minutes inclusive of one stop, but the majority make at least two stops and are scheduled to make the run in the level hour. Some travellers might expect faster running. The route is, however, constantly subject to a variety of temporary speed restrictions : it runs through a mining area, and slacks have often to be imposed because of subsidences. In the most favourable running conditions an end-to-end time of 50 minutes would be possible ; but with the numerous temporary restrictions there would be long periods when such a time could not easily be maintained, and in the interests of punctuality a slower schedule is preferable.

Among purely Scottish services some of the fastest daily running is performed on the Glasgow to Aberdeen route of the former Caledonian Railway, later LMS. For many years the fastest start-to-stop run anywhere in the British Isles was made from Forfar to Perth, 32·5 miles in 32 minutes ; it was initiated some sixty years ago during the time that Irvine Kempt was Superintendent of the line, and the tradition of fast running north of Perth has been maintained all down the years. Today the 3.30 p.m. up from Aberdeen, allowed 34 minutes, often regains one or two minutes with loads far heavier than in Kempt's day. In 1905 the Caledonian, then as usual in hot competition with the North British, put a most palatial train on to the Glasgow–Aberdeen service, the *Grampian Corridor Express*. Some very fine 12-wheeled carriages were specially built at St Rollox works, and the train became a great favourite. But after World War I the naming of trains was not revived until 1933, when the LMS bestowed upon the 10 a.m. from Buchanan Street and the 5.30 p.m. up from Aberdeen the name of the *Granite City*.

But these trains, like the Caledonian expresses of former years, could not show really fast overall times, as so many intermediate stops were included. Even the fastest of them called at Stirling, Gleneagles, Perth, Forfar, Bridge of Dun, Laurencekirk and Stonehaven, while some others added Guthrie, Alyth Junction, Coupar Angus and Larbert. It was in 1937 that the experiment was tried of running two fast expresses between Glasgow and Aberdeen in the even 3 hours, an overall speed of 51 mph. These trains called only at Perth and Stonehaven on the outward trip, but coming south one of them called at Forfar instead of Stone-haven. On the north-bound run it was necessary to cover the 73·7 miles from Perth to Stonehaven in 76 minutes start to stop, but the loads were strictly limited and no difficulty was experienced in keeping time. These trains were officially named the *Bon-*

Accord and the *Saint Mungo*, and ran only during the summer service ; reintroduced in 1938 and again in 1939, these fast services have not been revived since the war. The names *Bon-Accord* and *Saint Mungo* were reintroduced in the summer time-table of 1949 on the then 1.35 p.m. and 5.0 p.m. departures from Buchanan Street to Aberdeen, but the trains themselves continue to make the usual intermediate stops. For a time the down postal train, to which a passenger portion was attached at Perth, had a comparable timing, and with an 8-coach train—five postal vans and three carriages—I have recorded a time of $76\frac{1}{2}$ minutes to passing Stonehaven. This was in 1947, and was quite up to pre-war standards on the *Bon-Accord*.

The LMS had some further picturesque names for its Scottish expresses. There was the *Lewisman*, the 5.5 a.m. boat train from Kyle of Lochalsh in connection with the Stornoway steamer. When it ran, this train provided a day service from Kyle of Lochalsh to London ; connection was made with the *Midday Scot* and Euston was reached at 9.30 p.m.—a remarkable time for such a route of 16 hr 25 min. Another train on the Inverness–Kyle of Lochalsh service was named the *Hebridean*, though apart from the *Royal Highlander* and the *Highlandman* no trains running over the southern section of the Highland main line were named. In the days before World War I the Highland Railway had two named trains that achieved popularity, if not the fame of the *Grampian* or that of the English expresses. One of these trains was the *Strathpeffer Spa Express*, which ran in connection with the noon tourist express from Perth ; it started from Aviemore and ran non-stop to Dingwall, passing Inverness on the avoiding line without stopping.

The second of these named trains was the *Farther North Express*. I have referred earlier to the infrequency of the train service north of Inverness ; to alleviate this to some extent at week-ends in the holiday season a special express was run in connection with the noon tourist train from Perth. This left Inverness at 4.10 p.m. and called only at the principal stations ; there were some quite lengthy non-stop runs such as Inverness to Tain, 44 miles, Bonar

Bridge to The Mound, 23 miles, and Helmsdale to Georgemas Junction, 45.9 miles. Like many of the Highland trains of those days, however, the *Farther North Express* was all very well if it kept time ; but it was frequently delayed at crossing-places by the late running of other trains, and in such circumstances the non-corridor carriages of the day, with little chance of refreshment at intermediate stations, were apt to be wearisome in the extreme. This train was revived during the period between the wars, and in the flood-tide of railway publicity was officially named the *John o' Groat* ; another of the ' Farther North ' trains was named the *Orcadian*.

6

But from the fastnesses of Sutherland and Caithness we must return to Glasgow Central, to St Enoch and to Waverley, for up to now I have said little except by inference of the most famous of all trains running north of the Border, the day Anglo-Scottish expresses. Until quite recently departures for the south were always to be found in two well defined groups, one around 10 a.m. and the second between 1 and 2 p.m. The *Flying Scotsman* at 10 a.m. from Waverley to King's Cross, and the *Royal Scot* at 10 a.m. from Glasgow Central to Euston are times that have become hallowed by tradition. Nowadays, however, while these particular expresses still leave at the same times as of old, they no longer form the centre-pieces, as it were, of a group of trains running at relatively close headway. On the East Coast route, quite apart from the summer non-stop service of the *Elizabethan*, leaving Waverley at 9.45 a.m., there are first-class expresses to London leaving Waverley at 8.30, 10.10 and 11.0 a.m. ; 12.5, 1.30 and 4 p.m. Of these, the 8.30 a.m. and 4 p.m. departures—the morning and afternoon *Talisman* service—are little slower than the *Elizabethan*, both making the journey in less than 7 hours.

On the West Coast route the changes are more in the make-up of the trains than in the times, for except on Saturdays the once heavy *Royal Scot* is now a limited train, with all seats reservable. The formation is now restricted to a regular formation of eight cars, and in the busiest times considerable relief is necessary in the way of subsidiary trains. It is interesting to recall the variations that have occurred from year to year in the running arrangements of the 10 a.m. up from Glasgow Central. In the last years of the Caledonian, through traffic between Glasgow and London was a good deal less than that of today, and a six-coach restaurant-car set was sufficient. Then the Birmingham coaches were taken on the 10 o'clock train and conveyed by it throughout to Crewe. At the same time the *Flying Scotsman* had a keen rival for the through Edinburgh–London traffic ; there was another 10 o'clock from the Caledonian station, Princes Street, and this train, joining the main line at Carstairs, ran ahead of the Glasgow 10 o'clock all the way to Crewe. When the 10 o'clock departure was named the *Royal Scot* in 1927 and received somewhat preferential treatment, combination of the Edinburgh and Glasgow sections took place at Symington, and Birmingham then had a restaurant-car express to itself. A war-time measure that still remains as a natural outcome of nationalisation was to confine all through London–Edinburgh traffic to the East Coast route, though in the case of the morning group one can leave Waverley by the 10.5 a.m. for Carlisle and St Pancras ; but as the arrival in London is at 8.5 p.m. compared with the *Flying Scotsman's* 5.30 p.m. at King's Cross, the alternative is not very tempting.

A counterpart of the East Coast morning *Talisman* now runs from Glasgow Central to Euston in the form of the *Caledonian*, leaving at 8.30 a.m. This fine new express train, like the present *Royal Scot*, is an eight-car limited formation, and calling only at Carlisle provides a $7\frac{1}{4}$-hr service between Glasgow and London. The West Coast route between London, Liverpool and Manchester is just now in the throes of the conversion to electric traction, and the exceptionally heavy engineering work involved requires much running at very restricted speed. The strict limitation of the load on these two crack day expresses has been made to permit of very much faster running over the stretches unaffected by the engineering work, particularly in climbing the heavy gradients in the north, and so preserve a fast overall service despite the handicaps involved south of Crewe.

A deficiency in passenger-train services that has never been made good, even in the most highly competitive days before the first world war, is the provision of a really good morning service to Glasgow from the Yorkshire and Lancashire cities. On the East Coast route the good morning express, the *North Briton*, from Leeds due in Edinburgh at 1.44 p.m., affords time for a full afternoon's business before returning by the corresponding 5.15 p.m. from Waverley. But by the Midland route the earliest arrival in Glasgow is 3.53 p.m. from Sheffield and Leeds, and by the West Coast 3.5 p.m. from Liverpool and 2.45 p.m. from Manchester. In contrast to the East Coast express from Leeds, which stops only at York and Newcastle, these morning West Coast trains make a number of intermediate stops. As the last through return trains leave Glasgow at 4.30 p.m. for Liverpool and Manchester and 4 p.m. for Leeds, a business visit cannot be arranged within one day.

The morning Leeds–Edinburgh service, with its 1.44 p.m. arrival at Waverley, makes a series of important connections. The train itself continues to Glasgow, forming the 2 p.m. departure in the hourly series, but there are also trains at 2.3 p.m. to Perth, with a through portion for Inverness, and 2.10 p.m. to Aberdeen, with a series of connections to the ' Great North ' line. By this service it is possible to travel from London to Inverness in the day, as the semi-fast 4.0 a.m. from King's Cross connects with the Leeds train at York. Altogether, the 8.50 a.m. from Leeds, with its many connections at York, stands out as one of the ' key ' Anglo-Scottish services ; appropriately it is furnished with very fine rolling stock, and during the summer of 1948 it was one of the trains selected for display of the experimental new liveries. It is now named the *North Briton*.

At the height of their speed achievements both the *Flying Scotsman* and the *Royal Scot* completed their journeys in the even 7 hours, reaching Waverley and Glasgow Central respectively at

5 p.m. In the case of the *Flying Scotsman* the journey of 392·7 miles was made non-stop, at an average speed of 56·2 mph. The locomotive work required in running the *Royal Scot* was even harder, for not only is the distance from Euston to Glasgow greater —401·4 miles—but an intermediate stop was booked at Carlisle. This entailed a full 60-mph average over the 299·1 miles from Euston to Carlisle, and with a load of 13, and sometimes even 14, coaches, the effort demanded was much greater than that of working the 9-coach streamlined *Coronation Scot* from Euston to Glasgow in 6½ hours. Today, the *Elizabethan*, with its non-stop run of all but 60-mph average, is the hardest locomotive duty on the Anglo-Scottish services.

The zenith of Anglo-Scottish train speed was reached in the summer of 1937 with the introduction of the *Coronation*. This remarkable train was allowed no more than 6 hours for the London–Edinburgh run—an average of 65·5 mph—and on the north-bound journey this time included two stops. Although it does not strictly concern Scotland, the timing of this train from King's Cross to York at 71·9 mph start to stop made it the fastest in the British Empire. Only one locomotive was used throughout from London to Edinburgh, and Scottish enginemen from Haymarket shed took a share in the working north of Newcastle. The *Coronation* was to my mind one of the most beautiful-looking trains that have ever run in Great Britain. The handsome ' garter blue ' was introduced on the streamlined engines allocated to the working of this service ; the coach bodies were in the same colour, with Cambridge-blue upper panels ; and the striking beaver-tail observation car brought up the rear. To travel in one of these cars at over 90 mph was indeed a memorable experience. An arrival in Edinburgh at 10 p.m. after leaving King's Cross as late as 4 p.m. was certainly a great convenience to travellers. The south-bound *Coronation* left Waverley at 4.30 p.m. For the privilege of this extra-high-speed travel supplementary fares were charged, as they were also on the *Coronation Scot* of the LMS.

These streamliners were not the first Anglo-Scottish expresses on which supplementary fares were charged. Soon after the grouping in 1923 an all-Pullman train was introduced between London, Leeds and Harrogate ; this train proved a great success, and in 1927 it was extended to Edinburgh and Glasgow. Soon afterwards it received the pleasing name of the *Queen of Scots*. Post-war reconstruction had progressed far enough for this train to be reintroduced in the summer of 1948, and it now leaves King's Cross at 11.50 a.m. and reaches Waverley at 7.50 p.m. The time is longer than that of the *Flying Scotsman* on account of the detour via Leeds and Harrogate, and the train stops additionally at Darlington and Newcastle. It is continued through from Edinburgh at 8.38 p.m. to Glasgow. On the south-bound run the departure is at 11 a.m. from Glasgow and 12.5 p.m. from Edinburgh, thus conveniently dividing the interval between the 11 a.m. express to London and the *Heart of Midlothian* at 1.30 p.m.

This brings me to the afternoon London express from Glasgow Central. The celebrated lineage of the present 1.30 p.m. express has become rather obscured through the changes that took place at the time of the introduction of the *Coronation Scot* in 1937. Until then, whatever changes in departure time were made and whatever official names were given, to the staff the train was ' The Corridor.' It was in 1892 that the first all-corridor train was put on to this service, and for many years the departure time from Glasgow was 2 p.m. But during World War I, when conditions made it necessary to increase the running time, the hour of departure was made successively earlier till in 1918–19 it was 1 p.m. In the later London and North Western and Caledonian days this train could always be distinguished by the beautiful 12-wheeled coaches used, among the most comfortable and smoothest-riding stock ever to run in Scotland or England.

In former days this train and the competing 1.30 p.m. from St Enoch to the Midland line were essentially business men's trains, and both loaded heavily. But there has been a considerable change in the public taste. There is now no afternoon London train from St Enoch, and the 1.15 p.m. is not ordinarily heavy. Business men seem to prefer the night expresses, on which the lavish sleeping-car accommodation is always fully booked up.

7

And finally there is the south-western corner of Scotland, with two trunk lines leading to the important railhead and packet station of Stranraer. The line from Dumfries, which takes in its stride the southern uplands of Galloway, forms an important link in the mail route to Northern Ireland. Over this route there was once a day and a night service in connection with the steamers to Larne, but at the present time only the night service is in operation. The sleeping-car express from Euston leaves Carlisle at 2.26 a.m. and makes a fairly leisurely passage through Galloway in order to reach Stranraer at 5.38 a.m. Glasgow passengers for Ireland travel down overnight, leaving St Enoch at 9 p.m. and reaching Stranraer at 11.51 p.m. ; they can then secure a full night's sleep on the steamer before she sails at 7 a.m. next morning. The arrival in Belfast is at 10.5 a.m.

Inward bound, the steamer berths at Stranraer at 8.55 p.m. ; the mail train for Glasgow leaves at 9.15 p.m. and is due at Ayr at 10.53 p.m. and St Enoch at 11.42 p.m. The sleeping-car express for Euston leaves Stranraer Harbour at 10 p.m. ; this is always a very heavy train and requires to be double-headed over the severe gradients between Newton Stewart and Castle Douglas. When the morning steamer from Larne was in operation there was a through carriage from Stranraer to Euston, which was attached to the tail end of the up ' Corridor ' at Carlisle. Apart from the boat expresses the train service over both the Dumfries and the Girvan-Ayr lines from Stranraer is entirely in the ' all-stations ' category. The countryside is sparsely populated, and anything in the way of a local express service in the day-time would, one fears, receive scant patronage. On both routes there is, of course, a wild grandeur about the countryside, and observation rail-car trips might well prove popular with summer visitors to this very fine region.

A striking example of the way in which railway service is being kept abreast of the trends of the times is to be seen in the increasingly elaborate facilities provided for conveying motorists and their cars. Services are now available between Glasgow and London, Glasgow and Eastbourne, Perth and London, Inverness, Newcastle and York, and between Stirling and Sutton Coldfield. On each of these there is sleeping-berth accommodation for the car owner and any passengers who may be accompanying him, while the car is taken in a covered van on the same train. The general principle is to provide a comfortable overnight journey so that a motor tour or holiday can be commenced without the tedium of the long road journey between home and the holiday centres. These services, of course, operate also in the reverse direction, and have become very heavily patronised. For those who prefer day travel by train, a day Anglo-Scottish car-carrier service, with all the amenities of ordinary day express travel and full restaurant-car service, has also been put on between King's Cross and Waverley.

This is no more than a brief outline of the general build-up of Scottish main-line passenger-train services. The working of many of these trains requires not merely ample tractive power but first-class enginemanship ; even to a hardened traveller on locomotives they can provide some thrills of the first magnitude, especially to one whose love of the Scottish countryside is in-finite. In a later chapter some of these great runs will be des-cribed, while detailed particulars of the times, speeds and other technical data are included in the Appendix.

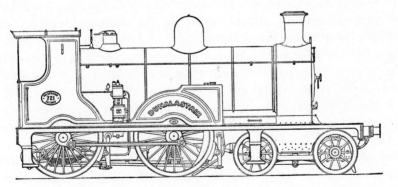

CHAPTER FOUR

MODERN EXPRESS FREIGHT SERVICES

I

THE entire railway network of Scotland was placed under one authority by the formation of the Scottish Region of British Railways consequent upon nationalisation in 1948. This opened up many possibilities for the integration of train services that had previously been duplicated, competitive and to some extent run over routes that were not ideal from the viewpoint of overall transportation. The existence, previously, of the LMS and LNER systems, perpetuating in many respects the old rivalries of the Caledonian and North British Railways, made this state of affairs largely inevitable. There are always hazards in changing the time-honoured routing of passenger trains. Travellers long accustomed to the use of certain stations, at certain times, usually have the most deep-rooted objections to going elsewhere, even if their point of departure is no more than a hundred yards or so farther down the same street. With freight, however, changes can be made more freely, and in Scotland a veritable metamorphosis has taken place since 1948.

The improvements and accelerations have been planned on the widest possible basis. The overriding consideration has been to provide evening departures from the principal centres of traffic, fast-running through the night, and the certainty of next-day delivery of goods. With freight traffic there is always the doubt among traders that even though consignments are handed over at the terminal stations in good time they may not get away on the fast services. In the past specific services have been known to have been cancelled when the traffic offered was poor and goods transferred to others ; but since 1948 it has been the aim of the operating authorities of Scottish Region to gain the complete confidence of traders, and to this end many of the more

Glasgow and South Western Railway: 4–6–0 express locomotive No 386 built 1903 by the North British Locomotive Company to the design of James Manson

important and speedy services are guaranteed—that is they will be run however small the business offered. A high standard of punctuality is maintained, not only on the main through runs, but on all the connecting and feeder services.

Although much has already been accomplished the major plan of development is only just unfolding, particularly with regard to the integration of marshalling-yard facilities. Prior to the grouping of the railways in 1923, the old Scottish companies had naturally laid in just those yard facilities that were needed for their own local needs, and for the needs of interchange with their neighbours. In Glasgow, Edinburgh and other centres where two or more companies operated there was inevitably a good deal of trip working between individual yards; but when Scottish Region was formed, and the problem of freight-train movement could be looked upon for the first time on a nation-wide scale, it was clearly evident that most of the existing work was uneconomical. Experience elsewhere had shown the immense advantage to be derived from the installation of single, large marshalling yards, capable of a through-put of anything up to 3,500 wagons a day. Not only is the operation greatly improved, but all the small local yards can be closed down, and much slow train and engine mileage eliminated.

Concurrently with the aim of running fast, fully fitted freight trains conveying block loads from one large centre to another, and the principle of substituting a small number of new, highly mechanised marshalling yards for numerous old ones, came the need to consider the routing of the modern freight trains. The stigma of unpunctuality unfortunately remains with British Railways, and so far as passenger services are concerned much of the late running that is prevalent all over Great Britain today arises from the interposing of slower trains with inadequate or impracticable margins in front of faster traffic. The need for express passenger-train punctuality is paramount, since it is by the running of such trains that much of the service as a whole is judged. At the same time there are very definite trends in passenger travel to be carefully regarded.

2

Nationalisation of the railways has tended to reduce the importance of the Waverley route from the viewpoint of through express passenger traffic. Prior to World War I the North British–Midland route provided a serious competitive service from Edinburgh to London, and even during the grouping era there were four through day services between the capitals, two West Coast and two Waverley, as well as the most direct route, namely that to King's Cross. Since nationalisation a very definite attempt has been made to concentrate the bulk of the passenger traffic on the King's Cross route, and there are now no through West Coast day trains, and only one on the old North British–Midland route. In consequence a good deal of line capacity has become available on the Waverley route, while on account of passenger-train policy it has become desirable to divert as much freight traffic as possible from the main line from Edinburgh to Newcastle. This factor has influenced the siting of the new marshalling yards.

Another factor has been the gradually changing pattern of Scottish industry. As on the railways, so in the coalfields the nationalisation of the mining industry and the replacement of many small individual concerns by a unified administration and centralised control have made possible an altogether broader outlook on the coal-mining activities in Scotland. In Fife in particular the introduction of new sinkings, as at Rothes and Seafield, and the closing of many smaller pits where the seams were almost worked out and the equipment in any case old and obsolete, have led to a reconsideration of marshalling-yard facilities. In consequence a new mechanised yard has been brought into operation near Thornton, in the very heart of the coalfield. This is actually the first of the new yards to be commissioned in Scotland, and it is situated to the west of the Edinburgh–Aberdeen main line, on the branch running westwards from the Thornton Junction triangle to Cowdenbeath and Dunfermline.

3

Before making reference to the details of working in a modern hump marshalling-yard, the position of Thornton in respect of the freight-train strategy of Scottish Region as a whole must be emphasised. The coalfields of Fife lie in two main groups, one lying east of the Aberdeen main line, and extending to the sea at Wemyss Castle, Methil and Leven ; the second is grouped roughly around Cowdenbeath. In addition to these there is the great new sinking on the coast south of Kirkcaldy at Seafield, where the workings extend out beneath the Firth of Forth. A central position was desirable for the new yard, but one of the great troubles besetting railway civil engineers in this area is subsidence, and travellers from Edinburgh to Aberdeen will be well enough aware of the serious effects of a major subsidence immediately beneath the main line at Thornton Junction. For years the ground has been gradually sinking and thousands of tons of material have been brought to the site to maintain the railway at its proper level.

On a main running line a gradual change of gradient over the years is of no particular consequence, though subsidence conditions naturally involve the imposition of a drastic reduction in speed over the affected area. But in a modern mechanised marshalling yard the gradients are designed with mathematical precision to suit the track circuiting, the automatic point-setting equipment, and the position and length of the wagon retarders, and any variation due to subsidence would throw the whole working out of gear. The site of the new yard near Thornton was chosen therefore in consultation with the National Coal Board, on ground where no colliery workings are contemplated in the future. From its central position trains from the new Thornton yard could be run direct to Dundee and Aberdeen ; to Stirling and Glasgow ; to Perth and the Highlands ; and to Edinburgh and the south. Although it is primarily a concentration point for coal traffic, a proportion of ordinary freight is also dealt with.

The second new marshalling yard to be built in Scotland is

57

that at Perth, where the entire railway layout provides a remarkable example of the developments that have taken place since the grouping of 1923, and more recently since nationalisation. Prior to grouping, three Scottish railway companies worked into Perth, and all three had their own locomotive sheds and goods yards. The Highland Railway was established at the north end, the Caledonian almost immediately beside the northern end of Moncrieff Tunnel, and the North British on a somewhat restricted site just to the south of the station. Now all motive-power facilities are being concentrated at the Friarton depot built by the LMS to co-ordinate the former Caledonian and Highland activities in grouping years, while the new marshalling yard is built on a site at Tulloch, covering the area once occupied by the old Highland running sheds, and extending northwards to Almond Valley Junction. At the same time the signalling in the whole Perth area is being modernised. No fewer than thirteen mechanical boxes are being closed and their work combined in a new power signal box situated near the station, and adjacent to the old North British running sheds.

The new marshalling yard at Tulloch will be a concentration and classification centre for traffic from every point of the compass. It is conveniently sited for receipt of trains from the Highland line, from Aberdeen, and from the ' Great North ' section, while coal and mixed freight trains from the south will be remarshalled for destinations on the North East coast, and in the Highlands. As modern marshalling yards are reckoned Perth is not a large one. There are thirty sorting sidings, as compared with thirty-six at Thornton ; and like Thornton it deals with traffic in either direction. Northbound and southbound trains arrive on one or other of the various reception lines, after which the train is drawn by a diesel locomotive to a head-shunt alongside the Almond Valley branch line. From the head-shunt, after examination, uncoupling and listing according to destination, the train is propelled over the hump, as at Thornton and other modern yards recently put into commission on British Railways.

The third of the new marshalling yards in Scottish Region,

one that is still under construction, is on the outskirts of Edinburgh, and is designed to deal with the entire flow of traffic into and out of the city, and passing through from all directions. This does not, of course, include the handling of block-load freight trains conveying traffic exclusively for Edinburgh, or departures of a similar kind, but includes the handling of all trains that require sorting or remarshalling. The new yard, which includes two separate humps and two groups of sorting sidings having between them a total of eighty sidings, is situated at Millerhill alongside the Waverley route main line to Carlisle, and some 6 miles out of central Edinburgh. From Millerhill, however, there is a connection to the East Coast main line at Monktonhall Junction near Inveresk, and trains to and from Berwick, Newcastle and the south can be run conveniently and directly to the new yard. From the north and west freight trains diverge from the main line at Haymarket West Junction, and take the Edinburgh suburban line via Craiglockhart and Blackford Hill, thus giving the additional advantage of minimising the passage of freight trains through Waverley station. On completion Millerhill will be one of the largest freight marshalling yards in Great Britain.

Closely allied with the modernisation work in Scotland itself and the altered flows of through freight-train traffic to and from England, is the construction of another very large double yard at Kingmoor, just across the Border, and some 3 miles north of Carlisle. Here the facilities will be much the same as at Millerhill, with two humps, two separate groups of sorting sidings for northbound and southbound traffic, and a total of eighty-five sidings in the two groups. These yards are situated so that they can deal with traffic directly from the Caledonian and Glasgow and South Western lines, though reversal of direction will be needed in the case of both arriving and departing trains on the Waverley route, due to the location of the yard just to the north of the point where the latter line enters the Carlisle area. On the other hand a high proportion of the freight trains now using the Waverley route consist of block loads that require little or no marshalling at Carlisle.

4

As the latest example of modern technique in freight-train marshalling particular reference may be made to Perth. After a train has been drawn into the head-shunt a list is made of the ' cuts ' into which it is divided, according to destination, and this list is sent by pneumatic tube to the elevated Control Tower. There an operator, reading the list, presses a series of keys to register the siding numbers on a punched tape. The actual principle of hump shunting is well known, in that a train already divided into cuts according to destination is propelled over the hump, and that the wagons in descending the steep gradient beyond separate out sufficiently to allow time for operation of the points between successive cuts, should this be necessary. In the process of acceleration, however, the speeds attained are such that if the wagons were allowed to continue unchecked they would cause widespread damage and derailment in the sorting sidings. Thus it is necessary to install retarders.

Until quite recently the degree of retardation in British yards was entirely under the control of an operator in the Tower. From this cut-list he had an approximate idea of the weight of the cut approaching ; from his observation point in the Tower he could make some estimate of whether it was running freely or not ; and he knew how full the particular siding into which it was routed happened to be at the time. From these factors he used his experience and judgment to decide upon what retarding force to apply. There is no doubt that the Tower operators in other British yards have attained a striking degree of proficiency in the operation of retarders. There are, however, many occasions when human judgment is not enough, and quite apart from the financial aspect of damage to goods arising from rough shunts or derailments, there is the time spent after a train has been humped in pushing wagons down to the foot of the sidings, when an operator, out of a natural caution and desire to avoid damage, is tending to apply a greater degree of retardation than is really necessary.

In consequence a great deal of research has taken place in recent years towards making the control of the retarders entirely automatic. The principles of the electronic computer have been utilised, and at Perth and elsewhere apparatus is installed to measure accurately the various factors that have to be taken into account in determining the retardation to be applied to each individual cut. The speed of an approaching wagon is measured by radar apparatus. Its running qualities—whether free or heavy —are also measured, while account is taken of how full the destination siding is. Another factor to be considered is the relative straightness or curvature of the route to be followed, as this can have a marked bearing upon how far a wagon, or cut, may run. A special weighing device is also installed in the track for registering the weight of the wagons in a cut. All these quantities are automatically registered as the cut is descending the hump, and duly 'fed' into the computer system. The complicated mathematical problem is worked out in a fraction of a second, in time for the correct air pressure to be applied at the primary retarder. Still more precise control is exercised when the cuts pass through the secondary, or group, retarders. At Perth there is one primary through which all cuts pass. Beyond the first sets of diverging points there are five group retarders, each regulating the running to a fan of six sidings.

The ideal condition for the marshalling of trains in sorting sidings such as these is for the wagons running down from the hump to arrive at such a speed that they gently buffer up with those already there. Fascinating as it is to watch the overall picture from the high vantage-point of the Control Tower in one of these modern yards, it is perhaps more impressive to one knowing something of the advanced modern engineering technique behind it, to stand down in the sorting sidings and see all sorts and conditions of wagons coming gently in, so that the shunters with their poles can slip the couplings of the arriving ones on to the stationary wagons without any fuss or further manoeuvring or shunting. Even in mechanised yards it was the usual practice for the humping engine to follow the last of the wagons into the sorting sidings, and to spend quite a time going from siding to siding pushing down wagons that had stopped short. Now nothing of that kind is needed, and once a train is humped the locomotive is free to deal with the next.

5

In all these new installations very careful attention is being paid to the architectural appearance of the major buildings, and at Perth in particular the new Control Tower is most striking. Above the rectangular ground floor, which houses all the intricate electrical equipment and the compressor plant to provide the compressed air supply for operation of the points and the retarders, rises a slender column supporting the Control Room. This room, which is polygonal in plan, is glazed from floor to ceiling on three sides, though due to the shape the glazing covers no fewer than seven facets on the sides facing the yard itself. The resulting lookout is extraordinarily good, not only from the extensive glazing, but from its height above ground level and from the absence of any intermediate storey in the building between the Control Room and the Apparatus Rooms on the ground floor.

6

From the underlying plan and the new policy in the siting and operation of the new marshalling yards, we come naturally to the trains themselves. In no region of the nationalised British Railways has the policy of speeding up freight services been more vigorously pursued than in Scotland. Concurrently with the policy of fitting wagons with continuous brakes, has been manifested a remarkable increase in the mileage run by fully fitted freight trains, so much so that as early after the launching of the modernisation plan as June 1957, the mileage run weekly in Scotland by such trains was more than double that in 1950, and the scheduled speeds were showing a steady increase. To give an added interest to staff and traders, and to foster that pride of

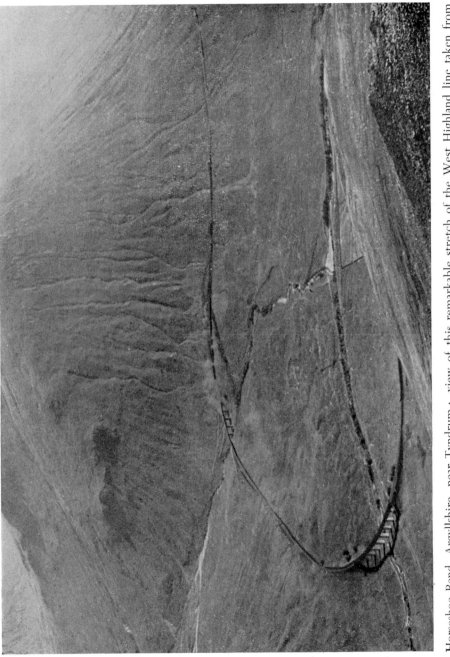

Horseshoe Bend, Argyllshire, near Tyndrum : view of this remarkable stretch of the West Highland line taken from the slopes of Beinn Dorain

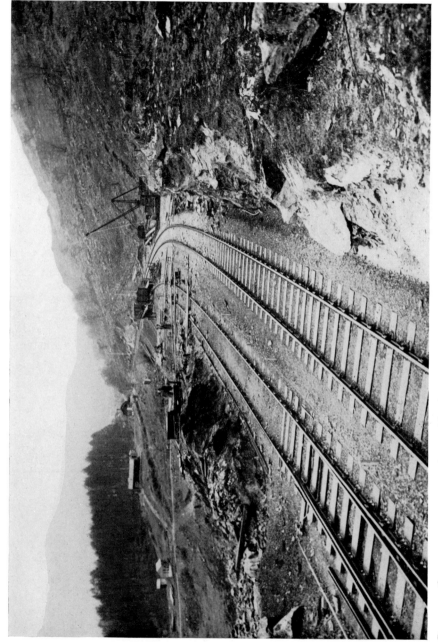

Recent railway construction in the Highlands: scene at Inveruglas where a new station has been built for the Loch Sloy hydro-electric scheme

On the West Highland line: a southbound freight ascends the grade beside Loch Treig

West Highland viaduct: characteristic example of Charles Forman's bridge work, with lattice girders supported on towers of masonry

achievement that inevitably leads to greater efficiency in working, a number of the more important trains have been given names— not in the high-sounding, old-established traditional style of the express passenger trains, but homely titles like *The Hielan' Piper*, *The Kitty*, *The Fifer*, and suchlike—not unreminiscent of those old but incomprehensible nicknames bestowed upon various broad-gauge goods services of the Great Western.

In 1948, when the first edition of this book was prepared, the total weekly mileage run by fully fitted freight trains in Scotland was less than 4,000 ; today there are no fewer than 729 such trains, and the weekly mileage is 78,877. The foregoing are trains working entirely within Scottish Region. Inter-regional traffic has also shown a notable increase. Today there are no fewer than 71 fully fitted freight trains crossing the Border daily, as compared with 53 as recently as three years ago. These are routed as follows :

Route	Trains		Total
	UP	DOWN	
via Berwick	12	14	26
via Hawick	8	5	13
via Carstairs	10	4	14
via Dumfries	11	7	18

The extent of the traffic from the larger centres can be judged from the nightly departures from Glasgow Buchanan Street Goods Station, namely :

5.42 p.m.	to	St Pancras
6.50 p.m.	to	Carlisle Kingmoor
7.5 p.m.	to	Carlisle Upperby
7.15 p.m.	to	Inverness
8.0 p.m.	to	Aberdeen
8.40 p.m.	to	Stirling
9.0 p.m.	to	Dundee
9.23 p.m.	to	Wolverhampton (Oxley Sidings)
10.45 p.m.	to	Carlisle Upperby

A most interesting feature of the freight-train development in Scotland is the extension of the fully fitted service to classes of traffic hitherto popularly considered to lie in the slowest grade of goods-train running. Now, express freight trains are run conveying iron ore in 33-ton wagons from Glasgow General terminus to two of Colville's great steel works, the Clyde Iron and the Ravenscraig works. Another new departure is the running of special wagons containing pallets of firebricks from Stirlingshire and Lanarkshire to the west of England.

In the winter service of 1960–1 the full list of named freight trains operating in and from Scotland is :

The Hielan' Piper	7.15 p.m.	Glasgow (Bell's Yard)–Inverness
The Killie	9.12 p.m.	Aberdeen–Kilmarnock
The Kitty	5.25 p.m.	Dumfries–Aberdeen (Kittybrewster)
The Galloway Piper	6.55 p.m.	Edinburgh–Stranraer
The Lothian Piper	6.0 p.m.	Stranraer–Edinburgh
The Fifer	8.20 p.m.	Irvine–Thornton
The Humber–Clyde	6.50 p.m.	Hull–Glasgow
The Condor	7.50 p.m.	Glasgow (Gushetfaulds)–London (Hendon)
	7.23 p.m.	London (Hendon)–Glasgow (Gushetfaulds)

In Scotland *The Condor* service is run non-stop in each direction between Gushetfaulds and Carlisle Citadel. The up train takes the Caledonian route, and has the sharp timing of 125 minutes for the 98·3 miles from Rutherglen Junction to Carlisle, pass to stop. When it is remembered that the now legendary 2 p.m. up West Coast ' Corridor ' express, hauled daily by the Caledonian 4–6–0 No. 903 *Cardean*, was allowed 135 minutes for the 102·3 miles from Glasgow Central to Carlisle, the remarkable nature of this modern freight-train booking will be realised. Over the 73·5 miles from passing Carstairs to Carlisle the allowance is only 83 minutes. On the down run, leaving Carlisle at 2.35 a.m., the Glasgow and South Western route is taken, and the overall average is not quite so spectacular, with 2 hours 33 minutes start to stop from Citadel station to Gushetfaulds Junction. Some of the intermediate timings, such as 69 minutes for the 58 miles from Dumfries to Kilmarnock, are practically equal to the best express passenger speeds. South of Carlisle the Midland route is taken throughout. These fine trains, diesel-hauled, are given a traffic priority equal to the West Coast passenger expresses, and the service as a whole forms an epitome of the enterprise of Scottish Region in developing freight-handling facilities on modern lines.

CHAPTER FIVE

The Great Scenic Routes of the West and North Highlands

I

THE *Waverley* was forging her way up the narrow fiord of Loch Long. It was a gloriously fine autumn day; the keen mountain air was tempered by the warmth of the sun, and the quiet broken by the rhythmical ' splash-splash ' of the paddles. My camera had been continuously ' at the ready ' since leaving Dunoon, and on this my first trip into the region I was keeping a look-out for a glimpse of the West Highland Railway, which I knew ran somewhere on the hills to our right. As the steamer turned out of Loch Goil and headed north I was attracted by an engine whistle; and a moment later I saw the train—yes, the train! From the deck of the steamer it looked like a tiny ' double-O ' gauge model, speeding along the skyline of the wild hills towering above us, and we watched it as it followed the curving track downhill, sometimes almost vanishing, then coming into full view, till it took the curve through Whistlefield and turned away downhill to Garelochhead. One of our party remarked what a marvellous ride it must be up there in the train, and to travel over the West Highland line became one of my great ambitions. That was in 1922, and it was not until nearly 10 years later that my ambition was realised, when, curiously enough, my first sight of the line was again from a steamer, though this time from the Portree mail boat berthing at Mallaig.

In the 140 miles of single track from Craigendoran, on the Firth of Clyde, to the dead-end on the jetty at Mallaig there are magnificent examples of practically every form of Scottish Highland scenery; what is more remarkable, in many places the railway provides unquestionably the finest viewpoint for seeing these noble prospects. For one thing the speed of trains on the West

66

Highland line is never very high: the maximum permitted at any point is 40 mph, as the curves are severe. But therein lies the almost indescribable fascination and charm of the route. The line, built to open up the country, was constructed as cheaply as possible; earthworks were kept down to a minimum, and the track twists and turns to follow the lie of the land. High above Loch Lomond it winds among the trees; up Glen Falloch it swings in and out of the ravines worn in the hillsides, and north of Tyndrum there is the celebrated Horseshoe Bend. In the country west of Loch Ailort the going is tougher still, with even the shallowest cutting revealing the naked rock, and the embankment sides sometimes bare of all vegetation.

The mountain prospects are sublime: Ben More and the half-circle of beetling crags behind Crianlarich as seen from the high altitude of Tyndrum station; the pine forests of the Black Mount seen across Loch Tulla; and above all the matchless picture of Ben Nevis while the train stands in Corpach station, with the white beacon-tower at the entrance to the Caledonian Canal and the seaweed-strewn shore of Loch Eil making so exquisite a foreground to the great massif across the water. But to appreciate something of the full majesty of the West Highland one must have seen it in many of its varied moods: in the fury of a mountain thunderstorm, in the dull haze of a Highland heatwave, or from the footplate of a snowplough engine when the snow is so deep in the cab that the young passed-cleaner who is firing the engine can hardly avoid shovelling a mixture of coal and snow into the firebox.

Just over three years ago at Eastertide I was making some locomotive observations up there, and one particular journey stands out as a vivid cross-section of West Highland operating. In the afternoon at Crianlarich the rain clouds had piled in from the west, though in the village itself the rain held off. But as I got into overalls and went out to join the 3.46 p.m. from Glasgow the clouds were touching down on the hills, and before the train arrived it was pouring. The passengers, most of them it seemed, made a concerted dash for the refreshment room directly the train stopped, while I climbed into the shelter of the engine cab to join the Fort William men who had taken over the working of the train at Ardlui. In those days engine troubles were not exceptional events, and on the gruelling climb up Glen Falloch the crew had had a somewhat rough passage; but the 10-minute halt at Crianlarich gave them a chance to do one or two jobs, and when we got the right-away they were ready for anything.

It was a wild thrilling occasion. I always find exultation in a mountain storm; the men set about their work with zest, and the very name of the engine, *Lord of the Isles*, could there have been one more appropriate on a train bound for Mallaig ? And so we drove out into the storm.

Up the exposed hillside towards Tyndrum we pounded away at 30 mph; over Charles Forman's slender viaducts, with the mountain streams below swollen into so many rampaging torrents, the wind and the rain caught us viciously, and although the cab of the *Lord of the Isles* normally provides excellent shelter in such a storm, to get the data I needed meant leaning out to sight and clock the quarter-mile posts—and on the windward side too! Leaving Tyndrum, with the mountains closing in on both sides of the line and the clouds down almost to rail-level, we fought our way uphill to the head of the pass, where at the Perth-Argyll County March the railway is 1,024 feet above sea-level. Then coasting downhill we came to the Horseshoe Bend. Expressions such as ' horseshoe,' when applied to the alignment of a railway, are usually picturesque exaggerations; but there is no exaggeration about the long detour from the slopes of Beinn Odhar, and on this April day the dark majesty of the glens was awe-inspiring in the extreme. Thick rain-laden clouds were drifting up the slopes of Beinn Dorain, the gloom in the corries was so intense as to suggest early nightfall. After the boisterous weather south of Tyndrum it was remarkably quiet and still in that mountain cul-de-sac, and we left a smoke trail that hung for miles behind us in the damp air. Red deer were feeding on the moorland just north of the Horseshoe; two big fellows with fine antlers

68

were actually on the railway track, and leapt nimbly over the fence as we bore down upon them.

But if rain and storm made more impressive than usual the ascent to the County March and the perambulation of the Horse-shoe Bend, the more open stretches northward from Bridge of Orchy are not seen at their best with the clouds low and the landscape seen but vaguely through a curtain of rain. Therein lies so often the fascination of the West Highland line, for a heavy storm is often followed by a quick clearing and hours of the most brilliant sunshine. From the windy expanse of Rannoch Moor famous peaks of the Atholl and Balmoral Highlands can be clearly distinguished on a good day. Then from Rannoch station, lying in the very heart of the moor, the track works its way to the summit, 1,347 feet above sea-level, at Corrour crossing, which takes its name from the shooting lodge in the Ben Alder country to the north-east. A lonely spot, but one of significance from the railway point of view, just as the equally lonely Aisgill on the Midland line southward from Carlisle, and Slochd on the Highland are important posts for the detaching of bank-engines. On the West Highland, if trains are heavy enough to require two engines, both work through from Glasgow to Fort William, or vice versa ; the spells of hard climbing are not confined to one particular stage of the journey, though in certain summer work-ings the crews of assistant engines are changed when the trains themselves halt to cross each other at Corrour.

Down the long grade on the hillside overlooking Loch Treig the railway descends from the bleak uplands of Rannoch and Corrour to the glens of Lochaber, and wheeling round at Tulloch to skirt the northern outlines of Ben Nevis, it comes soon to the Monessie Gorge where the Spean takes a spectacular course between rock-walls carved into fantastic shapes by the swirls and eddies of the torrent, and where from the engine cab one looks down sheer to the dark foaming waters. To anyone entranced with such a pageant of Highland scenery as we have passed through, Fort William is reached all too soon ; but for those travelling on to the west, or still farther to the Hebrides, this station on the shore of Loch Linnhe affords just a brief pause between the run over the West Highland Railway proper and the glories of the Mallaig extension.

At Fort William the co-ordination of rail, road and sea transport in the West Highlands is manifested. The MacBrayne bus station is at the pier-head, and while the train stands one can watch the coming and going of buses, and often see one of the stately red-funnelled steamers berthed alongside. But now, with a fresh engine attached to what has hitherto been the rear of the train, we are about to set off for the west. Seton Gordon has written: ' From Fort William west to Loch Ailort and Morar is as beautiful a country as can be found in all Scotland. . . .' Certainly it is threaded by a very notable piece of railway. There are, doubtless, strong differences of opinion as to what constitutes a beautiful country; and just as some would prefer the rich cultivation and fragrant woodlands of a southern English shire to the heathery wilderness and rock-bound tidal inlets of Moidart, so in railway affairs the winding, sharply graded track through that outstanding country, hewn for the most part from the solid rock, would be anathema to those who delight only in sustained high-speed running over a straight and almost level road.

For me, the character of the Mallaig extension railway was never more forcibly displayed than on a test journey made in that same Easter visit that I have mentioned earlier. On the day before I rode out from Fort William on the *Loch Laggan* I had been on a Pacific, the *Night Hawk*, riding over that incredibly straight and level road northward from York, with the country flat in every direction, and the engine purring along at 65 to 70 mph for half an hour at a stretch. On the second day, leaving Glasgow at dawn, we had seen snow lying on the heights of Argyll and Lochaber, but none remained on the hills west of Fort William, and the fine old birches by Loch Eil, with the leaves bursting, were a haze of pale green. It is beyond the head of Loch Eil that the railway assumes its most distinctive character: steeply downhill to the graceful concrete viaduct of Glenfinnan;

— O·S·NOCK —

London and North Eastern Railway: the *Flying Scotsman* in 1936, non-stop Edinburgh to King's Cross, on the cliffs overlooking the sea near Burnmouth. The engine is Gresley A3 Pacific No 2796 *Spearmint,* as well known in Edinburgh then as it is now

over the high pass and down again on a corkscrew alignment to the shores of Loch Eil, where the skill of the driver is displayed as much in his use of the brake as in securing maximum power output on the heavy ascents.

One feature of West Highland train working which always excites admiration is the smartness of the station working. No time is wasted in approaching the platforms; the drivers know the road to an inch, come in briskly, and make a clean stop dead on the mark. It is rare, too, for a train to stand as much as two minutes at a station. At Loch Ailort the line is high above that beautiful winding inlet of the sea, and in the next few miles even the most seasoned traveller might well be pardoned for losing all sense of direction as the train snakes its way through rock cuttings and tunnels, sweeps down to the concrete viaduct at the head of Loch nan Uamh, dives through another tunnel, and then, with the exhaust of the engine swelling into a rousing tattoo, enters upon the stiff climb through the birch woods to Beasdale. To me there is no more thrilling piece of railway in all Britain, and on this April day as the pace slowed down, and the exhaust of *Loch Laggan* developed into a positive roar, one could enjoy the sylvan beauty of the birch woods and see the carpet of fragrant mosses beneath the trees. The gradient is 1 in 48 here, and includes one particularly sharp curve; with a load of no more than five coaches speed fell to $17\frac{1}{2}$ mph.

Then once more there comes a swift change in the scene as the coast at Arisaig is neared, and framed in the ' V ' of a rock cutting is that most distinctive of West Highland summits, the Sgurr of Eigg. On the last stage, across the bleak moorlands of Keppoch, all eyes are towards the sea, where the inner Hebridean isles are displayed in all their strange ethereal beauty—Eigg, Rhum of the great peaks, and lastly Skye, on which keen mountaineers will identify one after another the splintered summits of the Cuillins. So to that tantalising viaduct over the River Morar, where one wants to look out of both carriage windows at once, seawards to the silver white sands, inland to the Falls of Morar; and finally to the stark, rocky shore of Mallaig, where on this same occasion the inhabitants were queued up at the station bookstall ready to buy the newspapers we had brought.

Like all these West Highland ports, Mallaig has its moments of intense activity. In the holiday season the arrival of the early morning express from Glasgow roughly coincides with the berthing of the mail boat from Portree, and on some days with the arrival of a steamer from the Outer Isles. On the quayside Scots fisher girls are busy gutting herrings; fish vans are alongside loading for the south-bound trains, and inward-bound passengers from the steamers thread their way through all this activity to the station. It was in this manner that I first came to Mallaig; and with some Highland journeys that I know, the tracing of the route in reverse ends with something of an anticlimax. But even in this respect the West Highland line is superb. One travels through the scenes of wonder on the Mallaig extension; then follow Monessie, Corrour, Rannoch, the Horseshoe Bend, and Crianlarich. By the time the train has wound its way down Glen Falloch and alongside the upper reaches of Loch Lomond, the traveller might well feel that journey's end was approaching, and that with a sigh of satisfaction he might sink into his corner and doze till Glasgow was neared. But to anyone with an eye for scenery, the stretch from Arrochar to Garelochhead is one of the finest of all, and inviting though the line may look from a steamer sailing on Loch Long, the sight of the loch itself from the high altitude of the railway usually provides one of the most memorable sights of the whole trip. So it was on that Easter journey of mine, three years ago, when, at seven in the morning, we came out on to the brink of the hillside at Whistlefield, saw the waters still as a mirror at the confluence of Loch Goil and Loch Long; snow lying deep in the high clefts of the mountains, and heather at the lineside bathed in hoar frost under a cloudless sky.

2

At Crianlarich the West Highland Railway crosses the one-time Caledonian line to Oban, but apart from the new service from Glasgow (Queen St) to Oban referred to in chapter three, there are no advertised connections, and it is indeed rare for trains on one line to be seen from the other. And while Crianlarich is of some importance as the half-way house between Glasgow and Fort William, on the Oban line it is a mere wayside station. The latter railway has forged its way up through the Pass of Leny, and alongside Loch Lubnaig to the charming village of Strathyre, and to Balquhidder, junction for the line to Crieff and Perth. It is on leaving Balquhidder that one of the great prospects of the Oban line opens out. The track mounts high up the hillside, and reveals the entire length of Loch Earn stretching away beyond St Fillans. Little by little this fair scene is cut off as the train pounds on into the wild and narrowing moraine of Glen Ogle. The Clan class engines of the former Highland Railway were transferred to the Oban line in the thirties, and their capacity for hard slogging was never displayed better than on this long 1 in 60 ascent from Balquhidder to Glenoglehead. I have vivid memories of fine runs with *Clan Munro*, with *Clan Mackenzie* and with *Clan Mackinnon*; best of all, however, was a run with *Clan Chattan* when a load of no fewer than ten corridor coaches was taken up the hill at a steady 17 to 18 mph.

From Glenoglehead the country traversed by the Oban line is for the most part wild and bare, and it is not until the train has passed through Crianlarich and Tyndrum and begun the steep descent of Glen Lochy that any appreciable change takes place. Passing through Tyndrum today, one cannot easily visualise the little place at the height of its glory. Before the coming of the railway it was an important coaching station lying at the junction of the routes to Fort William and Oban. Its importance was at first enhanced by the construction of the railway, for the line from Callander proved much more costly than had been expected and funds ran out when construction had proceeded only as far as Tyndrum. The one-time coaching station then became a railhead for the bulk of West Highland tourist traffic, and the remains of the old terminus can be seen today in what looks like a surprisingly large goods yard lying below the present

73

station. For a period of four years Tyndrum played its unforeseen role. In the meantime a new Act had been passed authorising
the extension of the line, and in 1877 the section to Dalmally
was opened.

It is in the steep descent of Glen Lochy that Cruachan first
comes into the picture. This great mountain, viewed in its
distant and dominating aspect from away to the west on the Firth
of Lorne, has two peaks; but from the Dalmally side no fewer
than five can be counted, all of about the same height, and this
grand prospect is seen to advantage in the railway approach to
Dalmally. The track passes near the fine ruin of Kilchurn Castle,
then winds round the head of Loch Awe, a broad lowland mere
by comparison with the majority of Highland lochs, nevertheless
assuming true western grandeur in the narrow outlet that stretches
far into the Pass of Brander. Here the railway is running on the
very slopes of Cruachan, on a stretch where precautions have to
be taken against falls of rock. Some little distance up the mountain-
side there is a fence of wires; these wires act as rock-detectors,
and if any one of them were broken by falling boulders, a series
of special semaphore signals on the railway would be put to
danger as a warning to traffic. Despite this precaution there
was an accident here in August 1946, when a large boulder crashed
on to the line just in front of the 6.5 a.m. train from Oban to
Glasgow. Although the driver applied the brakes promptly he could
not avert a derailment, though fortunately there were no casualties.

Emerging from the Pass of Brander one soon sees ahead Tay-
nuilt and the blue waters of Loch Etive. I have written the
word ' blue ' because I always seem to have been fortunate in
travelling along this next stage in brilliant weather, when sunshine has accentuated the vivid colouring of the loch, of the
distant hills, and, not least, of the saffron yellow seaweed on
the shore near Ach-na-Cloich. The railway follows the lie of
the land in this green countryside of Lorne, though even here
the slightest cutting reveals the naked rock, and there are several
short bursts of hard pulling on gradients of 1 in 50 or so. Along
this stretch the fine cantilever viaduct at Connel Ferry can be

seen stretching over Loch Etive; across this bridge passes the branch line from Connel Ferry Junction, which runs through the Stewart country of Appin to Loch Leven and Ballachulish. And so over the steep crest of Glencruitten to Oban itself, where the haunting air of a Hebridean port is mingled with the gay life of a popular resort. The little steamers come in from Barra and South Uist; in the summer another one makes the journey to sacred Iona, and for those who, in this age of hustle, can still find time to travel at leisure on their holidays, there is that choicest way to the north, by the MacBrayne steamer to Fort William.

3

The third railway port on the seaboard of the West Highlands is Kyle of Lochalsh. One could hardly imagine a more exquisite setting: a narrow waterway between high mountains; the picturesque fragment of Castle Maol beside Kyleakin village on the opposite shore, and at the railway jetty, the friendly red-funnelled MacBrayne steamers once again. The railway did not come to Kyle of Lochalsh till 1897, only four years before the Mallaig extension of the West Highland was completed. Until then Strome Ferry had been the western railhead of the High-land Railway, but that final extension of $10\frac{1}{2}$ miles, for the most part blasted from solid rock, brought the line almost to the shores of Skye. From the outset—even before the extension to Kyle—the railway was known as the 'Dingwall and Skye,' and the grand little 4–4–0 engines that worked the traffic were known as the Skye Bogies. As long as forty years ago they might have been thought diminutive machines, but they proved ideal for the Kyle road, riding the sharp curves easily and taking the heavy gradients in their stride. In their stride—yes, until developments consequent upon the merging of the Highland Railway in the LMS group put heavy corridor coaches on to the Kyle trains, and later added restaurant cars. Nevertheless as recently as 1927 I photographed the morning train from Kyle coming finely up the bank by Loch Luichart with a Skye Bogie.

I shall never forget a journey I made in 1932 in the company of an islesman, a shepherd in late middle age who at infrequent intervals made some laconic remarks on the trip. This was on the morning train from Inverness, and at Achnasheen we crossed the train from Kyle running in connection with the mail boat from Portree. The up train was made up of early London and North Western corridor stock with a clerestory-roofed Midland restaurant car in which passengers were at lunch. The old shepherd viewed the train dispassionately and then remarked: ' Ay; there's some swanky trains going to Kyle now.' The rigours of the old Highland non-corridor coaches had to be experienced to be fully appreciated; but once they were replaced it was not long before the gallant little ' Skye Bogies ' followed them to the scrap-heap.

Leaving Kyle for Dingwall the railway winds incessantly along the southern shore of Loch Carron, plunging through each successive hillock in a vertical-sided rock-cutting. Looking out over the sound one catches glimpses of the great hills of Skye, though from this angle the Cuillins are practically obscured by the smooth rounded heights of the Red Hills. Soon the broad expanse of Loch Carron, as seen from the train, contracts to a narrow kyle, and we come to Strome Ferry. For the next twenty miles or so from this point the railway follows a very characteristic piece of West Highland scenery: first the fiord between the mountains, the water becoming shallower till the point is reached where the loch is silted up; beyond this comes the green and level strath, with the surrounding mountains noticeably higher, and then the head of the inlet is reached, and ascent of the narrowing glen begins. In the Carron country the run alongside the upper reaches of the loch and up the pleasant levels of Strathcarron is accompanied to the north by a constantly changing panorama of mountain splendour: clouds above the nearby towering mass of Sgorr Ruadh, throwing an intense blue shade over her crest; a distant glimpse of the dazzling white quartz-tipped peak of Beinn Eighe, and then the railway swings over from the south to the north side of the valley and comes under the shoulder of the hills.

The crossing station of Achnashellach roughly marks the end of the level going, and trains take water here before tackling the heavy ascent of Glen Carron. As the train stands at the curved platform where pinewoods clothe the steep hillside above the railway, and where the fragrant scents of heather and peat mingle with that of the pines themselves, the traveller sees on ahead the magnificent grouping of the heights south-east of the glen—Sgurr Nan Ceannaichean, Moruisg and the outer range of the Glencarron Forest. Past these heights, seen in all the fascination of changing colours from the constant play of light and shade from the sun and clouds, the train pounds its way up the glen, rarely doing more than 25 mph, and as the summit of the pass is neared the railway enters a high region where the hill forms are smoother, and the prospect is more open and bleak. The watershed is passed, and a brisk downhill run brings the train to the intermediate station of Achnasheen, an important exchange point for mail and tourist traffic.

Achnasheen stands at the road junction leading to the celebrated regions of Loch Maree, Glen Torridon, and Gairloch—a paradise alike for fishermen, rock climbers and lovers of wild nature in all its forms. Coaches connect with the Kyle trains, and altogether Achnasheen is one of the busiest intermediate stations on the route. Up the glen leading to the head of Loch Maree is another of those startling glimpses of snow-white Beinn Eighe. Eastwards the line leads through the windswept, treeless expanse of Strath Bran, beneath the volcano-like cone of Sgurr A'Mhuilinn and the fringe of Loch Luichart to Garve, the second road junction for the north-western seaboard. From here a road strikes off on a long desolate run that leads ultimately to some further magnificent districts, Dundonnell, Loch Broom, Ullapool and the wild coast road to Lochinver. In the meantime the Dingwall and Skye Railway, nearing its eastern end, passes through some rugged country which, though not spectacular in itself, afforded ample difficulties in construction, and has left one severe handicap to train operation.

Loch Garve is 220 feet above sea-level. The Black Water

issuing from it falls 150 feet in 2 miles, and whereas the main road follows this river in its descent, the rough intervening country in the neighbourhood of the picturesque falls of Rogie evidently deterred those who built the line, for they carried their track to the north of the Raven Rock and came down practically to sea-level by a 1 in 50 gradient 4 miles long through Achterneed. Thus came the inconvenience of having the Highland spa of Strathpeffer at the terminus of a short branch line from Dingwall instead of on the main line to Skye. Achterneed serves as the station to and from the west, but it is one mile away, and there is a certain amount of service duplication between Strathpeffer and Dingwall. This could have been avoided if the main line had been carried through Strathpeffer, and onwards to Garve up the glen past the Falls of Rogie. So far as one can judge from a study of the contours, the gradients would have been easier than the present toilsome ascent to the Raven Rock. But the necessary way-leave could not then be obtained and the route through Achterneed was the second choice.

4

And so at Dingwall we come to the Highland main line at a point 18½ miles north of Inverness. It is good to pause here for a moment before continuing to the far north. Personal acquaintance with this furthermost chain of British railway communication, so relatively long, so slender, yet always so virile, came at a fairly late stage in my railway exploration of Scotland. I was getting to know other Highland routes fairly well; I had ridden West Highland and Oban engines in all weathers, but the Far North was known to me only from a distance. I had studied the gradients, and from large-scale contoured maps the lie of the land; from Nairn on the Moray Firth I had often seen the mountains of Sutherland and Caithness, and had painted them in water colours. But still there remained that lack of personal experience. When the opportunity did eventually come the experience was one never to be forgotten. It came during a spell

of some of the finest and clearest weather I can ever recall in
Scotland, and in setting out for Wick I enjoyed once again that
privileged ' front seat '—in the engine cab.

Leaving Dingwall for the very ' back of beyond ' as it were,
the single-tracked railway runs at first through the strip of good
farming country lying between the sea and the smooth rounded
hills of Easter Ross. Even amid such gentle undulations the line
follows the lie of the land, and changes in gradient are frequent.
Alongside the Cromarty Firth there are some fine prospects, but
after the grandeur of the western end of the Skye line the scenery
is placid, though none the less delightful. There is a hint of
something wilder in store as the train, in crossing the isthmus
between the Firths of Cromarty and Dornoch, swings round
north-westwards and the mountains of Sutherland come into view,
again with that variety that provides the almost endless charm
of a Scottish journey.

One could hardly imagine a greater contrast than between
Loch Carron and the Dornoch Firth; both long winding inlets
of the sea and both supremely beautiful, but Dornoch has something of the air of those wide smiling Devon estuaries while Loch
Carron has that dramatic west coast beauty of great crags, deep
clear water, and of the Hebrides lying across the sound. But
even on the east coast communication is mostly by leisurely
means. From Tain, 44 miles from Inverness, Dornoch itself can
be seen only 5 miles across the water, but the journey is more
than 29 miles by road, and no less than 44 by rail. The road
takes the shortest cut, round the head of the firth at Bonar Bridge,
but in constructing the railway other considerations had to be
borne in mind. This northern main line was the result of a series
of different enterprises, the line as far as Bonar Bridge being an
extension of the Inverness and Aberdeen Junction Railway, and
was opened in 1864. In the following year the Sutherland Railway was incorporated, which authorised the continuation of the
route to Golspie on the coast some 8 miles north of Dornoch
in a direct line.

It would have been a comparatively simple matter to construct this stretch of railway through the level country on the north side of the Dornoch Firth, putting Dornoch on the direct line to the south, but the promoters wished to serve the hinterland of Sutherlandshire as well, possibly with an extension to the north-west coast later. So instead of taking the easy and obvious route, they carried the railway up the glen of the River Shin to Lairg, where junction was made with roads leading through the north-west Highlands to Laxford Bridge, to Durness and to Tongue. As to possible branch lines, the need for developing rural areas in the Highlands by the provision of better transport led to a suggestion in 1918 for the construction of a line from Culrain to Lochinver, among others; but the rapid advance in facilities that could be provided by road transport killed such a suggestion, and today Lairg remains the railhead of western Sutherland—often quite busy with tourist traffic in the summer, and at all times a focal point for traffic arising from the sheep-farming industry.

Whatever other considerations may arise from the circuitous and heavily graded route taken by the old Sutherland Railway from Bonar Bridge to Golspie, this inland deviation provides some of the finest scenes on the farther north main line. The great single-span viaduct over the Kyle of Sutherland at Invershin marks the entry to real ' Highland ' country once again; from its height one looks westward up the richly wooded Strath Oykell, and through the other carriage window to Dornoch and the sea. When I came south the last time, in the cloudless weather of May 1948, I was again riding in the engine cab, and at Invershin station we drew up with the engine and tender actually on the viaduct. The brilliant weather was accompanied by extra-ordinarily clear visibility, and we looked down to the shimmer-ing waters of the Kyle, to the rich greens of new foliage in the nearby forests and away to the blues and purples of distant ranges. The ' right-away ' from our guard came all too soon for me!

We are, however, travelling north now rather than south, and at once the railway bears away to the right from Strath Oykell, and on a heavy gradient works its way up the glen towards Lairg.

To a measured thunderous beat from the engine, fighting a 1 in 72 gradient, we climb slowly through a profusion of lovely old birch-woods; even in May the earth was carpeted with prim-roses, and there were many glimpses far below of the brawling, tossing River Shin. At Lairg the track turns eastward again through bleak moorland country, over which to the north-west can be glimpsed the jagged peaks of Ben Klibreck. The summit point, 488 feet above sea-level, is reached 3 miles west of the crossing-loop of Acheilidh, after which the line follows the River Fleet downhill through Rogart to the Mound Junction. This station takes its name from the embankment, or mound, con-structed by Telford in 1815 across the estuary of the River Fleet. The branch line to Dornoch runs alongside the highway over the Mound. Here again the prospect from a main-line train is very fine, with the almost landlocked Fleet estuary spread out below, and beyond the water the crag of Creag Amaill imparting almost a west-coast touch to the scene.

After leaving the Mound Junction the Highland Railway for the first time comes in full sight of the open sea, and looking through the cab glasses I thought involuntarily of other stretches of that long line of communication through from the south of England, where the tracks are carried on or near the cliffs of the North Sea: Alnmouth, Beal, Goswick and Scremerston at the gateway to Scotland; the Border, by Lamberton Toll, and then Burnmouth. There are some great stretches on the Aberdeen main line, too, at Lunan Bay, and from Stonehaven to that dramatic rounding of the curve by Girdleness Lighthouse, to the final entry into Aberdeen. And here again, heading north from Golspie and pounding away up the 1 in 60 gradient towards Dunrobin, one has the same feeling, that eagerness to press on, to see what lies beyond the next headland, and with all the greater eagerness here as we are now getting within measurable distance of John o' Groats. There is a glimpse of Dunrobin Castle near at hand as we pass through the Duke of Sutherland's private station, and then after emerging from the woods we bowl along over the narrow stretch of farming and grassland between the flanks of

Ben Uarie and the brilliant blue sea. Very soon now wilder hills begin to extend towards the coast line, and then on a steeply rising gradient the railway turns inland into Helmsdale Station.

Actually Wick is now no more than 30 miles ahead, following straight up the coast; but here again as between Bonar Bridge and Golspie, those who built the railway had to satisfy as many districts as possible in carrying the one line to the far north. Thurso had claims almost as great as those of Wick, fortunately so in view of its immense strategic importance in two world wars, and again communication with the north coast had to be provided. So instead of going straight on from Helmsdale, the line was carried almost due west at first up Strath Ullie, alongside the road to Golval and Reay Bridge. The track mounts gradually through a rough and increasingly bleak countryside, through Kildonan and Kinbrace till it reaches Forsinard, an inn about halfway between north and east coasts. Forsinard is a mere oasis, set in surely the bleakest moorland country it is possible to see anywhere in Scotland, and from here the track, now un-accompanied by any road, climbs to an altitude of 708 feet at the Sutherland-Caithness County March.

In this cloudless May weather the deep brown of the moor-land had a warmth, a golden tinge, and the sweet reek of the peat bogs mingled with the composite smells of the engine cab. But even on so fair a day there was something about that slender ribbon of a railway, stretching over so seemingly boundless an expanse of heathery, utterly depopulated countryside, that sent a slight shiver down the spine. For mile after mile, from Forsinard over the County March and on to the north of Alt-na-Breac, there was ranged that ominous double line of snow fences, standing well back from the line of railway, and one thought of times when the moor is scourged by snow, visibility is just nil, and the train is fighting against an elemental fury of driving snow and sleet. As the train came down the gradient now the wilder-ness gradually gave place to some signs of cultivation, and—striking the passenger with perhaps complete surprise—this northernmost tip of Scotland is almost dead flat! The whole landscape, in the late afternoon sunshine, is green and smiling, with smallholdings dotted as far as the eye can see and soon after 4 o'clock the train draws into Georgemas Junction, barely 7 miles from Thurso. The branch train is waiting to take the through carriage we have brought from Inverness, and the main portion turns away south-east now to run the final 14 miles into Wick.

As a spectacle the journey's end is a complete anticlimax. Here is no magnificent finale, like that of the Great Western at Penzance, or of the old London and North Western at Holyhead. Where one might perhaps expect to run alongside Wick harbour, with all the activities of the fishing industry displayed, the Highland Railway instead reaches its dead end in a rather humdrum covered-in little station on the outskirts of the town. But then one realises that the arrival at Wick is not after all the finale, but the close of the penultimate act. High tea is waiting in the hotel, and having done ample justice to that, we find the warm spring evening ideal for the final run, 17 miles over dead-level roads to John o' Groats. Here indeed was a finale, beyond the range of Scottish railways it is true, but a finale of utter magnificence, with the evening sun gilding the heights of distant Orkney and the blue waters of the Pentland Firth turning to green as the colour paled from the sky overhead. No words of mine could describe the beauty of that northern evening.

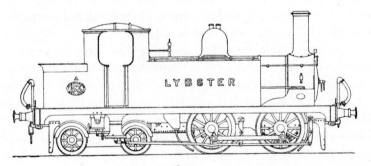

CHAPTER SIX

THE CLYDE COAST

I

THE Cloch promontory, round which the Clyde wheels to the final and most majestic reach of the firth, was from ancient times a key point in western Scottish transportation. There was no township there, nor even a natural harbour; it was just the nearest point to the opposite shore. There were good reasons too why traffic to that opposite shore, of Cowal, was not great. The coast of Renfrewshire was ' front-line ' territory when Lowland Scotland had to keep an exceedingly wary eye on the Highlands, and dreadful stories of the days of clan warfare lingered and made the shores opposite the Cloch forbidding to all except the few Highland lairds that were in the habit of coming to the mainland, and an occasional merchant who ventured westwards by way of Cowal. An old mail coach brought those hardy travellers to Greenock, and from there they had to make their own way over the eight miles to the Cloch. For more than 150 years the charter for the right of ferry over this waterway was held by the Campbells of Ballochyle, one of the conditions being that they should have an eight-oared galley ready at any moment to convey the Marquis of Argyll to the Renfrew shore. The ferry terminus on the Cowal shore was a Highland clachan, and in 1822 it consisted of a church, a manse, three or four slated cottages and a few thatched huts. Its name was Dunoon.

From the Cloch travellers awaiting the ferry looked out on one of the greatest prospects in Scotland: the great sweep of the Firth itself, from Helensburgh to Kilchattan and the lighthouse on Little Cumbrae, and those dark mysterious-looking sea-lochs winding away northwards into the mountains; the smooth hills of Cowal opposite, with the loftier, steeper and wilder peaks beyond the Holy Loch. And over this whole scene in all but the

84

most exceptional weather the colours are constantly changing; the ceaseless play of light and shade is fascinating to watch, as squall follows sunshine and a brilliant scene re-emerges from behind a dense curtain of rain. But even as those travellers of 125 years ago waited for the ferry, the stage was already set for a transformation without parallel in any region of Great Britain. In August 1812 the people of Glasgow went to the Broomielaw to witness the departure of the quaint little ship *Comet* on her first trip to Helensburgh; few, if any of them, realised the supreme significance of what they saw—certainly the first British steamship, but far more, the pioneer of passenger steamship services in the Firth of Clyde. The *Comet* was not a commercial success, and in the unrest following the end of the Napoleonic wars little development took place; but from 1825 things began to move more rapidly, and by 1840 there were several companies operating ships on the Firth. Then in March 1841 came the completion of the Glasgow, Paisley and Greenock Railway.

2

Fifty years later, in taking that splendid walk from Gourock to the Cloch, a keen-eyed observer could count at least ten piers, and would see the steamers of three railways and of many independent steamboat companies plying in those waters. Older residents on the Renfrew shore, recalling the deserted ferry at the Cloch, might well rub their eyes as they saw the rival railway steamers putting out from Greenock, while another competitor, outward-bound from Helensburgh, left a snowy wake to the north as she too raced for Dunoon. Raced! The competition of those halcyon days does indeed seem incredible when studied in retrospect; no less incredible in these expensive times seem the fares, such as 2s 6d return from Glasgow to Rothesay. Most of the piers in the Firth of Clyde are picturesque little wooden jetties, heavily built it is true, but large enough to take only one steamer at a time. The first boat to arrive would gain anything up to ten minutes on her rivals, and in that breathless competitive period when in running the rival services even minutes counted, the steamers raced pell-mell for the piers. Quite apart from the racing, the spectacle of a lovely Clyde paddle-steamer sweeping in to call at a pier in one of the fiords adds a touch of rare distinction to the most beautiful of scenes: the dark heather-clad hillside; the shore so steep that the jetty extends for no more than fifty yards from the water's edge; that expectant little group of people on the pier, and then the steamer with its trim lines and gaily painted funnel, a fine Scots name, and the ever-fascinating ' splash-splash ' of the paddles as they churn the clear water into pale-green foam.

From the earliest days of railway service to the Clyde coast, when the Glasgow, Greenock and Paisley Railway, and later the Wemyss Bay Company, plunged with more enthusiasm than discretion into the running of steamer services, competition blazed away like fire on a parched heathland. One company would gain the advantage and the traffic; another would build a new line, new piers and new steamers and turn the tables on its rival. It was a case of all against all, cut and thrust without quarter, for close upon fifty years; and, as the competition grew, so did the magnitude of the new works undertaken, until the climax was reached in the million-pound extension of the Caledonian Railway from Greenock to Gourock pier. In view of earlier references to the sparsely populated regions of the Highland shores of the firth it might well be wondered what was the object of all the competition; but, having discovered the charms of the firth in many a day's sail, the folks of Glasgow began to build summer residences at such places as Kilcreggan and Cove; business began to spring up at Dunoon and Rothesay, for the multitudes coming for the day by boat must needs be fed and otherwise entertained during their brief sojourn. And then of course the English partners of the Scottish trunk railways began to develop the tourist traffic from the south. From their earlier and rather amateurish efforts at steamboat-operating the railway companies gradually developed the most perfectly co-ordinated train and steamer services that have ever been seen anywhere.

London Midland and Scottish Railway: the celebrated 3-cylinder 4–6–0 express locomotive No 6100 *Royal Scot* built 1927 by the North British Locomotive Company. The engine carries the bell presented in commemoration of the North American tour 1933

The Glasgow, Paisley and Greenock Railway being first in the field had the choice of route, and naturally took that with the easiest gradients. From Paisley the line struck out through relatively flat country straight for the firth, and so was able to skirt the range of hills lying immediately behind Greenock and Port Glasgow. The terminus was at Cathcart Street station, but was some little distance from the Custom House quay whence the steamers sailed. Passengers had to make their own way between station and quay, and, although sailings were arranged in connection with the trains, the arrangements for transfer devolved largely upon the passengers themselves. But with the recollection of the Cloch ferry still in mind, the arrangements at Greenock were accepted by the public, at any rate until something better was provided. That ' something better ' did not, however, come from the Caledonian Railway, which powerful company had absorbed the Glasgow, Paisley and Greenock in 1851; it was the Greenock and Ayrshire line, an associate of the Glasgow and South Western, that forced the pace. Leaving the Glasgow-Ayr main line well to the west of Paisley, this new route headed for Greenock through the hill country, and on heavy gradients reached a summit point high above Port Glasgow. As the train breasts this summit the prospect that opens out to the north is magnificent, with the firth immediately below, and the varied scene blocked in on the northern horizon by Ben Lomond and the Glen Falloch mountains.

Down this hillside the Ayrshire Railway carried its line steeply into Greenock; more than that, it continued almost to the water's edge, and a first-class railway passenger port was established at Princes Pier. The pier itself was, however, the property of the Greenock Harbour Trust. The resulting slump in Caledonian Railway business was followed by a spectacular reply in the form of the Gourock scheme. It was certainly a conception in the grand manner, this extension of the line through Fort Matilda to the western arm of Gourock Bay. The little stone pier that served the handful of houses had been acquired in 1866, but the scheme envisaged then had been abandoned in 1869. Under the new project a port was constructed which could compete at least on level terms with the Princes Pier. The construction of the railway involved some very heavy engineering work including massive retaining walls and the longest tunnel in Scotland—all in addition to the port itself at Gourock Bay. Although following a sinuous course the track was aligned for fast running, and it was not long before that facility was being exploited to the utmost. For the completion of Gourock in 1889 put the Caledonian and Glasgow and South Western strategically on almost equal terms, and henceforth the fight for the traffic was to be conducted on the relative convenience, speed and comfort of the rival services. For a time, at any rate, it seems that comfort was the least important of those three considerations, for when trains and steamers are racing, passengers are apt to be hustled in a manner that can be a little disconcerting.

It was not as though the fight was a straight one between the Caledonian and Glasgow and South Western. In 1866 the North British obtained control of the Glasgow and Helensburgh Railway, and while the two fierce rivals on the south side of the firth were jockeying for position, the ' interloper '—for so the North British was regarded in the west of Scotland—was building a new railway port at Craigendoran, at the eastern end of Helensburgh. There the Clyde coast traffic could be handled independently of the profitable residential business in Helensburgh itself, which the North British was actively fostering. The establishment of a first-class passenger port at Craigendoran and its opening in 1883 attained an added significance very soon afterwards when the North British gave active support to the project of building a railway through the West Highlands to Fort William. The first scheme—the Glasgow and North Western Railway Company, which proposed the construction of a line from Maryhill and through Strathblane to the eastern side of Loch Lomond—was rejected by Parliament in 1884; but the second contained the stroke of inspiration that eventually knit the entire North British workings west of Glasgow into a well-co-ordinated organism.

This second proposal, which received Parliamentary assent in

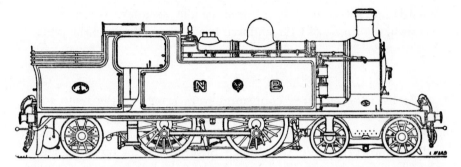

1889, was for the construction of a line northward from Craigendoran. At that time transport in the West Highlands was in
a very primitive state; tourist traffic was catered for locally, by
coach services in the Trossachs and more frequented beauty spots,
but the establishment of the new West Highland Railway on a
Clyde coast port like Craigendoran opened up the prospects of
very attractive combined railway and steamer tours, all under the
direct aegis of the North British Railway. Craigendoran itself is
one of the pleasantest of the railway ports. At the entrance to
the Gareloch, it lies away from the main shipping route to the
Glasgow docks and the industrialism of Greenock; the Highland
hills close at hand make an impressive background, and yet from
this relative seclusion the North British steamer services were
able to compete on level terms with those of the other two railways in the daily race to Dunoon. The run down from Glasgow
is over a fairly easy road, through Clydebank and Old Kilpatrick
and round the sweep of the river at Bowling, where some of the
North British steamers could usually be seen lying up during the
winter months. Then comes Dumbarton, and the widening firth,
with broad views across to Greenock and beyond, and then the
fast final run along the water's edge till a curve in the line at
Ardmore brings Helensburgh itself into the picture. Then only
the veriest dullard could fail to be thrilled by a scene wherein
the animation of the steamer port has as its background the constantly changing lights and colours on the mountains and the vast
expanse of sky, or fail to experience the eager anticipation of going

aboard the splendid gaily painted paddle steamer, which even in this first glimpse of Craigendoran can be seen alongside the pier.

3

So by 1889 all three companies were armed to the teeth for the battle of the Clyde resorts. The Caledonian, profiting by earlier misfortunes in the steamer business, had launched a subsidiary enterprise, the Caledonian Steam Packet Company, and the Glasgow and South Western countered the building of Gourock by putting on a fleet of new steamers, some of the most luxurious ever to sail the Clyde. The competition reached its greatest heights of intensity in the residential services, morning and evening. In the morning one could stand on the hill above Gourock and count as many as twelve steamers at once converging upon the mile and a half of waterway that separates Renfrewshire from the Kilcreggan shore, all racing in to berth to Craigendoran, Princes Pier or Gourock as the case might be. In the evening the Glasgow terminal stations between them dispatched eleven trains in the half-hour following 4 p.m., and with these were associated no fewer than thirteen steamers. The Caledonian permitted no luggage on its Clyde coast expresses, and a modest two minutes was allowed at Gourock between the arrival of the train and departure of the boat. The allowance at Craigendoran was three minutes. In later years the Caledonian built some most luxurious coaching stock specially for these trains; these coaches were carried on six-wheeled bogies and were generally

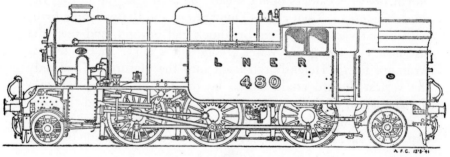

the same as the celebrated ' Grampian ' stock, except that they were non-corridor. While every effort was made to provide everything possible in the way of comfort, weight-saving was equally important. The use of corridor stock would have seriously reduced the seating capacity and made it necessary to run extra coaches.

There was a striking individuality about the engines working the coast trains. Although the duties were generally similar, and all three companies constructed special engines for the job, the designs were in great contrast to one another. In early days the North British Railway had three very handsome 4–4–0 tank engines for the boat trains, and they were duly named *Craigendoran*, *Roseneath* and *Helensburgh* in great gilt letters on the tank sides, after the Brighton style. The Caledonians of the 1880–1900 period were 4–4–0 tender engines, in the Prussian blue then standard, and generally similar, save for their smaller driving wheels, to the main-line engines that so distinguished themselves in 1895 in the racing of the night expresses to Aberdeen. The Glasgow and South Westerns, perhaps the least distinctive in outline and colour, long outlasted their contemporaries; indeed James Manson's ' Greenock bogies ' were still on the job in 1930, and still doing yeoman work. By that time the world-famous ' Dunalastairs ' had come and gone from the Gourock route, and the massive six-coupled bogie tanks were pounding up the grade from Port Glasgow towards Wemyss Bay. On the north side of the firth Clydebank, Dalmuir and Dumbarton were echoing oft-times to the quick syncopated tattoo of the Gresley V I 2–6–2 tanks, and the big English ' Moguls ' essayed the West Highland trains. By the middle thirties the old Scottish individualism on the Clyde railways was passing rapidly away— at any rate so far as locomotive power was concerned; but the working lost nothing of its old smartness, even though Gourock and Princes Pier were by then in close alliance.

The Caledonian had its share of heavy gradients, though not on the most hotly competitive route. The Wemyss Bay Railway was built to secure a monopoly of the Rothesay traffic by the establishment of a railway port on the mainland almost opposite to Toward Point, the entrance to Rothesay Bay. To cut across the hilly country inland from the Cloch, the Wemyss Bay line climbs at the steep inclination of 1 in 67½ through Upper Greenock, giving views from the carriage windows that bid fair to eclipse that ' best walk in Scotland,' from Gourock to the Cloch. Then, turning southward into the hills and with the going much faster, the line comes to the shore at Inverkip, and soon after to the fine, dignified and—yes, beautiful terminus at Wemyss Bay. Whatever may with justification have been said, and written, about the dirt and dismal atmosphere of British railway stations in general, such a stigma could rarely be applied to the Caledonian, least of all at Wemyss Bay: a glass roof over the concourse with white timberwork and hanging floral baskets, clean spacious platforms and a fine covered way leading to the pier, this station, whether in Caledonian or later days, was a credit to Scotland.

In former times one came down from the train to find those lovely paddle steamers *Duchess of Rothesay*, *Duchess of Fife* or the *Marchioness of Breadalbane* berthed alongside. The transfer was never made in such hectic style as at Gourock or Craigendoran, for the Caledonian with the longer rail journey had a flying start on its rivals for the Rothesay traffic. Nevertheless, one crossed the firth smartly enough, and after a brief halt at Craigmore pier, the steamer came alongside at Rothesay, a veritable ' Crewe ' of the Clyde coast services—to use a railway metaphor. There are times when the quay resembles nothing more nor less than a busy railway junction: there is room for five steamers to berth at once, with Glasgow and South Western, North British and Caledonians calling frequently throughout the day. When to these are added the steamers of the independent companies, and the famous red-funnelled mail boats of David MacBrayne & Co., with the pier itself crowded, and the esplanade thronged with sightseers, Rothesay certainly partakes of a character and vigour that is worth going far to see. The holiday-maker has an almost bewildering choice of trips, and not only in fine weather. Except at the special holiday seasons, when every boat is loaded to its utmost capacity, there is ample room in the saloons to shelter from a sudden characteristic Clyde downpour. Many years ago in his grand book *The Highlands and Islands*, A. R. Hope-Moncrieff dubbed the steamers 'arks of escape from a hopeless deluge.' But West Highland weather, although fickle, is not always quite so hopeless as to drive visitors to the steamers out of sheer boredom.

The railway steamers did not at one time penetrate into the fiords so far as MacBrayne's, but they sailed the Kyles of Bute, calling at little piers in the back of beyond like Colintraive and Ormidale, and then turning southward down the western kyle to the charming little villages of Tighnabruaich and Auchenlochan, nestling under the crags of Beinn Camull. The ordinary service steamers turn about at Auchenlochan, but the Caledonian turbine *Duchess of Argyll* used to continue southward and make a complete circuit of the Isle of Arran. This was no trip for a rough day, except to those with strong stomachs; for despite protection from the west in the form of the long Kintyre peninsula, the firth between the east coast of Arran and the mainland is some twenty miles across. Similarly the passenger and mail service to Campbeltown, at the foot of Kintyre, was not until recent years maintained by the railway steamers; Williamson-Buchanan put their fast turbines *King Edward* or *Queen Alexandra* on to that run, but since the taking over of the Williamson-Buchanan business by the former LMS Railway, steamers have sailed to Inveraray as well as to Campbeltown.

The islands of Great and Little Cumbrae, lying out in the fairway, divide the firth into its inner and outer reaches; and whereas traffic in pre-grouping days was a glorious 'free for all' in the inner waters, the region south of the Cumbraes was nearly, though not quite, a Glasgow and South Western preserve. Here residential traffic to the coast towns was interwoven with the boat trains; timing at some of the junctions was very close, and the running often very fast. Competition rose to fever heat after the Caledonian opened its line from Glasgow to Ardrossan in 1890: the piers from which the Arran steamers sailed were no more than

100 feet apart. More than this, for the last six or seven miles the two lines were little more than shouting distance away from each other, and tales are told of the rival boat trains racing neck and neck along this stretch with the drivers shaking their fists at each other! One Glasgow and South Western driver was pounding his engine with such vigour that the blast from the chimney blew one of the flooring boards out of a station footbridge! The other bone of contention between the Glasgow and South Western and the Caledonian was the Irish cattle traffic. Some of the beasts were landed at Ayr harbour and some at Ardrossan, and the running that ensued sounds today more in the streamlined passenger style than the working of loose-coupled freight trains. Just imagine a train of nine loaded cattle-trucks worked over the $40\frac{3}{4}$ miles from Ayr Harbour to Saltmarket Junction, Glasgow, in 43 minutes!

A study of the map would seem to suggest that the steamer ports of Fairlie and Largs are awkwardly placed for direct participation in the traffic from Glasgow to Rothesay, though the sea passage from Largs is not much longer than that from Wemyss Bay. The high massif of Waterhead Moor just inland from these two ports precludes a direct line of railway, and the wide detour via Ardrossan, to join the main line as far south as Kilwinning, results in a route 43 miles in length from Largs to St Enoch, compared with the 31 miles from Wemyss Bay to Glasgow Central. Nevertheless first-class express services long outlasted the fiercest competitive days, and even in the restricted period between the end of the first world war and the grouping of the railways in 1923, the Glasgow and South Western regularly operated two morning expresses from Largs and one from Fairlie pier, none of which made any stops on the Glasgow side of Saltcoats until Paisley. On Monday mornings these three regular trains were supplemented by no less than six more, including one non-stop from Largs to St Enoch and a second running non-stop from Fairlie pier.

The stretch of coast southward from Ardrossan to Ayr, itself quite flat, and with its hinterland no more than gently rising, is

Between Grantshouse and Berwick: typical scene in August 1948 when many bridges were swept away by the great floods

Ayton 'Dam': scene on East Coast main line after the great floods of August 1948, when the railway embankment acted as a dam for a large volume of flood-water, and urgent measures had to be taken to prevent its collapse

After the landslips on the Cockburnspath Bank: to fill the breach in the line a heathery knoll was bulldozed into the gap. The effect is clearly seen on the level ground beyond the line of railway

Temporary bridge on East Coast main line: streamlined Pacific engine testing
new structure near Grantshouse

nevertheless most attractive. Apart from this being a regular paradise for golfers, the view across the broad firth to Arran is always, or nearly always, invested with the charm of a West Highland seascape in its limpid air and vivid colouring. In their last independent days the Glasgow and South Western and the Caledonian had various working arrangements, largely as a result of war conditions, which on the face of it would seem to indicate a more co-operative spirit. The veteran Sou' West paddle steamer *Glen Sannox* and others working on the packet service to Arran used to serve both piers at Ardrossan, collecting passengers from Caledonian boat trains as well as those of her own company. And what a stately ship she was, with her two red funnels, pale grey and white hull and the ornamented splashers over the paddles. As with all the Clyde steamers her carrying capacity was enormous, though not quite equal to that of the immortal MacBrayne mailboat *Columba*, registered to carry 2,000. The present railway steamer *Queen Mary II* is registered to carry 2,086.

4

South of Ardrossan the passenger-train service is residential, with a heavy increment at week-ends, and purely railway traffic too. There were never any regular passenger sailings from Troon or Ayr. But although the incentive of competition from another railway was not present here, the residential expresses had, over the major part of their runs, to be dovetailed into the time-table with the boat trains to Ardrossan and Largs, while from Paisley inwards the Greenock traffic was superimposed upon this ensemble. The importance of strict punctuality in the most competitive services placed an obligation upon all concerned, and if a train suffered delay at any point the driver seemed to make it a point of honour to recover the lost time. The spirit of those stirring days of 45 to 50 years ago bred a generation of hard-running enginemen, and great are the tales told of speed exploits with the Manson 4–4–0 engines—larger wheeled and very fast versions of the Greenock bogies. Nowhere was the spirit of enterprise more prevalent than at Ayr itself, as the writings of David L. Smith have so vividly revealed. One story must suffice, told in a racy trilogy of articles in *The Railway Magazine* some years ago: ' G & SW Nights' Entertainments.' Smith writes:

' Big Jock Clark! What a man he was—big hearty soul, as well known in Ayr as the town steeple. When the 50-minute non-stop expresses were put on between Ayr and Glasgow, Cowan and Jock Clark got the jobs to themselves, 8.25 a.m. from Ayr and 5.10 p.m. from Glasgow, with engines 238 and 239, the last of the small-boilered Manson 4–4–0s, brand new out of the shops. For a period of months no-one else got a turn on the flyers, and the speeds recorded in the enginemen's bothy at Ayr sheds at night were terrific! Then one day Cowan was absent attending a funeral, and the choice of a substitute fell on one Davie Smith, no relative of the writer, but a very great friend. It was the 5.10 job, and before Davie left Ayr sheds he was given to understand by his fellow drivers—Mackie and McGarva and Munachen and Tom Barry—that unless he should that night lower Jock Clark's record he need not show his face in Ayr again.

' Now the 5.10 of those days was quite a big proposition, for it ran out to Elderslie via Paisley (Canal), a line infested with curves, and with short-sighted signals. Cowan's regular mate Jock Taylor was firing, engine 238, and a tare load of about 140 tons. Out they thundered over the Canal road, and had almost got quit of its tortuous length when Ferguslie box dead-stopped them for a train crossing their path at Elderslie. Davie said the train was not in sight when they stopped, which infers a stop of at least 2 minutes. Then they got away, and arrived at Ayr at 5.54—44 minutes from Glasgow, 41·9 miles by the Canal route, and about 40 minutes net, a performance which I have not known surpassed in those days of 45-minute schedules and 5X 4–6–0s.'

This certainly was a grand piece of work in itself, but no less thrilling is the spirit that inspired it. Smith was writing in 1938, at the zenith of Ayrshire speed history, and the 5X engines, which he mentions in the last sentence, were not stationed locally, and were certainly not entrusted to one, or even two sets of men, as in the old G & SW days. These modern engines did their trips between Glasgow and Ayr as part of a complicated round of duty based on the Patricroft shed at Manchester; in the course of this round they would be handled by half a dozen different crews. This complicated arrangement was one outcome of the grouping, and it was devised in order to obtain a greater weekly mileage out of individual engines. The implications of this policy will be discussed in more detail in a later chapter, but so far as the Clyde coast is concerned the arrangement is now at an end. The modern successors of the old Manson 4–4–os on the G & SW and of the Pickersgill 'pugs' on the Caledonian are the efficient standard LMS 2–6–4 tanks; they are well looked after, kept very smart and run like greyhounds. The old Scottish locomotive men who used to add little touches of their own in ornamenting their engines—decorative metal-work on smoke-box doors, and so on—would no doubt applaud their successors who even in these austere days find time to adorn their black engines by painting in coloured backgrounds to the number plates on the smoke-boxes, some red, some blue and some yellow.

Paisley is the grand junction of the Clyde services. Through it pass trains to all resorts, except the few which used to take the Caledonian route to Ardrossan and of course those on former NB routes. The main line out of Glasgow to Paisley, quadruple-tracked, was owned jointly by the Glasgow and South Western and the Caledonian; to avoid what would otherwise have been congestion at Gilmour Street, the principal Paisley station, some of the old non-stopping G & SWR trains took the alternative route from Glasgow—what is known as the 'Canal road,' rejoining the Ayr main line at Elderslie, well beyond Paisley, and clear of any complications arising from the joint use of Gilmour Street station by the Caledonian. There is no doubt that in the highly competitive days many of the facilities provided were on an unduly lavish scale, and the incorporation of the G & SW and the Caledonian within the LMS group led to some weeding out.

Today, the Clyde services are in process of complete moderni-

97

CHAPTER SEVEN

Scottish Railway Engineering and Architecture

I

THERE are not many countries where the natural beauties of the landscape have in many places been dignified by the building of a railway. The time of construction is one of sad tribulation to the immediate neighbourhood; the countryside is disfigured by spoil banks, roads are churned into morasses by the constant passage of vehicles bringing up supplies, while at all times the peace is shattered by hordes of navvies swarming everywhere. It is small wonder that the time of construction caused many an outcry, particularly when it came to the building of some major work in a famous beauty spot, like the long curving viaduct at Glenfinnan.

But turning once more to the present day, and to our original point of entry into Scotland, it is good to walk on the riverside path above Berwick, and look upon the final majestic sweep of the Tweed, and to look also upon those three great bridges. The loftiest and most beautiful of the three, the Royal Border Bridge, standing like some immense and finely proportioned Roman aqueduct, carries the East Coast main line at a height of 126 feet above high-water mark. This great viaduct, mellowed with the years, would ennoble the fairest of river scenes, and it stands, indeed, symbolically at the gateway to a country that includes such notable items of railway engineering as Killiecrankie, Ballochmyle and Culloden Moor; as Loch nan Uamh, where Sir D. Y. Cameron accentuated the effect of the concrete arches to the enrichment of a fine picture; and not least at the Firth of Forth, where engineering artistry touched one of its highest peaks in Sir Benjamin Baker's supreme creation. Of Glenfinnan Viaduct J. J. Bell was moved to write: ' Sailing up the loch one sees a thing so delicate that the fairies might have built it.'

Those who built the early Scottish railways used largely indigenous material for the construction of the bridges. Once the stone had weathered, and the immediate traces of construction had been obliterated by the growth of new vegetation, these bridges came to harmonise most pleasingly with the surroundings. Nowhere is this fact more evident than on the Highland main line, in the work of Joseph Mitchell. Nearing the gorge at the head of Killiecrankie pass the single line of railway is carried high across a ravine. Lying deep among the trees the viaduct of ten graceful arches will rarely be seen by the traveller; for although it lies on a curve, the train emerges from the woods, sweeps over it and then immediately enters a short tunnel, so that there is only time for a tantalisingly brief glimpse of the pass itself. One needs to scramble over the steep path by the side of the gorge to see the arches in all their beauty.

Where long single spans had to be taken Mitchell did not display that same unity of design. Over the Tilt at Blair Atholl he adopted the simple expedient of using deep lattice girders— of no distinction—but to adorn the structure he added a curious battlemented gateway at each end. The same technique is used at Ballinluig on the Aberfeldy branch. These bridges are of the ' through ' type—that is, the deck carrying the rails is fixed to the bottom booms of the girders. At Invershin the same combination of lattice girder and masonry is used, but to infinitely more pleasing effect; there are no fancy turrets or battlemented gateways; the approach viaducts are finely proportioned arches, and between the piers on either side of the Kyle of Sutherland are slung the main girders—230-feet clear span—and the track in this case is carried on the upper booms.

Of continuous arched viaducts there are some very fine examples in Scotland. That by which the Inverness Direct Line crosses Strathnairn near to Culloden Moor is magnificent, in red sandstone. The centre-piece of the viaduct is a most graceful semi-circular span of 100 feet, and the remainder of the arches, 28 of them, are 50-feet span. This beautiful work is set in the green valley of the River Nairn, in full view of the battlefield of 1746. The tragic episode of the ' Forty-five ' has been so romanticised that pilgrims visit Culloden Moor to brood over the scene of that overwhelming Jacobite disaster. Few going there in the summer can derive much satisfaction from their visit when the place bears so much evidence of charabanc parties, litter and souvenir buying. But as tourists go out from Edinburgh to see the Forth Bridge, so they might equally visit Culloden from Inverness to see one of the noblest Scottish arched viaducts.

There is another picturesquely situated arched viaduct over the South Esk at Montrose. The start, south-bound from Montrose, is on a heavy gradient of 1 in 88, and to anyone watching from the waterside the fine aspect of the viaduct is frequently made intensely vivid by the spectacle of a lengthy train, passenger or goods alike, fighting its way up the grade. If this viaduct by the Montrose estuary is distinguished by the spectacular passage of south-bound trains, another, situated in the heart of the Burns country, amid the ' Braes o' Ballochmyle,' has the rare distinction of including the largest semi-circular stone railway arch at least in Europe if not in the world. On the main line of the one-time Glasgow and South Western Railway, between Auchinleck and Mauchline the glen of the River Ayr is bridged by a single arch of 181-feet span, carrying the railway no less than 167 feet above the river. The situation is superb, but owing to the dense growth of the trees on both sides of this deep glen the full extent of the viaduct can scarcely be seen from any point, and it is not often realised that the much-photographed central arch is approached on either side by three auxiliary arches of 50-feet span. To through travellers Ballochmyle Viaduct must be practically unknown; the speed in both directions of running is high, the line is only slightly curved, and one is over the glen almost before realising it. This grand piece of work was completed as early as March 1848.

2

When the time came for the building of the West Highland Railway steel was coming into general engineering use, and on that line an economical yet handsome design of viaduct was generally used, wherein latticed-steel girders were supported on piers of masonry. The same style of construction can be seen in the Tomatin viaduct on the Inverness Direct Line, built about the same time, and also in the approaches to the Forth Bridge. Sir John Fowler, a member of the famous firm of consulting engineers Barlow, Harrison and Fowler, was consultant for both the Forth Bridge and the Inverness Direct Line, and Charles Forman, in designing the bridges for the West Highland line, adopted the same principle. Compared with the massive stone viaducts of Joseph Mitchell on the Highland main line, Forman's bridges look almost fragile; but although at the time of their construction the West Highland engines were no larger than the bogie four-coupled type of the North British, weighing with their tenders only $75\frac{1}{4}$ tons, the viaducts are adequate for the modern 3-cylinder engines of Sir Nigel Gresley's design, of which the largest used on the West Highland line weigh 113 tons, inclusive of their tenders.

When riding in the engine cab it is a thrilling experience to approach and cross those slender-looking viaducts. There are two of them in the middle of the Horseshoe Bend, and, with the gradient stiffening, and the engine going hammer and tongs on the climb from Bridge of Orchy to the County March, the viaducts, as one approaches, look somewhat narrow. The main girders are approximately under the rails, and the footwalk is on steel plates with open hand-railing at the sides. This construction is, of course, an excellent engineering job; but from a viewpoint whence the main girders are generally out of sight, well. . . . The feeling one gets is perhaps accentuated by the existence of only a single line of railway, and the viaduct itself is therefore narrow in proportion. But the most vivid experiences are reserved for the descent of Glen Falloch. Here the track winds in and out, conforming generally to the rugged contours of the hills on the western side of the glen; frequent brake applications are necessary to keep the speed within the limit of 40 mph, and to come gliding round one of those curves, through

Caledonian Railway: the Neilson 4–2–2 express locomotive No 123, preserved by the LMS at St Rollox Works. As depicted here the engine has a more modern boiler than that originally fitted

a rock-cutting on a blind corner, and then suddenly to be confronted by one of those slender lattice viaducts, on a reverse curve, certainly provides a supreme thrill.

The West Highland Railway proper was completed in 1894. Apart from the viaducts some of the greatest difficulties in construction arose from the inaccessibility of much of the country traversed. Over long stretches of the line where no road existed, as between the head of Loch Treig, over Corrour summit and on across Rannoch Moor, materials had to be conveyed by pack horse. But on the Mallaig extension there was no point more than 6½ miles from the sea. On Loch Eil the contractors built a pier, and laid a temporary railway for the conveyance of stores. Apart from purely engineering difficulties caused by the hardness of the rock and the amount of blasting necessary in the cuttings, the major factor governing the construction of this line was the difficulty of obtaining and retaining suitable labour. The navvies were principally Irish, and were constantly coming and going; and the larger items of engineering construction were so designed as to permit of their erection by what was largely inexperienced and unskilled labour.

All the viaducts are built in concrete, made from crushed stone excavated from the nearby cuttings, and cement. There are fine examples at Morar and at Loch nan Uamh, though nowadays it is difficult to appreciate the handsome proportions of the Morar Viaduct as it is almost completely surrounded by trees. But finest of all, of course, is the 21-arch structure at Glenfinnan, situated on a sharp curve, from which there is a wonderful view of Loch Shiel winding away to the south-west. The viaduct is 416 yards long, and has a maximum height of about 100 feet. It is difficult to conceive of a more picturesque and romantic situation: approached and left through deep vertical-sided rock-cuttings, set among lofty mountains, and looking down to the marshy flat where Prince Charles Edward Stuart raised his standard in 1745, Glenfinnan is certainly one of the ' lions ' of Scottish railway topography.

This construction of railway viaducts with largely unskilled labour had an interesting parallel more than 30 years later in Northern Ireland. When the Greenisland direct line of the Northern Counties Committee section of the LMS was built the work was done partly for the relief of unemployment, which was severe in Belfast at the time. The lofty viaducts near Bleach Green were, once again, constructed in concrete.

3

Within sight of Dundee stand the grim remaining ruins of perhaps the greatest tragedy in British engineering—the one well-nigh incredible case where a fundamentally unsound design was combined with makeshift workmanship. There, out in the firth, stand what is left of the piers of the first Tay Bridge. The engineer was Thomas Bouch, whose rather superficial ways and flair for speculative administration were in very striking contrast to the innate caution and solid reliability of contemporary engineers like Robert Stephenson, Locke and Cubitt. A good deal of his reputation as a bridge builder was derived from the painstaking work of certain of his subordinates, and particularly that of Robert H. Bow; but when the time came for the construction of the first Tay Bridge he seems to have been less fortunate. At what was still a relatively early stage in railway construction design was apt to be based upon rule-of-thumb methods, and there was definite ignorance upon matters such as wind pressure. Stephenson made careful allowance for what might be termed the ' factor of ignorance ' by using generally massive proportions. In the construction of the famous tubular bridge over the Menai Strait he admits that if his calculations showed that one bolt, or one rivet or one chain would be adequate for a particular function, he made a practice of providing two. By modern standards his work would probably be regarded as unduly heavy; but it has endured for nearly a hundred years, and has proved amply strong enough to carry the far heavier traffic of today.

Bouch on the other hand used very much lighter construction. At the Firth of Tay this lightness need not have been fatal in itself, but the girder work was insufficiently braced against the effect of heavy side winds. This was bad enough, but the diagonal members were connected to the main vertical columns in a manner that must inevitably make any modern engineer raise his eyebrows, if nothing more. For those vertical columns were of cast iron, with small lugs cast integral for the attachment of the diagonals. Those small cast-iron lugs were in *tension*, and to make things worse—if such were possible—the bolts securing the diagonals were made a loose fit in the lugs. So during the passage of a train there would always be a certain amount of slogger. This was just asking for trouble.

To crown all it is terrible to relate that the workmanship put into the bridge was very bad indeed. Those cast-iron stanchions on which so much depended were not well cast. The centre cores were not accurately held, they shifted during the pouring of the molten metal, so that in some of the resulting columns the metal was thick on one side and perilously thin on the other. The lugs for the attachment of the diagonals were in some cases so flimsy that they broke off altogether. Bouch, who should have arranged for the most stringent supervision of this critical work, was apparently unaware of what was going on in the contractor's works, and where faulty columns were cast the man responsible saved the expense of casting new ones by the expedient of ' burning on ' the lugs, that is, welding them to the columns. This latter is a process one would hesitate to apply even with all the advanced modern technique in welding practice—let alone in so critical a member as on the first Tay Bridge. With all this in view it is little short of a marvel that the bridge stood as long as it did. It was opened to traffic in May 1878, and was hailed unwittingly as one of the greatest works of the day. In the summer of 1879 Queen Victoria travelled over it on her way to Balmoral, and while in Scotland she knighted Thomas Bouch. The end came only a few months afterwards, on the evening of 28th December, when at the height of a gale the high girders over the navigable part of the firth collapsed under the 5.27 p.m. mail train from Burntisland to Dundee. The moon shone through a break in the flying clouds, and those who had seen a strange flash of fire as the train fell with the ruin of the bridge then saw a great gap in the middle of the firth, and no sign whatever of the train.

The imagination turns from this appalling yet almost inevitable disaster to the project Bouch was engaged upon at the time. If his Tay Bridge was unsound his proposal for bridging the Firth of Forth was nothing short of fantastic. The need for a bridge was urgent, for the Granton-Burntisland ferry, well equipped though it was, could not cope with the volume of traffic offered, and the English partners in the East Coast route took the drastic step of sending their through traffic to the north of Scotland via Larbert and the rival Caledonian line, rather than risk the delays and hazards of the North British line through Fife. In a busy month more than 17,000 wagons would be transported across the ferry, but it was not unusual for 100 wagons or more to be detained in a single day. Several proposals had been put forward by Thomas Bouch for bridging the Forth. One of these, for a lattice-girder bridge of 62 spans from Blackness Castle to Charlestown, received Parliamentary sanction in 1865, and some preliminary work was done. But further investigations as to the nature of the river bed at this site revealed a soft soil, very unreliable and treacherous, and quite unsuitable for the foundations of so great a bridge.

The third scheme, authorised by an Act of Parliament passed in August 1873, provided for the construction of a bridge on what is practically the present course of the railway, over the narrow stretch of the firth at Queensferry. There were to have been four immense towers, among them supporting two spans of 1,600 feet on the suspension principle. The idea of carrying railway traffic over a suspension bridge, and moreover one having so colossal a span, does not commend itself; but then there were those towers. The loftiest point on the great cantilevers of the present bridge is 361 feet above high-water-mark; in Bouch's design of 1873 the four towers were to have been 550 feet above high-water-mark! Yet doubtless on the strength of the great reputation Bouch then enjoyed the design was accepted and work was begun. One of the piers on which the towers were to rest had actually been completed when the Tay Bridge disaster occurred. All public confidence in Bouch vanished utterly, and work was stopped on the Forth Bridge. The one pier stands intact today, and is now crowned by a lighthouse.

The bridge ultimately built across the Forth ranks as one of the greatest engineering works of the world, as much today as when it was first completed in 1890. The nature of the river bed at the Queensferry passage dictated the length of the two largest spans—1,710 feet—which were very much the same as Bouch's projected suspension bridge; but the three great cantilevers were built out from the central pier on the rock of Inchgarvie and from the two landward piers, each being self-supporting at every stage in the construction. Then from the central arms of these cantilevers the connecting viaducts were built out till the sections met in the middle of the two great spans. In all some 52,000 tons of steel was used in the construction of the bridge; some of the tubes constituting the main columns are 12 feet in diameter, and at many times during the constructional period as many as 5,000 men were employed. In work of so great a character, in so exposed a situation and involving scaffolding at great heights above the waters of the firth, it is hardly likely that the task could be completed without any fatalities, and yet in the seven years during which the work was in progress 56 lives only were lost. The lesson of the Tay Bridge disaster had gone deep. Not only was very great care taken in the design, and in every detail of the workmanship, but it was scrutinised at three-monthly intervals by an inspector of the Board of Trade.

The bridge was constructed and maintained under the aegis of a separate concern, the Forth Bridge Railway Company, for which the bulk of the capital was furnished by the four railway companies interested. The Great Northern, the North Eastern and the North British were directly interested as partners in the East Coast Route to Aberdeen and the far north. The fourth company concerned was the Midland, which, in collaboration with the North British, was preparing to run a through express service to the Highland line via the Waverley route, the Forth Bridge, Dunfermline and Perth, and to run through carriages from its own system to Aberdeen. The completion of the bridge in 1890 gave the East Coast allies a route from London to Aberdeen 16½ miles shorter than that from Euston, and the way was thereby paved for the very exciting ' Race to the North ' of August 1895. From whatever aspect it is seen, at whatever time of the day or night, the Forth Bridge is impressive beyond words: the exquisite grace of the cantilevers when seen broadside; the bizarre appearance when seen from the footplate end on, as the train emerges suddenly from the cutting at Dalmeny; and then the thrilling passage over it in the dead of night, with a hollow reverberation as the engine steams across, each successive overhead girder lit by the glare from the fire, and all the time the mast-lights of ships far below.

Not long after the completion of the Forth Bridge another very fine Scottish viaduct was constructed on the cantilever principle at Connel Ferry, Argyllshire, over Loch Etive. This carries not only the Ballachulish branch of the former Caledonian Railway, but in addition a roadway of restricted width, over which all public traffic is subject to a toll. Before the construction of this viaduct the only alternative to a long detour round the head of Loch Etive was a very primitive ferry rowing boat, by which early motor cars were conveyed athwartships in a somewhat hazardous manner, supported on baulks of timber improvised to suit the dimensions of the vehicles in question. The viaduct at Connel Ferry is an interesting and handsome structure, especially in the method of support for the cantilevers. The towers slope outwards from their foundations. If this had not been done the length of the straight connecting girders between the two cantilevers would have been excessive.

4

The magnitude and majesty of the engineering work involved in these great bridges is there for all to see, but on the railways of Scotland there are some great works that with familiarity and a less romantic situation become commonplaces to which hardly a thought is given. One such work was the extension and re-construction of Glasgow Central Station, undertaken from 1899 onwards. At that time the station contained nine platforms and was approached by a quadruple-tracked bridge over the Clyde. There were no half measures about that extension. It was to consist of thirteen reconstructed platforms and a new bridge across the Clyde carrying nine tracks abreast. Not the least intricate part of the work lay in the crossing of Argyle Street, as there the foundations had to be carried to a depth of 40 feet below street-level in order to avoid difficulties from the drainage system of the Glasgow Underground Railway. The new bridge over the Clyde is a massive and imposing structure of five spans. The river piers consist of steel caissons sunk to a depth of some 68 feet in one case, and 71 feet in the second, below high-water-mark. The main girders of the three river spans are of the open-web lattice type, and entirely under the flooring, one span having nine, and the other two spans ten of these main girders abreast. The piers are massively constructed in stone, with towers continued upwards for carrying signal gantries spanning all nine roads on the bridge.

The reconstruction of the station itself represented a very pleasing and successful piece of engineering and architectural design, in which a lofty and spacious concourse is surrounded in such a way that the whereabouts of all important offices can be seen at a glance, and in which the train arrival-and-departure indicators are of exceptional size and clarity. Generally speaking, Scotland has good reason to be proud of its principal stations. In late Victorian days, when early layouts were proving cramped and inconvenient, the Caledonian, the North British and the Glasgow and South Western in turn took the proverbial bull by the horns and carried out very thorough reconstructions. In Glasgow, St Enoch Station was greatly enlarged in 1901, and in Edinburgh the North British completely rebuilt Waverley in 1899. If their English allies had adopted the same methods Euston, for example, might have been a more appropriate headquarters for a railway that was styled ' The Premier Line.' But to return to Scotland, Waverley is to my mind the very model of what a large through station should be, built on the island platform principle with all the offices contained in the large central block. Its situation, deep in the glen between the old and new towns, is central and yet entirely unobtrusive.

In referring to the extension of Glasgow Central Station I mentioned the Underground Railway. This, to give it the correct title, was the Glasgow Central Railway, and was promoted by the Caledonian to give direct access from the main line at Rutherglen to its interests west of the city on the north bank of the Clyde. The central portion of the line ran under the very heart of the city, and its construction involved some exceedingly difficult engineering. Where it ran beneath streets, underpinning of the buildings on either side had to be carried out on a vast scale; sewers had to be diverted, and on some sections the nearness of the river caused trouble, in that the tunnels were made through sand that was affected by the rise and fall of the tide. Charles Forman was the engineer, and he had this unsavoury task on hand at the same time as he was building the West Highland Railway.

Travelling on the underground, still steam worked, provides an excellent reproduction of conditions on the Inner Circle in London in pre-electrification days ; but in Glasgow the railway company tried to make up for the gloom of the stations themselves by giving very special consideration to the design of the buildings at street-level. The task was entrusted to noted Scottish architects of the day, but after the lapse of some 60 years one cannot regard their efforts with other than mixed feelings. At Botanic Gardens, for example, the designer might possibly have been thinking of the pagoda in Kew Gardens when he produced the curiously incongruous oriental design. Hamilton Ellis's description cannot be bettered: ' The oblong station building is surmounted by two tapering towers, each crowned by a thing like a huge golden onion. In the rude nineteen-twenties it would doubtless have been referred to as a station " with knobs on.'' But the place has an air about it, a rakish look, that is delightful amidst the prim greys and greens of Kelvinside, and it deserves to become an ancient monument some day.' The architect was James Miller F.R.I.B.A. R.S.A.

5

In recent years the railways of Scotland have provided little opportunity for new constructional work. The departments of the respective chief civil engineers have been concerned with maintenance work, improvements in permanent-way design and methods of maintaining the road, and of course the perennial local troubles, such as mining subsidences, erosion of sea walls, deterioration of timber work, and so on. But in August 1948 the newly constituted Scottish Region of the British Railways was suddenly confronted with a task the magnitude and urgency of which has so far no parallel in the history of railways in this country. The torrential rainstorms that swept south-eastern Scotland on the afternoon of 12 August 1948, reaching their maximum intensity over the Lammermuir Hills, were followed quickly by flood devastation of the direst kind imaginable. Small rivers leading from the hills to the sea changed within an hour or so to torrents of such volume and violence as to suggest that a reservoir dam had been breached. Water poured down open hillsides as over a weir, and while many districts experienced severe flooding, as at Kelso, where 6 inches of rain fell within 24 hours, one of the main outlets for this deluge proved to be the course of the Eye Water, which strikes the East Coast main line at Grantshouse station.

The results were almost incredible. The flood waters sweeping rightward to follow the valley towards Reston and the sea carried all before them. Water flowed deep over the railway, leaving over the permanent way a thick deposit of earth, debris and rooted-up vegetation. North of Grantshouse station a large volume of water from the Blackburnrig Burn began to pass northward along the railway through Penmanshiel Tunnel and down towards Cockburnspath. Between Grantshouse and Reston the main line crosses the Eye Water seven times, and every one of these bridges was swept away and the rails left hanging in mid-air, while at the height of the disaster it is alleged that the flood water was running within four feet of the crown through Penmanshiel Tunnel. This veritable cataract was augmented by numerous smaller torrents charging down the steep hillside to west of the railway, and a tremendous landslip occurred roughly halfway between Grantshouse and Cockburnspath stations. Near Ayton, following the collapse of a culvert, the high railway embankment acted as a dam for flood water from the neighbouring hills. In all, within the 28 miles of railway between Dunbar and Berwick the line was completely breached at seven bridges and three large slips, in addition to being severely damaged at several other places by scouring of bridge foundations, slips, landslides and wash-outs, not to mention the critical embankment at Ayton.

When, in past years, main-line bridges have been destroyed or damaged, the recognised engineering procedure has been to erect as quickly as possible a temporary bridge supported on piles so as to reopen the line. Over such structures traffic must necessarily pass at slow speed, but the possibility of a slight loss in running time is of no consequence compared with the need for restoring through communication as soon as possible. I know of a case in central Wales where the line was reopened within a week of the complete destruction, by flooding, of a stone-arched bridge. But the destruction of seven bridges within a small area is another matter, and between Berwick and Dunbar the circumstances were rendered far more difficult, since the Eye Water valley section was sealed off by a major slip at each end. At the Dunbar end the great slips on the Cockburnspath Bank were the most spectacular breaches of all, while at a point just north of the Border the collapse of an embankment effectively prevented the use of the up line.

It was decided to construct temporary bridges of the military type, and a railhead for receipt of the necessary steelwork was set up in the goods yard at Tweedmouth Junction. Contracts were let, not only for the bridge-construction work, but for the road haulage of supplies from Tweedmouth to the various working sites, and for the restoration of the embankments where the great slips had occurred. For some days after the original disaster 'Ayton Dam,' as the 52-feet embankment came to be known, gave cause for acute anxiety. The embankment had been weakened and it was feared that the great volume of water impounded would force a breach, and if that had occurred little or nothing could have saved the town of Eyemouth from disaster. A trench fitted with sluice gates was cut through the embankment, and some of the water released; 9-inch pipes were laid over the embankment and also over rising ground to a culvert that had withstood the flood, and more water from the artificial lake was pumped to safety; so, gradually, the danger of complete collapse was averted.

The great slip between Grantshouse and Cockburnspath provided a major problem. In the construction of new railways the gradients are arranged so that the spoil excavated from cuttings will provide enough filling for the embankments, and the alternation from one to the other is designed so that haulage of material can be kept down to a minimum. But on the Cockburnspath Bank much of the hillside, and the railway embankment with it, had glissaded down into the deep glen of the Pease Burn, and it would have been a colossal labour to try to reclaim the material that had slipped away. Much of the surrounding land consisted of rough heather-clad scrub: with the ready co-operation of the landlord concerned, permission was obtained to use some of this adjoining land and to explain the operation in a single phrase, large knolls lying between the railway and the burn were bulldozed into the gaps to form the new embankments. The employment of such rapid methods inevitably recalls the laborious means on which the earliest railway engineers had to rely; no more formidable tools than picks and shovels for dealing with earthworks, and no other means of transport, in those days, than by horse.

Between Berwick and Dunbar in 1948 the major items of reconstruction were divided between the two famous firms of Scottish civil engineers, Sir Robert McAlpine (Scotland) Ltd., and Balfour Beatty and Co. Ltd. McAlpines, who nearly fifty years ago built the Mallaig Extension of the West Highland Railway, had the Cockburnspath Bank slip and the three Eye Water bridges nearest to Grantshouse, while Balfour Beatty had the remaining bridges and the two landslips between Burnmouth and the Border. With such a diversity of work on hand careful co-ordination was needed, and no greater tribute to the way in which the Civil Engineer of Scottish Region and his staff handled the whole affair could be found than the astonishingly short time taken to reopen the line. When the full extent of the havoc caused on 12th August had been assessed, the most sanguine expectations of reopening the line did not at first come much below six months; in actual fact the line was opened to goods traffic on Monday 25th October, and just a week later passenger service was resumed, the first train through being the south-bound *Flying Scotsman*. Speed was, of course, limited to 15 mph over all the temporary bridges, and equally severe restrictions were in force over the sites of the slips and at Ayton embankment. In the meantime construction of the new permanent bridges has proceeded. All in all, the restoration of traffic on the line between Dunbar and Berwick in less than three months ranks as a great achievement in Scottish railway history.

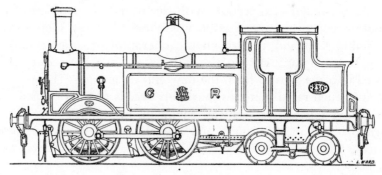

CHAPTER EIGHT

Traffic Control and Signalling

I

SINCE railways north of the Border came under the unified administration of the Scottish Region of British Railways, progress was rapid in co-ordinating the closely integrated operational organisations which had been set up during the twenty-five years of the grouped railways ; and while at the time of writing consideration of traffic working in Scotland tends to fall more or less naturally into two divisions represented by the former LMS and the former LNER lines, the complete revision of the old district boundaries has resulted in the unification of control at places where the two former companies adjoined each other. The methods of the two former companies in exercising control over traffic movements differed in certain details of procedure, and without indicating any preference for one method or the other, one may add that controversy often raged quite fiercely over their respective merits as it has done over many other aspects of railway working in the past. But I am anticipating a little, for the principles of Traffic Control, let alone the details of working, are not so widely known as to justify any assumption of familiarity with them on the part of readers.

The day-to-day working of a railway can be likened to a gigantic military operation, in which movements can be planned to the last detail beforehand, but which nevertheless includes innumerable hazards. Analogous to the resistance of an enemy, counter attacks and the sustaining of casualties are the receipt of unexpectedly heavy freight for conveyance, delays on the line due to locomotive casualties or failures of other equipment and the onset of exceptional weather. The secret of success in both classes of operation is for the command, at successively higher levels, to be constantly informed of the position—in the railway case so that locomotives, carriages and wagons may be disposed to meet varying needs and running arrangements controlled so as to ensure a constantly smooth flow of traffic. For that purpose District Control offices are set up at various key locations, to which stations, marshalling yards and other centres of activity can report: in turn the District Control offices report to Divisional Control. The District Controls are connected by telephone to every signal box and every goods yard in the particular area. This practice was adopted by both LMS and LNER, so that train working in Scotland was covered by a chain of District Controls reporting back respectively to the old LMS Scottish Divisional Control in Glasgow and to the LNER Scottish Area Control in Edinburgh. The latter control is now much more than divisional: it is Regional, under the direct supervision of the Regional Operating Superintendent. The degree of co-ordination is not materially affected by one section of the Regional Control being in Edinburgh and the other in Glasgow.

Apart from the general supervision over train movements that is exercised through the agency of these control offices, an extremely important feature of the work concerns the loading of freight trains. One has only to consider the fluctuations in the fish traffic south-bound from Aberdeen. I have told, in chapter two, of what ample provision is made for the conveyance of this perishable freight; but it is clear that the organisation must be most flexible, so as to cope economically with day to day variation in the amount of business offered. In the event of small catches or of the trawlers being delayed in making port, arrangements must permit of the ready cancellation of a train or group of trains, just as it must equally be capable of transporting without delay an unusually heavy catch. In the District Control offices staff are allocated to duties such as the provision of motive power, the provision of passenger and freight rolling stock and arranging of duty rosters for train crews. In this latter branch of the work the controller responsible must work in close collaboration with the controllers engaged in the surveillance and regulation of train movements; for with freight trains the arrangements for relieving trainmen on their outward workings and the taking up of return trips is a facet of the working that is constantly under examination.

The controllers are in touch with the various out-stations, yards, running-sheds and so on through a system of selective telephones. Each control desk is equipped with a telephone keyboard, by means of which the controller can communicate with any point in his sphere without leaving his desk. The difference between the LMS and the LNER method of working lay in the control of train movements. In the LMS District Control offices a track diagram of the line is mounted on the wall in front of the controllers. The track layout throughout the controlled area is completely depicted down to the last siding. The controllers receive reports of the running of trains from certain key signal boxes as a matter of routine; if, on account of some special circumstances, they require a report of the movement of a particular train at other localities they can inquire by their telephone line from the signal boxes in question. The passing times of the regular passenger and fast freight trains are merely noted on the record sheets for the day, but the slower moving freight trains are given special attention. While on the move the last occupy the running lines for longer periods, and while regulating their movements from place to place, in order to afford the minimum of interference to faster traffic the controller concerned must see that they are not unduly delayed waiting in refuge-sidings, running-loops and so on.

Each of these trains is represented by a ticket, this ticket, bearing full particulars of the load, destination, type of engine and any other relevant data, being hung on a peg corresponding to the siding or other refuge where the train is temporarily berthed. Thus the disposition of tickets on the diagram at any moment shows the general freight-train position, apart of course from those trains that are actually on the move. The illustration facing pages 30–31 shows a portion of the track diagram in the District Control office at Polmadie, Glasgow, and each of the white tickets represents a stationary freight train. The communication side of the Control system is not, of course, confined to the controllers themselves. Goods stations, yards and individual signalmen ring up the controller for their section, not only in cases of routine reporting, but for guidance in the handling of traffic matters under their immediate eye or in giving priorities to the different trains on the line. Generally, however, the signalmen, in following through the various movements scheduled in the working time-table, carry on without any reference to Control except at those signal boxes from which regular train reports are sent. But when late running occurs Control, with a general picture in front of them of the traffic position on the line, may step in and alter the regular arrangements; and although such a change might possibly mean delay to one or more individual trains the all-line position would be improved by such improvisations. This is one of the principal advantages claimed for the Control system: that the regular reporting of movements, and the up-to-the-minute picture of traffic conditions thus presented, enables traffic as a whole to be kept flowing more freely.

2

In control offices on the former LNER lines the 'picture' was derived in a different way. When the time-tables are planned originally the 'path' of each train is plotted on squared paper, vertical lines being drawn to represent each minute of the day, and horizontal lines to represent position of stations, junctions, intermediate signals and so on. The time-table is worked out, allowing what experience has proved to be adequate margins between trains. In the former LNER control offices, as reports of train movements were received from the key signal boxes, the positions of the trains were plotted on squared paper corresponding to the original time-table graphs. As the day progressed the controllers on succeeding shifts could see at a glance how traffic was flowing and how close to schedule regular passenger trains were running, and they could also see clearly the locations where freight trains were berthed. The day-to-day graphic

Highland Railway: northbound special express composed of L&NW and Caledonian stock leaving Blair Atholl, hauled by Highland engines Nos 91 *Strathspey* and 30 *Dunvegan Castle*

record, studied over a period of months, also served to show up any ' black spots ' that might have existed—places where certain trains were frequently delayed, due perhaps to insufficient time-table margins behind the preceding trains. At the present time modifications are being made that will eventually bring traffic control in all the regions on to a standard basis.

The Scottish railway network is covered by District Control offices at Polmadie (for the Glasgow, Clydesdale and coast lines of the former LMS, including the G & SW line from St Enoch to Kilmarnock); Balornock (for the line northward from Buchanan Street); Perth; and Inverness. At Kilmarnock another District Control covers the G & SW lines other than those controlled from Polmadie. The former LNER control offices, using graph recording, are at Glasgow, Edinburgh and Burntisland, while a further one, put into commission during the war to assist in the handling of the greatly increased traffic over the former Great North of Scotland line, is at Aberdeen. This last control office provides one of the first instances of integration between the former LMS and LNER lines since the formation of Scottish Region. The first instance of control integration was in Glasgow, early in 1948, when the former LMS controls at Polmadie and St Rollox were placed under the former LNER Control at Queen Street and their territories placed under the supervision of the District Operating Superintendent, Glasgow. At Aberdeen there was an LMS control office covering the line southward to link up with Perth control, but the work of this office has now been merged with that of the former LNER control covering the GN of S line. This change provides an interesting example of how traffic working may be more closely knit following an amalgamation, and a more detailed reference to present-day operation at Aberdeen will help the function of control to be better appreciated by the reader.

The great uncertain factor in railway working at Aberdeen is the fishing industry. Very heavy traffic originates at the Buchan ports of Peterhead and Fraserburgh; further traffic originates at Buckie, Macduff and elsewhere, and the problem of providing engine power, in view of the considerable day to day variations, will at once be appreciated. But the factor overriding all others is the situation of the two major fishing ports of Peterhead and Fraserburgh at the extremities of long single-tracked branches. Although the overall traffic, taken year in and year out, would not justify doubling any part of those lines or even the construction of intermediate passing-places in some of the longer sections, the most careful regulation is needed on busy days to ensure that the fish is conveyed expeditiously to Aberdeen for marshalling in the south-bound express fish trains, and that its working over the Great North line does not cause any dislocation of north-bound traffic. The emphasis in the last sentence ought perhaps to have been put the reverse way round. The need for punctual departure of the trains from Peterhead and Fraserburgh has long been appreciated in the fishing industry and every effort is made to co-operate. But the running of north-bound passenger trains is dependent upon arrivals from the south, some from the English sleeping-car expresses, and the Aberdeen controller must constantly watch the running on the Peterhead line, and if necessary alter the crossing-places of north-bound and south-bound trains.

The main line of the Great North section is double-tracked to Grange Junction, 49 miles north of Aberdeen; the line from Macduff joins in at Inveramsay, and that from Peterhead at Dyce Junction, only $6\frac{1}{4}$ miles short of Aberdeen, by which time traffic from all converging routes of the Great North system—excepting the Deeside branch—is concentrated upon the double-line bottle-neck. It is here that the co-ordination of control between the main lines north and south of Aberdeen is so necessary. Quite apart from fish a good deal of freight traffic for the south is concentrated and remarshalled in the Craiginches yard, just south of the Dee Viaduct; the siding capacity of this yard regulates the amount of ordinary freight traffic that can be accepted from the Great North line, and constant scrutiny of the position at Craiginches enables this flow of freight traffic from the north to be carefully controlled so as to avoid congestion in the northern approach to Aberdeen. Control has also to keep a close watch upon locomotive power. The fish trains are worked by express engines, and during the night every north-bound train from Aberdeen is usually double-headed, not from immediate necessity but for the need to have additional engines at the northern termini for the south-bound express fish trains. Such are some of the day-to-day problems that are dealt with by Control.

3

While Control exercises a general supervision over traffic handling and train movements all over Scotland the actual progress of trains along the line is regulated by the wayside signals, and responsibility for the correct operation of these signals rests entirely with the signalmen. The basic principle of the block system, wherein the line is divided into a number of sections, or blocks, and only one train permitted in a block at any one time, is widely known. Experience in the art of railway working, extending now over a period of more than a hundred years, has resulted in the standardising of a code of block regulations, in which the procedure to be adopted in the signalling of trains is clearly laid down. Local conditions have led in some cases to the adoption of additional rules applying to the particular place. The observance of the block regulations is the responsibility of the signalman, just as the observance of signals is the responsibility of enginemen. No mechanical or other aids are provided. Within station limits, however, at junctions, and indeed at all localities where there are points, the actual setting of the road is very carefully safeguarded.

From an early date in railway history, when levers for working signals and points were grouped together and mounted in a single framework, the Board of Trade required some positive safeguard against the setting up of conflicting routes. From this requirement the now familiar mechanical interlocking mechanism was devised, making it necessary for the signalman to pull the various point-levers to set the road before he can pull the levers to set the signals; and once the road is set it is impossible to

121

pull levers to set another road that would conflict with the first. As the art of interlocking developed, so the size of installations increased. Among purely mechanical plants, that put into commission at Waverley Station, Edinburgh, when that station was completely reconstructed in 1899, ranked as one of the finest of its kind. There were two large signal boxes, one at each end of the station, having locking frames of 260 and 205 levers respectively; and in addition to these centrally located boxes there were various smaller ones on the approach lines, like those in the Princes Street Gardens and at Abbeyhill Junction, as well as three small additional ones in the station area, the North Central and South Central to control the scissors-crossing in the centre of the long outer platform roads, and Waverley suburban.

About the turn of the century it began to be felt that better co-ordination of control in signalling operations would result from concentrating the work of large stations or junctions in as few signal boxes as possible. The introduction of electric or electro-pneumatic motors for point and signal operation enabled the manual work to be reduced, and so it was considered practicable to bring the control of more functions than hitherto into one signal box. In Scotland two remarkable installations of power-signalling were put into commission during the first decade of the present century. With the enlargement of Glasgow Central Station, as described in Chapter Seven, the signalling was modernised so as to bring the entire control of this now very large station under the jurisdiction of only one signal box. This entailed the use of an interlocking-frame having no fewer than 374 miniature levers. It was built by theMcKenzie, Holland and Westinghouse Power Signal Company, and even today it remains the largest power interlocking-frame ever constructed in Great Britain. Since its installation in 1908 the plant has been modernised to include track circuiting, regarding which further reference will be made later in this chapter. The enlargement of another Glasgow station, St Enoch, was accompanied by a notable installation of the Sykes system of electro-mechanical interlocking. The operation of points by electric or compressed air motors is relatively expensive, and where all the points concerned are conveniently near to the signal box an economical solution can be reached by operating the points manually and using electric control for the signals. This was done at St Enoch. The inter-locking-frame consisted of a row of full-sized levers for point operation, and above them a row of miniature slides for electrical control of the signals. A degree of compactness was achieved in that the frame was less than half the length of an all-mechanical apparatus doing the same work.

The use of power in these plants as first designed was confined to the physical work of moving points and lowering signals. But the development of the track circuit enabled point levers to be track-locked and signal levers to be electrically locked if the section of line ahead was occupied by another train. These additional safeguards were added to the original power plant at Glasgow Central about 1930–1, and shortly afterwards the electro-mechanical plant at St Enoch was replaced by an all-power inter-locking and day colour-light signal system. The use of track circuiting and the provision of an illuminated track diagram showing the whereabouts of every train make it possible for signalmen to control an area extending far beyond the tracks that can actually be seen from the signal box. In the Sykes installation at St Enoch additional signal boxes had to be provided at Clyde Junction and Gorbals Junction, whereas in the new plant points and signals at the latter place are power-worked from St Enoch signal box, one mile away Another interesting example of remote control is at Galashiels, where signal boxes at the outlying junctions have been dispensed with and the functions at these locations operated from a central control panel. There is no lever inter-. locking in the ordinary sense in this plant at Galashiels; small thumb-switches replace the conventional levers, and if a signal-man should try inadvertently to initiate the movement of a pair of points that would involve a conflicting route, electric interlocking would prevent that pair of points from being thrown.

Just a short time before the outbreak of World War II the

signalling at Waverley was completely modernised. The mechanical plant previously mentioned was replaced by an all-electric installation, with two power-locking frames of 207 and 227 levers, colour-light signals and all points operated by electric motors. By the use of complete track-circuiting with illuminated diagrams, it was possible to bring the extensive approach lines under the direct control of the Waverley boxes. On the west side the area indicated on the illuminated diagram extends through the Princes Street Gardens and Haymarket tunnel to Haymarket Station, while on the east side Abbeyhill Junction box has been dispensed with and the junction put under remote control from Waverley East box, even though the actual layout is 0·6 mile away and well out of sight on the far side of the Calton Hill Tunnel. Such concentration of control tends to improve the working by obviating the need for many messages by block-bell between formerly adjacent signal boxes, and by giving the signalman in the large station boxes a broader picture of the traffic situation as a whole.

At Waverley, as in the all-electric signal box at St Enoch, there is no block-working in the ordinary sense of the word, and a reference to the previous working on the west side of Waverley is necessary to an appreciation of the new arrangements. Before the introduction of the electric colour-light signalling there was an intermediate signal box in the Princes Street Gardens; a block section existed from Haymarket Station, through the tunnel, to this box, and a second section extended from Princes Street Gardens to Waverley West. Trains were belled from box to box under the ordinary block regulations. There are now several sets of colour-light signals on each of the four running lines between Waverley and Haymarket, so that it is possible to have two or three trains on each line between these two stations at the same time, following one another at intervals regulated by the working of the colour-light signals. Under ordinary block-working the signalman passing a train forward to the next box describes it on the bell code, and the signalman at the receiving end knows that this will be the next train to arrive on that particular line, since the block regulations do not permit more than one train to be in the section at a time. But to take the North Up Main Line as an example there are now three colour-light signal sections between Haymarket and Waverley, and if each train passing Haymarket was described purely by audible means, such as a block-bell, the men at Waverley would have to rely on their memories for the description of trains coming through from Haymarket, and with all but the lightest of traffic the position would be unworkable.

A system of train description has therefore been installed whereby the class of train and its route is displayed on an illu-minated indicator in the signal box at the receiving end. To take the previous example, as incoming trains pass Haymarket Central box the signalman there registers the class of train, and its route, on his train describer, and corresponding indications are displayed on the receiver in the Waverley West box. There the indicator shows the class and route of the first, second and third trains on each running line, and when the first train indicated duly arrives its description is automatically cancelled; the train previously shown as second thereupon becomes first, and the third goes up to second. There may come a time when trains are following one another so closely that there is one train in every colour-light signal section between Haymarket and Waverley, another waiting to leave Haymarket, and perhaps yet another following close behind. Even though the indicator at Waverley can only display the descriptions of the first three trains the signal-man at Haymarket Central can register up to six on his describer. The indications are ' stored,' as it is termed, by means of electrical apparatus, and when one train arrives at Waverley and is auto-matically cancelled, the fourth train registered by the describer at Haymarket Central, now the third to arrive at Waverley, has its description brought ' out of storage,' so to speak, and dis-played on the indicator in the ' third ' place for the particular running-line concerned. Where train description is installed there is no need for any other communication between these all-electric signal boxes and their neighbours, though of course there are times when the telephone is used for inquiries as to the whereabouts of certain ' key ' trains and so on.

Since nationalisation some remarkable schemes of resignalling have been carried out in Scotland. The use of track circuiting, colour-light signals and comprehensive illuminated cabin diagrams has permitted the replacement of groups of small signal boxes by one central box controlling large areas, with consequent improvement in the general regulation of the traffic. An out-standing example of this principle is to be seen at Cowlairs, where branches to the western residential districts north of the Clyde, and the important freight line through Springburn connect with the Glasgow–Edinburgh main line of the former NBR. Prior to modernisation there were no fewer than eight signal boxes between them controlling this complicated group of junctions. These have now been replaced by one control panel working on the route-relay interlocking principle with one control switch for each route.

Still more recently the famous installation of electro-pneumatic signalling at Glasgow Central has been replaced by a similar, but much larger relay interlocking than that at Cowlairs. At Glasgow Central it was not merely a case of signal-ling and traffic-control modernisation. In Chapter Seven reference was made to the original four-tracked bridge over the river Clyde. Until the completion of the nine-track bridge, commenced in 1899, all traffic into the station was conveyed over the old bridge, and in recent years it had become evident that this bridge would soon need to be replaced. In the light of modern signalling developments, however, the problem of traffic working into and out of the Central Station was studied afresh, and it was ascertained that if each road over the newer bridge was signalled so as to permit of traffic working in either direction, as required, the nine tracks over the newer bridge could cope with the entire traffic of the station. Even though a considerably increased density of service was to be expected from the electrification of the Cathcart Circle and the lines south of the Clyde to Greenock, Gourock and Wemyss Bay the actual number of train and engine movements in the station itself was not expected to increase due to the elimination of the majority of light-engine movements, through the substitution of multiple-unit electric trains for locomotive-hauled stock.

The resignalling of the station to deal with the altered track layout, and to provide for reversible road working on the six running lines across the Clyde bridge has resulted in what is believed to be the largest in the world route-relay interlocking operated from one control desk. At the time of its completion in 1951, the installation at York created world-wide interest ; that installation includes 825 routes. The new plant at Glasgow Central has more than 1,000 routes. The signal box is situated at the junction of the main lines to the south with the lines to the Clyde coast, near the site of the former Bridge Street Junction. It replaces not only the original power box at the Central Station, with its 374 miniature levers, but also two mechanical boxes previously at Bridge Street Junction and Eglinton Street.

4

As yet, however, colour-light signalling has been used only to a very limited extent in Scotland, and for many years to come manual-block will remain the basis of train working. Yet even here there are some changes in evidence. The LMS and LNER both adopted as standard the upper quadrant type of semaphore signals, and this is gradually replacing the older types of arm. At a first glance all lower-quadrant semaphore signals look much alike, but it was really astonishing to see how greatly the arms of the old Scottish companies varied in detail, among themselves as well as in comparison with those of the English companies. The North British had the triangular-shaped spectacle glasses in which the old signalling firm of Stevens and Sons specialised ; the Caledonian arms had adjustable spectacles, and in the ' clear ' position they came off to a much steeper angle than those of most other Scottish railways. The Highland used the McKenzie and Holland pattern semaphore in conjunction with those very elaborate 4-foot-high pinnacles that looked as though they might have been designed to match the adornments of Indian and Burmese temples. But from the operational point of view one of the most salient characteristics of Scottish signalling, as practised on the Caledonian, North British and Glasgow and South Western Railways, was the use of a truly green glass in the spectacles. There is, of course, a good deal of yellow in the light from an ordinary oil-burning signal lamp, and many railways sought to counteract this by using a strong blue-green glass in order to display an orthodox bright-green light. On the Scottish lines the light displayed at night was often quite a pale yellow-green.

On the Highland Railway maintenance of the oil lamps was made easier by a device that enabled the lamp to be lowered to ground-level for refilling and general attention. This winding-gear was for a time used also on the Great Western Railway, and signals so fitted could always be recognised by the pulley-wheel at the top of the mast, just below the pinnacle. As it was generally unnecessary for Highland linesmen to climb the signal posts no ladder was provided, merely a set of open rungs up which one could swarm if any special attention was needed at the top. The Highland also made a practice of carrying the signal wires from cabin to mast, at a height of about 6 feet above the ground, so that they would be unaffected by all but the most exceptional snowfalls. Under grouping many of these pleasing individualities were disappearing, and although in signalling as in everything else it is impossible to devise ' standards ' that will meet every individual case, there is bound to be a good deal more levelling-out to bring Scottish working into line with the general code of signalling practice now being formulated.

A recent scheme of signalling modernisation that may well prove to be the forerunner of many more in Scotland is to be seen at the south end of Aberdeen Joint Station. From all outward appearances this is a mechanical plant, with the upper-quadrant type of semaphore signals and points worked manually ; but the whole layout is track-circuited, and electric locking is applied to the full-sized signal and point levers. This plant indeed possesses all the modern safeguards in operation afforded by a complete all-electric interlocking, and the signal-box equipment includes a fine illuminated diagram. One very interesting feature can be observed from the station platforms : from most of the platform roads alternative lines are available for a train or light engine proceeding towards Ferryhill Junction ; previously a separate semaphore arm was provided for each of these alternative routes, whereas now only one arm is used, working in conjunction with a route indicator. These indicators are electric, and are of the 'multiple lamp' or 'theatre sign' type. A number of electric lamps are mounted on a display board, and when a particular indication is required only those lamps needed to make up the figure or letter signifying the route are lighted.

5

In the Highlands, and on stretches of the lines leading to Stranraer, a high proportion of railway mileage is single-tracked. Over many of these routes express services are run, with maximum speeds sometimes exceeding 70 mph, and there single-line working has been reduced to something of an art. The Block Regulations require a positive safeguard that a section is unoccupied, and before a train can proceed the signalmen at each end of the section concerned must carry out, together and in proper sequence, a series of operations on the special single-line block instruments ; at the conclusion of this procedure the man at the entering end of the section can extract a token from his instrument. This is handed to the driver ; without it he is not allowed to proceed. The instruments at the ends of the section are electrically interlocked in such a way that once a token is obtained both the instruments for the section are locked up and unusable until the token is reinserted in one or other of the two instruments. This is normal practice in Great Britain and Ireland, and on all railways where full single-line block-working is in force.

It was James Manson, famous afterwards as Locomotive Superintendent of the Glasgow and South Western Railway, who invented apparatus for the mechanical exchange of tokens. In the ordinary way it is necessary, when exchanging tokens at a non-stopping station, to slow down to 15 mph or thereabouts for the fireman to catch the loop of the token pouch on his arm. The Manson apparatus enabled this exchange to be carried out at speeds up to 60 mph, though generally speaking a speed restriction to 40 mph has to be observed when exchanging tablets with this apparatus. It was first installed on the Great North of Scotland Railway, where Manson was Locomotive Superintendent at the time, and later it was adopted on the Highland. On the Glasgow and South Western, a somewhat different form of the same apparatus was introduced by W. Bryson, the Signal and Telegraph Superintendent, whose son was at one time Signal Engineer of Scottish Region, British Railways.

CHAPTER NINE

LOCOMOTIVE BUILDING IN SCOTLAND UP TO 1922

I

FROM the earliest days of the Industrial Revolution, Glasgow and the Clyde came to be recognised as one of the greatest centres of shipbuilding and marine engineering anywhere in the world. Adjacent to the shipyards there grew up establishments specialising in marine engines, and in the late twenties of last century those enterprising pioneers saw that there was close affinity between marine steam engines and the locomotive engines used on the new railways that were then being constructed. There were a few such railways in the Glasgow district by the year 1835; there was the Monkland and Kirkintilloch, largely a colliery line, and the Garnkirk and Glasgow. Even so when the firm of Neilson and Company started business in 1837 in Hyde Park Street, Finnieston, it was for the construction of stationary and marine engines. Shortly afterwards, however, they added to their activities the construction of railway locomotives. The founders were W. M. Neilson, Henry Dübs and James Reid. Railway and marine engineering were well and truly mingled in those early days, and between the founding of Neilsons and the end of 1853 some personalities destined to be very great had entered the world of Scottish mechanical engineering.

In 1837 a young lad of 17, Patrick Stirling by name, began his apprenticeship at the Dundee Foundries; Robert Sinclair arrived from France to become Locomotive Superintendent of the Glasgow, Paisley and Greenock Railway, and a particularly tough young gentleman named Dugald Drummond was living his boyhood at Bowling, where the working of early railways was to be seen adjacent to the fascinating prospect of early steam navigation on the Clyde. Another engineer who was to have a profound influence upon Scottish locomotive practice had by this time served his apprenticeship in Scotland, and was busily engaged in obtaining a wealth of experience in various English appointments—this was Alexander Allan, who was born at Montrose in 1809, and returned to Scotland in 1853.

Although there were certain offshoots of the industry with the first North British Railway works at St Margaret's, Edinburgh, and the GPK & A with their works at Kilmarnock, Glasgow grew to be more and more the focal point. The Caledonian set up their principal shops at St Rollox; those of the Edinburgh and Glasgow near by, at Cowlairs, ultimately became the locomotive head-quarters of the North British Railway, and in 1862 Neilsons established their new Hyde Park Works at Springburn, roughly midway between Cowlairs and St Rollox. Two years later Henry Dübs, one of the founders of Neilsons, formed a new company, Dübs and Co., and the ' Glasgow Locomotive Works ' of that firm were established in a part of the city lying south of the Clyde and adjacent to what became the Caledonian main line to the south. With the extension of railways in all parts of the world the art of designing and building locomotives grew and prospered; the Scottish railways were in frequent con-sultation and collaboration with the two Glasgow firms, and gradually the industry grew until in the years before the out-break of the first world war Glasgow was the largest locomotive building centre in Europe, and its overseas trade in steam loco-motives was the largest of any in the world. A little before that time, in 1903, Neilson, Reid and Co.; Dübs; and Sharp, Stewart and Co. had amalgamated to form the North British Locomotive Company, and the combined capacity of the three works— Hyde Park, Atlas and the former Dübs works, then renamed Queen's Park—was approximately 800 main-line locomotives per annum.

Naturally activities at St Rollox and Cowlairs, and, 25 miles to the south, at Kilmarnock, were on a smaller scale, as these three works were concerned with the maintenance of locomotives in addition to some new construction. But progress continued to a large extent on parallel lines, and the world-wide fame achieved by engines of Neilson, Dübs and Sharp, Stewart build during the nineteenth century to some extent reflected the exacting demands that were made, and the magnificent performance achieved, on the home railways of Scotland. By 1910 one could scarcely go into any part of the British Empire without encountering engines built in one or other of the works of the North British Locomotive Company. It was perhaps natural too to find them in large numbers on the then British-owned railways in South America; but large numbers were also built for France, and some even for Canada, where competition from the great American firms must have been severe.

2

While the great works were being established, and manufacturing facilities developed, the design of Scottish locomotives was beginning to follow one or two marked trends. The most striking, in the fifties and sixties, was due to Alexander Allan. It was while working in England for the Grand Junction and later for the London and North Western at Crewe that Allan evolved the celebrated layout of engine framing that was so widely adopted in Scotland. The ' Old Crewe ' passenger locomotives were of the 2–2–2 type; the leading and trailing wheels were given outside bearings, and the cylinders placed outside and rigidly encompassed by the outside frame plates. The sides of the smokebox were swept outwards in a graceful curve to meet the cylinders. The Caledonian Railway was built largely as an outcome of Grand Junction enterprise, and when the time came for provision of motive power for the Scottish line it was not surprising that Joseph Locke should have recommended the type of locomotive that was proving so successful on the English part of the West Coast route. The position was further consolidated in 1853 when Alexander Allan left Crewe to become General Manager of the Scottish Central Railway. From his headquarters at Perth his duties included direct supervision of the locomotive department. Although Allan himself resigned in 1865, when the

Scottish Central was absorbed by the Caledonian, the locomotive department of the enlarged railway remained faithful to the Allan front-end for more than thirty years—in all until 1884.

It is remarkable to recall that for the greater part of this long period the main-line express services of the Caledonian were operated by engines having a single pair of driving wheels, many having the exceptional diameter of 8 ft 2 in. Such large wheels were appropriate enough on railways where the booked speed was high and gradients not severe; but on the Caledonian, having such an obstacle as the Beattock Bank with its 10 miles of 1 in 75 ascent, these single-wheelers regularly required to be double-headed. The engineer under whose direction they were built was Benjamin Conner, and he certainly built some very imposing machines. The splashers over the great single driving wheels were slotted like the paddle-boxes of a Clyde steamer; they had tall stove-pipe chimneys, while the distinctive shape of the framing and the fine Prussian blue livery rendered them conspicuous anywhere. There were smaller variations of the same general design with 7 ft 2 in wheels, and from 1867 onwards engines of the 2–4–0 type having similar proportions were constructed. There were 38 of the 7 ft 2 in class of 2–4–0, and of these 11 were constructed by the Caledonian Railway at St Rollox, 18 by Neilsons, 7 by Dübs and 2 in the Perth works of the former Scottish Central Railway.

The Allan front-end was also adopted on the Highland Railway, and 2–2–2 passenger engines of almost identical design to those of the Caledonian were built by Hawthorns of Leith from 1855 onwards. Indeed the picturesque double-framing with inclined outside cylinders remained a standard feature of all passenger engines on this line until 1894. To the Highland Railway in the early days of his great career came William Stroudley, to succeed Barclay as locomotive superintendent in 1865. The Hawthorn 'singles' and the slightly larger ones built in 1863–4 by Neilsons were even at that time inadequate for a road with such long and severe gradients, and Stroudley began converting some of these engines into 2–4–0s in order to

Great North of Scotland Railway: 4–4–0 express locomotive No 115 built by Neilson, Reid and Company in 1899 to the design of W Pickersgill

increase their adhesion weight and thus to increase their ability to handle a load. But in these rebuildings Stroudley did more than a mere utilitarian piece of work; he revealed himself as a true artist among railway engineers. A large canopied cab was provided; the tall chimney was adorned with a handsome copper cap, and a superb finish was given to every part of the engine. Above all they were painted in a bright gamboge shade of yellow, with rich crimson-red underframes.

Stroudley's stay at Inverness was brief, and there would be no point in imparting to it any particular prominence, despite the fame he achieved later at Brighton; but it so happened that during that brief stay Dugald Drummond was appointed as foreman erector, and very soon afterwards he was made works manager. Dugald Drummond and his younger brother Peter were to play a great part in Scottish locomotive engineering, and this early association with Stroudley, and its continuance at Brighton from 1870–5 was to prove exceedingly fruitful. At this stage, however, I must leave the Highland for a while in order to trace development on the other railways.

3

From 1853 to 1866 another Scottish engineer who was to win even greater renown than Stroudley was locomotive superintendent of the Glasgow and South Western Railway; this was Patrick Stirling. He founded a great tradition at Kilmarnock, for he was succeeded by his brother James, who reigned there for a further 11 years. The tradition was continued unbroken for a further 14 years by the third engineer of the lineage, Hugh Smellie, till he, like the Stirlings, sought advancement elsewhere. Those were the days when locomotive engineers moved freely from one railway to another. Patrick Stirling went to the Great Northern at Doncaster, and then James Stirling went to the South Eastern. In earlier days Robert Sinclair had moved from the Caledonian to the Great Eastern, and Stroudley from the Highland to the London, Brighton and South Coast. It is notable that so many eminent positions in the English locomotive world were filled by Scotsmen.

On the Glasgow and South Western the Stirlings and Hugh Smellie followed the cult of the domeless boiler. Patrick Stirling encased the safety valves in a tall brass column beautifully shaped and burnished to the last degree, but although he took this design with him to the Great Northern and used it on every engine he built at Doncaster, his brother reverted to open Ramsbottom-type valves on a simple flat mounting for subsequent G & SWR engines. While at Kilmarnock, Patrick Stirling earned distinction by being one of the very first engineers to provide a proper cab for the men; the side-sheets were extended upwards in a continuous sweep, and a large circular hole in each side was provided for a lookout. After he went to the Great Northern he reverted, at the request of the enginemen, to a more attenuated form of shelter, which his brother and Hugh Smellie duly copied on the G & SWR. As with the Caledonian, some of the engines for the ' Sou'-west ' were built at Kilmarnock, while Dübs and Neilsons between them supplied the rest. During the Stirling-Smellie era the Glasgow and South Western possessed some of the finest and fastest express engines. In that dark handsome blue-green livery that remained unchanged from Patrick Stirling's days to the time when the G & SWR became merged in the LMS group in 1923, those tall domeless engines were outstanding among all Scottish express designs of their day.

4

The Great North of Scotland Railway was, as readers may have gathered from my previous remarks, a rather singular concern in its earliest days, and the locomotive department was not the least singular part of it. The first locomotive superintendent was Daniel Clark, whose famous book, *Railway Machinery*, is perhaps better known than the locomotives he designed for the GN of S. He worked from an office in London, and under his direction the railway was exceptional for those days in that its orders for locomotives were placed outside Scotland. Fairbairn of Manchester, Beyer Peacock and Co. and Robert Stephenson and Co. all had their share, and it was not until 1866 that an order went at last to Neilsons. But in a more important and practical aspect the early locomotive stock of the Great North was unique in Scotland, in that the 'single' type of engine was completely absent. Daniel Clark's very first engines, delivered from Manchester in 1855, had four wheels coupled; but it is still more remarkable that in later years the Company never used anything more than four-coupled engines, even for goods traffic.

Clark's first engines set a fashion in locomotive lineaments to which the Great North was to be faithful for nearly thirty years. The cylinders were outside, and in the 2–4–0s there was something reminiscent of the Allan framing in that the leading wheels had outside bearings, and that the outside framing encased the slide bars. But on the Great North the encompassing of the cylinders by the outside framing was discontinued when later engines of the same general type were built having leading bogies. The driving-wheel splashers were slotted, and the chimneys were copper-topped and bell-mouthed; but externally the most marked characteristic of all these early engines was the placing of the huge brass dome and Salter-type safety valves on the fire-box. An interesting feature, used from the outset by Daniel Clark, was the raising of the fire-box above the line of the boiler. This was a good point in design, as it provided additional steam space above the water-line, and thus reduced foaming at the point where the steam was collected and passed by way of the regulator in the dome to the cylinders. Difficulties due to water passing direct from the boiler to the cylinders—priming, as it is termed—were greatly reduced by this arrangement. Daniel Gooch used the same device on his broad gauge 4–2–2 express engines for the Great Western Railway.

All these Great North engines, from Clark's cab-less 2–4–0s of 1855 to Cowan's C class 4–4–0s of 1879 were finished in most ornamental style. The copper-capped chimneys and polished brass domes have already been mentioned; deep brass bands

137

covered the joint of the fire-box with the boiler, and that of the boiler with the smoke-box, and the lining-out on the basic emerald green was most elaborate. The later engines of this general design were built by Neilsons, and they made a characteristically fine job of them. It must, however, be recorded that their potentialities as motive power units were not put to a very serious test. The time-table allowances for all Great North trains of those days were exceedingly liberal and the traffic working equally haphazard, so that anything in the way of sustained express running was quite unknown north-west of Aberdeen.

5

But in bringing the story forward to 1879 we have already entered a phase of greatly intensified development. Dugald Drummond was back in Scotland, acting vigorously as locomotive superintendent of the North British; with David Jones in command at Inverness, Highland engines were at last assuming the massive proportions that should, from the first, have been appropriate to the formidable road over the Druimuachdar Pass. It was the completion of the Midland route to Carlisle in 1876 that put all companies concerned in the Anglo-Scottish traffic on their mettle, though for some years the Caledonian continued to work its share of the traffic with the out-dated single-wheelers and large-wheeled 2-4-0s of Benjamin Conner's design. The shape of things to come, however, was seen in 1876, when Dugald Drummond brought out a powerful class of 4-4-0s, built by Neilsons, specially for working the through Midland expresses over the Waverley route from Carlisle to Edinburgh. This class, most of which received names appropriate to the Border country through which they ran, formed the prototype of a long series of very successful designs, serving not merely the North British Railway but the Caledonian, the Highland, and later, in England, the London and South Western Railway. A direct derivation of this same design was built in large numbers for Belgium.

The keynote of the original design of 1876 was its extreme

simplicity, and good mechanical engineering practice. The cylinders were inside, and spaced so that the slide valves could be placed between them; the valve motion was driven direct from the eccentrics without the need for any rocking levers; the steam passages were large and direct, and in consequence the engines ran very freely. In external lineaments there were several points in evidence of Drummond's association with Stroudley, in the lines of the cab, the shape of the chimney and not least in the vivid gamboge livery; but over the winding track of the Waverley route there was not much opportunity for their speedworthiness to be displayed. In 1882, however, Drummond resigned his appointment with the North British to become locomotive superintendent of the Caledonian, and very soon a larger version of his ' Waverley ' 4–4–0 was being constructed. As with the North British Railway engines, Neilsons built the first examples of the new class, but after the first ten a further eighteen were built by the Caledonian at St Rollox works. Drummond brought to the North British Railway the Brighton idea of naming engines after places along the routes they worked; this, however, was not one of the ideas he took over to St Rollox, and wisely too he made no changes in the beautiful dignified style of painting standard on the Caledonian.

But within a dozen years his new 4–4–0 engines had made railway history. An account of the racing to Aberdeen in 1895 appears elsewhere in this book; night after night the 49¾ miles from Carlisle—practically sea-level—to the 1,014-foot altitude of Beattock summit were covered in well under the hour; the engines climbed as well as they ran freely on the level and downhill stretches. But in mentioning these highlights in the career of the Drummond 6 ft 6 in four-coupled engines I have skipped another important event in Scottish locomotive building, the construction of the celebrated ' single-driver ' express engine No. 123 by Neilsons in 1886. One would have thought perhaps that the Caledonian would have had enough of ' single-wheelers ' after the long innings of the Conner eight-footers; but No. 123 was in a different class altogether. She was designed in the

Drummond tradition, with a boiler very little smaller than that of the record-breaking 6 ft 6 in 4–4–0s and having the same excellent design of cylinders, valves and motion. She was exhibited by Neilsons at the Edinburgh Exhibition of 1886, and was immediately hailed as being one of the most beautiful engines ever built in Scotland.

In her early days No. 123 had a strenuous and distinguished career. She was the sole representative of the Caledonian in the first 'Race to the North' in 1888; in later years, while stationed at Carlisle, she regularly made two return trips to Glasgow each day—a remarkable daily mileage of 409; many years afterwards she was retired from ordinary traffic and allocated to work the directors' saloon carriage. But she was at all times an isolated engine, and so rather awkward to fit into regular working links. Still more so, she was non-standard, and not likely to fit in with the rationalisation schemes initiated after the Caledonian had been merged into the LMS group in 1923. Her days might well have been numbered but for the energy and enthusiasm of a number of locomotive connoisseurs who lost no opportunity of pressing their claim for her preservation. The LMS authorities eventually agreed; not only so, but from the utilitarian black in which she had been running in passenger service between Perth and Dundee, with the number 14010, she was restored to a large measure of her original beauty. The Drummond boiler had been replaced by a more modern one; but Mr Leech's colour photograph of her, taken in 1948 at St Rollox, shows that most of her original beauty has been retained. The blue livery is that of later Caledonian days, and is a little lighter than the Prussian blue of Drummond's time.

6

Returning now to the four-coupled engines, before tracing how far and wide the influence of Drummond's North British and Caledonian 4–4–0s spread, we are obliged to side-step for a moment to the Highland Railway to follow the traditional Alexander Allan design to its highest development in David

Jones's Strath class of 1892. These grand engines, of which No. 91 *Strathspey* is seen in the colour plate facing page 118, were the culmination of some twenty years' progress. In 1874, from being a railway with generally inadequate motive power, the Highland stepped into the forefront of British locomotive practice. In that year Dübs and Co. delivered the first ten of the powerful 4–4–0s at one time known as 'Jones bogies.' For their time they were massive engines, and the general appearance of solidarity was enhanced by the appearance of the outside framing round the cylinders. Most of the Highland passenger engines were named, a custom that was continued until LMS days, and the new locomotives of 1874 were mostly named after counties—*Perthshire, Morayshire, Caithness-shire*, and so on.

On these engines, and on many older ones which he rebuilt at Inverness, David Jones installed a device for deflecting the exhaust steam clear of the driver's look-out. While a great deal of running on the Highland Railway involved heavy collar work when the steam would be lifted, by the vigour of the exhaust, high and clear of the cab, there are many stretches on the down gradients and on the more level lengths of the line north of Inverness where the engines would be steaming more easily and where the blast would be softer. To counteract the effect of steam beating down in such conditions of running Jones fitted an outer casing to the chimney in the front of which were a series of louvres; through these openings air entered when the engine was in motion, and emerged as a strong upward draught at the back of the column of exhaust steam from the inner—the real chimney. The louvres are prominently shown in the picture of the engine *Strathspey*.

A somewhat larger version of the 'Jones bogie' of 1874, and introduced just ten years later, is of note as the eight engines of this class were the first locomotives to be built at the newly established Clyde Locomotive Works. On the Highland Railway these particular engines were in consequence always known as the 'Clyde bogies.' As an independent concern this new firm did not survive long, for in 1887 it was absorbed by Sharp,

Stewart and Co., and their establishment in Glasgow further paved the way for the amalgamation of 1903, by which the North British Locomotive Company was formed. The Strath class of 1892 had the same machinery and chassis as the ' Clyde bogies,' but had considerably larger boilers; they were built by Neilsons, and with this class the dazzling yellow livery bequeathed to the Highland engines by Stroudley gave place to a bright apple-green, though still plentifully adorned with red lining, and set off with crimson underframes. But this gay colour scheme did not remain long after the retirement of David Jones. His successor at first adopted an olive-green with plain black-and-white lining, and later the lining was dropped altogether, while on some engines colour was banished even to the extent of painting the buffer-beams green instead of red. At the very conclusion of the Highland Railway's existence as an independent concern a rather lighter green was used on some engines, though still without any lining, and it is in this guise that I have depicted *Strathspey* and *Dunvegan Castle* in the colour plate facing page 118.

7

It is difficult to maintain a strict chronological order in a chapter such as this, and while dealing with 4–4–0 engines it is time once again to take up the Drummond saga before returning to the Highland to describe the outstanding creation of David Jones. Now Dugald Drummond had a younger brother Peter, who like the younger Stirling followed very much in the family tradition. He was with his brother at Brighton, Cowlairs and St Rollox in succession, and when Dugald resigned from the Caledonian in 1890, Peter stayed on as Works Manager, and was there during the great days of the second ' Race to the North ' in August 1895 and during the following year when J. F. McIntosh built the first of the famous Dunalastairs. But the end of 1896 saw Dugald Drummond in command at Nine Elms on the London and South Western Railway, and Peter taking up the reins in succession to David Jones at Inverness. Thereafter the Drummond influence was to extend greatly; it persisted throughout McIntosh's tenure on the Caledonian, where the various Dunalastair classes were little more than successive enlargements of the 1884 class of 6 ft 6 in 4–4–0, while at Cowlairs, first Matthew Holmes and then W. P. Reid built upon the sure foundation of the 1876 Waverleys designed by Dugald Drummond.

On the Highland, delivery was taken from the Dübs works in 1898 of the first eight engines of the Small Ben class, while in London, at Nine Elms works of the L & SWR, eight express passenger engines were built so like the Small Bens that they might almost have been made from the same drawings. There is no doubt that the Drummond brothers were in very close consultation, and while one might perhaps be inclined to criticise the younger for lack of originality he was a sound enough engineer to appreciate that his brother's design was a magnificent job, and one that needed only minor changes to render it almost ideal for the northern section of the Highland Railway. While the layout of the machinery was well designed and the boilers were good, the whole construction was massive. Engines of the generic Drummond type, whether of Caledonian, North British, Highland or London and South Western build, have outlasted most of their contemporaries; indeed on the Southern Railway even such a thoroughgoing modernist as O. V. S. Bulleid considered the 4–4–0s of the 1898–1900 series good enough to warrant their conversion to oil-firing in 1947. I rode on several of them working from Portsmouth and found them as game as ever. A further link with Scotland is provided in that thirty of these famous LSWR engines were built by Dübs in 1899.

The closing years of the nineteenth century witnessed a marked increase in train loads. Competition for traffic between the rival companies did not only take the form of higher speeds. Increased amenities were provided, particularly on the long-distance trains; corridor coaches and dining cars were introduced; the conventional straight-sided flat-roofed carriage began to give place to wider vehicles extending to the limit permissible by the loading gauge, and having lofty elliptical or clerestory roofs.

These developments increased the loads to be hauled, and to avoid as far as possible the need for double-heading several varieties of very large passenger locomotives were built in Scotland. In this respect David Jones, on the Highland Railway, was actually the pioneer, though the remarkable engines he put on the road in 1894 were not primarily intended for passenger traffic. These engines were the first in the British Isles of the bogie six-coupled type—the now familiar 4–6–0, 'maid of all work' on the Scottish railways. But in 1894 their appearance caused something of a sensation. They were built in Glasgow by Sharp, Stewart and Co., and although having relatively small coupled wheels, 5 ft 3 in diameter, they were very successfully used in both goods and passenger traffic. In them the traditional Allan front-end framing was at last discarded, though Jones wisely retained the excellent Allan straight-link valve gear.

On passenger work, however, it seems clear that the use of these great engines was regarded only as a stop-gap measure. Jones's resignation in 1896 came as a result of an untimely accident and he left with his successor the design for an express passenger version of the famous 'Jones Goods.' Peter Drummond accepted this excellent design almost in its entirety, changing it only to the extent of including the typical Drummond cab and chimney, the steam reverser, and the double bogie tender, with inside bearings, that his brother had largely standardised on the London and South Western Railway. Such was the origin of the Highland Castle class, of which the first six were built by Dübs in 1900. To the basic robust Jones design were added those touches of elegance that bore clearly the Drummond imprint; in service they were among the best hill-climbing engines in the pre-grouping days of Scottish railways. The names were all splendid, and are worth quoting in full:

Number	Name	Year built
140	Taymouth Castle	1900
141	Ballindalloch Castle	,,
142	Dunrobin Castle	,,

Number	Name	Year built
143	Gordon Castle	1900
144	Blair Castle	,,
145	Murthly Castle	,,
146	Skibo Castle	1902
147	Beaufort Castle	,,
148	Cawdor Castle	,,
149	Duncraig Castle	,,
30	Dunvegan Castle	1910
35	Urquhart Castle	1911

Some further engines of the same general class were built later, and included detailed modifications.

When shortly before the first world war the French State Railways (the one-time Western system) were in urgent need of mixed traffic locomotives, the Castle design was chosen, and fifty engines of this class were built by the North British Locomotive Company, identical with the Highland engines even to the extent of being equipped with the Drummond double-bogie tenders.

8

On the Caledonian at the turn of the century the great success of the Dunalastair class 4–4–0s in handling heavy loads at express speed had the undoubted effect of postponing for a short time the construction of six-coupled passenger engines. The obstacle of the Beattock incline only affected north-bound trains, and bank engines were always available at Beattock station to provide rear-end assistance when needed. The first 4–6–0 class built by the Caledonian was designed to cope with the severe mountain gradients of the Oban line; no high speed was possible owing to the constant curvature of the track, and so the coupled wheels were made quite small, thus providing a high tractive effort for hill-climbing. They fulfilled their function admirably, and then, in 1903, with the experience gained in the building of bogie six-coupled engines, McIntosh and his staff at St Rollox proceeded to construct two of the most imposing, beautifully proportioned locomotives that have ever run on Scottish metals, the express passenger 4–6–0s 49 and 50. The second of these engines was named *Sir James Thompson*, and is illustrated in the colour plate facing page 4. A further batch of five 4–6–0 engines, with still larger boilers, was built in 1906, the first engine being the famous No. 903 *Cardean*, which worked the 2 p.m. Corridor express for so many years.

That indeed was an age in which appearance counted for much in a locomotive. Little has happened during the intervening years to change the fundamental design. The ingredients of the modern general utility B1 4–6–0 of LNER design could be incorporated in an external form as neat as that of the Caledonian No. 50; but now accessibility is the watchword, and the cylinders, valve chests, connecting rods and motion, which are between the frames in the McIntosh engine, must be outside, where they can be attended to without the need for getting over a pit or getting between the frames from the level of the running plate. But while No. 50, and other McIntosh 4–6–0s of the Caledonian that were roughly contemporary, would now be regarded as ' period pieces ' among locomotives, they performed for many years very fine work on the Anglo-Scottish expresses, on which each of these big engines had its own special round of duty maintained year in year out. For a long period No. 50 was stationed at Balornock shed on the north side of Glasgow, and worked to Perth, while the sister engine No. 49 nightly took the 10.45 p.m. ' sleeper ' from Glasgow down to Carlisle.

McIntosh will perhaps be remembered best as the man who started the twentieth-century fashion for big boilers. In 1895–6 there was a tendency, particularly on some of the English railways, to increase the nominal power of locomotives by fitting larger cylinders, but without a commensurate increase in boiler power. In Scotland this trend was not so clearly marked; the Drummond engines were well proportioned, and there was certainly no lack of boiler capacity on the later Highland engines of David Jones's design. Be that as it may, in the first Dunalastairs, although the cylinder volume was increased by only 3 per cent over that of the Drummonds, the heating surface was increased by 18½ per cent. The Dunalastairs could therefore be worked much harder without the risk of their running short of steam; indeed, in running the down night Tourist express they often averaged a full 60 mph non-stop over the 117¾ miles from Carlisle to Stirling with loads varying between 140 and 170 tons. Successive developments of these engines were in the same tradition, while very similar practice was being followed on the North British Railway to culminate in the Scott class express passenger engines and the smaller-wheeled Glens designed specially for the West Highland line.

9

On the Glasgow and South Western Railway a pronounced change had come over locomotive practice since Smellie had been succeeded by James Manson in 1891. The new locomotive superintendent had been connected with the G & SWR since his boyhood; he was born at Saltcoats, his father was at one time district superintendent at Ayr, and he was at Kilmarnock works under both Patrick and James Stirling. Later, after a spell of marine engineering, he returned to become works manager under Hugh Smellie. It might now have seemed that he had only to wait for the chieftainship; but after only five years in this second spell at Kilmarnock he was appointed to succeed William Cowan as locomotive superintendent of the Great North of Scotland Railway. There he set about the modernisation of the locomotive stock, following the gay highly embellished outside cylinder 4–4–0s in the Daniel Clark tradition with a neat, perhaps undistinguished 4–4–0 design of his own. But the management of the locomotive department of a railway involves a good deal more than the mere building of new engines, and the most successful man is not necessarily he who makes the most spectacular showing. On the Great North, Manson quietly and systematically changed the locomotive department from its former airy-fairy confusion to a closely knit well-organised entity, so that when the management of the railway did awake to the need for a great improvement in the train services the locomotive department was ready to take the much-accelerated schedules practically in its stride.

Manson was a very modest and altruistic man, and when he returned to Kilmarnock in 1891 to succeed Smellie, his locomotive-building activities were at first on a modest scale, even though the working of the through expresses to and from the Midland line involved the Glasgow and South Western Railway in a good deal of double-heading. In 1903, however, while the Caledonian was turning out the celebrated 4–6–0s 49 and 50, Manson produced a 4–6–0 design which was no less of a masterpiece for that period. Technically these G & SWR engines differed from the Caledonian in having outside cylinders driving on to the middle pair of coupled wheels; but the valve gear was inside, and the appearance of the engine as a whole was one of balanced symmetry that was very pleasing. The first batch of ten was built by the North British Locomotive Company. But these engines, one of which is shown in the colour plate facing page 54, were not merely elegant to look upon; they were good on the road and extremely fast runners. It was traditional among South Western drivers of that period to run economically; on the main line at any rate they rarely indulged in uphill pounding, but relied on the swiftness of their engines on the favourable stretches to maintain end-to-end times. In the years before the first world war the Manson 4–6–0s were frequently timed at speeds up to 85 mph.

10

The North British Railway was the last of the Scottish companies to adopt ten-wheeled engines for heavy passenger traffic, and their justly famous Atlantics of 1906 stand so much outside the general trend of Scottish locomotive development as to raise various questions. Why, for example, with gradients of the length and severity of those on the Waverley route should the 4–4–2 type have been chosen in preference to the 4–6–0? Why, again, in view of the frequent slacks, and the need for rapid acceleration afterwards, should the 4–4–2 type have been chosen in preference to the 4–6–0 for the East Coast route from Edinburgh to Aberdeen? Although the North British was at one with its English allies in adopting the Atlantic type, the new engines of 1906 were no mere Scottish adaptation of an existing design; in their final form they proved themselves the most powerful Atlantics that have ever run in Great Britain, and in the gruelling conditions of day-to-day service in Scotland they long outlasted their contemporaries of the 4–6–0 type on the Glasgow and South Western and the Caledonian. In this respect they amply justified their construction; how much better they might have been as 4–6–0s is a matter for conjecture.

In the naming of them was shown that magical touch that suggests romance, and that synthesis of Scottish character, dignity and power that gave to every single engine an individuality. Here is the complete list, including those built after 1906 :

868	Aberdonian	879	Abbotsford
869	Bonnie Dundee	880	Tweeddale
870	Bon-Accord	881	Borderer
871	Thane of Fife	901	St Johnstoun
872	Auld Reekie	902	Highland Chief
873	Saint Mungo	903	Cock o' the North
874	Dunedin	904	Holyrood
875	Midlothian	905	Buccleuch
876	Waverley	906	Teribus
877	Liddesdale	509	Duke of Rothesay
878	Hazeldean	510	The Lord Provost

11

Deeply impressive as all these great engines of the 1900–10 decade were, Caledonian, G & SW and North British alike, it seems now when viewing the period in retrospect that they were more the consummation of the older school than a step in

the gradual evolution of locomotive practice. In the Caledonian
4–6–os of J. F. McIntosh the ultra-simple design propounded so
ably by Drummond had been enlarged practically to its limit,
and if in the future improved performance was to be realised,
means other than the mere enlargement of cylinders and boilers
would have to be sought. It was a problem that was to be felt
acutely in all countries where fast and heavy traffic had to be
worked. The introduction of superheating postponed the demise
of the basic Victorian design of locomotive for a few years, until
indeed the first world war came and developments in express
passenger locomotives had in any case to be shelved. How the
old Scottish companies would eventually have met the problem
remains a matter for conjecture, for by the time the war was
over the prospects of amalgamation in one form or another over-
shadowed everything else. So it befell that the last ten years
of the independent Scottish railways produced only a very few
locomotive developments of any significance.

There was a general change round in personnel. McIntosh
and Manson retired; Pickersgill moved from the Great North to
the Caledonian, and Peter Drummond, by then a relatively old
man, came to the 'Sou' West,' and Kilmarnock experienced a
taste of the new broom that had swept so cleanly where the
Drummonds had been before. He introduced several new classes,
all in the family tradition, but his greatest work—a huge 4–6–0
with four cylinders, somewhat on the lines of his brother's well-
known 'Paddle-boxes' on the London and South Western—had
not been constructed at the time of his death in 1918. To Robert
Whitelegg, who succeeded him, fell the difficult task of trying
to rehabilitate the locomotive stock from the arrears of maintenance accumulated during the war years. It was largely a case
of 'patching up,' pending the formulation of new designs, and
there was time only for one of these to be constructed before
grouping came in 1923. This was a very large express tank engine
design of the 4–6–4 type for the Clyde coast services, and will
be noticed in more detail in the next chapter. It was in some
ways a counterpart of Pickersgill's 4–6–2 tank design for the

London and North Eastern Railway: one of Sir Nigel Gresley's 2–8–2 express locomotives, No 2006 *Wolf of Badenoch*, designed specially for use on the Edinburgh-Aberdeen route and built 1936 at Doncaster Works

Caledonian, of which the first examples were built by the North British Locomotive Company in 1917.

Pickersgill's regime on the Caledonian also witnessed a certain break with tradition. The need for considerably more powerful engines than the McIntosh inside-cylinder 4–6–0s was felt keenly, and in 1916 some new bogie six-coupled locomotives were built, which, by all outward appearances, should have given a good account of themselves. But they did not prove anything like as strong as they might have been on the hills, and were sluggish on the level. If the 60 class, as these latter engines were known, seemed handicapped by its valve gear, Pickersgill's final design for the Caledonian was virtually killed by the extraordinarily complicated valve motion with which it was saddled. The engines themselves, great 3-cylinder 4–6–0s, were magnificent to look upon, but as motive power units they can only be classed as failures.

These large new engines were, however, few in number, and after the war years the standard of Scottish locomotive performance rose once more to a high level. Especially was this so on the North British, where the Reid 4–4–0s of the Scott and Glen classes worked with almost unfailing reliability and the Atlantics seemed to gain in prowess as the years went by. On the Highland, after the departure of Peter Drummond, an interesting project for some large new 4–6–0 locomotives ended in a fiasco. Six engines were built by Hawthorn Leslie and Co. of Newcastle, and the first two were actually delivered at Perth before it was discovered that on account of certain engineering restrictions it would be inadvisable to run them. This was during the war, and the Highland found a ready purchaser in the Caledonian, which like all other British companies was in urgent need of engine power. But on the Highland, with rapidly increasing traffic on its long line to Thurso, the need was perhaps greatest of all, and the blunder that led to the loss of six large and powerful engines was inexplicable. But from this grievous set-back the Highland made a very fine recovery, so much so that almost alone of the old Scottish companies the new locomotive classes built in the last few years of its independent existence were not merely an immediate success, but put in some twenty years of arduous service in the stringent economic conditions of the post-grouping era.

Of three classes designed by C. Cumming, the Clans as main-line passenger engines are perhaps the best known. The first four of them were built by Hawthorn Leslie and Co. in 1919, and four more followed in 1921. They were a sturdy straightforward 4–6–0 design, with a good boiler and an infinite capacity for hard slogging; they took trains of 350 tons unassisted out to Blair Atholl, and could bring the same load south-bound from Aviemore over the Druimuachdar summit. On the far steeper inclines from Struan up to Dalnaspidal, and from Inverness to the Slochd pass, they needed assistance with such loads as this. But perhaps one of the finest tributes to these engines came after 1935, when they were transferred to work on the Callander and Oban line; the old Caledonian drivers, who for some years past had not been too well served with engine power on this route, took to them at once, as indeed any engineman would to a locomotive that would steam under the heaviest pounding. Although the maximum tonnage laid down for the Clans over the Oban line was 245 tons, the men would cheerfully take 300 tons if need be, *and* keep time. The eight engines were named after the clans Campbell, Fraser, Munro, Stewart, Chattan, Mackinnon, Mackenzie and Cameron. *Clan Mackinnon*, the engine illustrated in the colour plate facing page 167, was the last to remain in service, and was not withdrawn until March 1950.

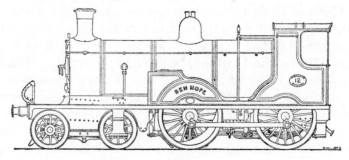

CHAPTER TEN

SCOTTISH LOCOMOTIVES AFTER THE GROUPING

I

By the terms of the Railways Act of 1921 the Scottish lines were grouped variously with English companies, so that instead of five wholly Scottish concerns there were, for the twenty-five years from January 1923 to January 1948, only two main-line companies operating in Scotland—the London Midland and Scottish and the London and North Eastern. So far as locomotives were concerned, grouping came to be felt in a variety of ways, though throughout the twenty-five years the Scottish constituents of the LNER—the North British and the GN of S—were affected much less than their confrères on the western side of the country. This was in part due to both the Scottish companies having their locomotive departments in very good order at the time of the grouping; but it was in a greater measure due to the policy and personality of the great engineer who was appointed Chief Mechanical Engineer of the LNER in January 1923—Mr, as he then was, H. N. Gresley, previously Locomotive, Carriage and Wagon Superintendent of the Great Northern Railway.

Sir Nigel Gresley, as he became in 1935, was a Crewe man by training, but otherwise almost the whole of his professional career had been spent in the service of the Great Northern. Although his direct associations with Scotland had not so far extended beyond the provision of motive power for the East Coast Anglo-Scottish expresses between London and York, he had already shown himself a man of wide interests, and above all as an out-and-out ' locomotive man.' In recent years, through contact with some of those most intimately associated with him, I came to know that he was not only a great designer, a great railwayman and a man of immense stature, but that he was also a real *lover* of the locomotive as such. He had a great regard

153

for the work of his predecessors, not only on the Great Northern but on all other constituent companies of the LNER, and he maintained in good order the pre-grouping engines, keeping them based as far as possible upon their original spheres of activity. As a result standardisation came very slowly on the North British and on the GN of S.

2

On the London, Midland and Scottish matters were not so clear-cut. The first years after the grouping witnessed a period of prolonged controversy on technical points of locomotive practice, resulting from differences of opinion upon high policy. The traffic department and the department of the Chief Mechanical Engineer were continually at variance in their views as to the most suitable form of motive power. While this controversy lasted, no progress could be expected in the urgent task of providing enhanced locomotive power for the principal express services from Glasgow to the south. Added to this was the vexed question of the style of painting. Three railways having such highly individualistic natures as the Caledonian, the Glasgow and South Western and the Highland were not going to take kindly to grouping in any case; and to have their distinctive engine liveries superseded by an alien colour, and red into the bargain, was not likely to go far by way of appeasement! At first, however, the Highland lay outside the area most affected; the locomotives were repainted and kept in spotless condition, but the workings remained practically unchanged. It was on the Caledonian and the G & SW that the hand of grouping tended to press more heavily.

On the Caledonian it might have pressed more heavily still but for the strong advocacy of Caledonian practice put up by John Barr, the Locomotive Running Superintendent, who became Motive Power Superintendent of the Scottish Division of the LMS. He had excellent grounds for his advocacy. In spite of the rather abortive attempts to produce a successful large express

engine of modern design—described in the previous chapter—
Caledonian motive power was generally in a healthy state; what
was perhaps more impressive, due to the robust construction of
the locomotives themselves, the running costs were low. The
Glasgow and South Western Railway was, however, caught fairly
on the wrong foot. Manson's good, though moderate-powered
engines were ageing; Drummond had not been long enough at
Kilmarnock to exert any appreciable influence, and Robert
Whitelegg's work of rehabilitation after the first world war had
not brought locomotive affairs beyond a stage of ' betwixt and
between.' Whitelegg, still a relatively young man, found himself faced with the prospect of being little more than a glorified
works manager, and when an opportunity to leave the railway
came he took it. His services to the British locomotive industry
as a whole were fortunately retained in the important capacity
of the General Managership of Beyer, Peacock and Company.
This change was of course Scotland's loss, and the engines of
the former Glasgow and South Western were thenceforth no-
one's babies.

Before he left, however, Whitelegg had put on the road one
of the most imposing classes of engine ever to run in Scotland.
In earlier years he had been Locomotive Superintendent of the
London, Tilbury and Southend Railway, a line having an extremely
heavy passenger traffic operated entirely by tank engines. In 1912
some 4–6–4 tank engines of his design had been built for this
road, and on coming to Kilmarnock, with the Clyde coast lines
of the G & SWR presenting a network somewhat analogous to
that of the Tilbury, he prepared a design of 4–6–4 tank engine.
They were huge machines, grand to look upon, with the tank
sides and cabs in the traditional green of the G & SW, the underframes red and the boiler cleading sheets unpainted blue planished
steel. In working order they turned the scale at no less than
99 tons. Unhappily they cannot be ranked among the most
successful of engines; they were prone to roll in the most alarming way, and gave trouble with heated bearings. There was little
work on the Clyde coast heavy enough to justify the use of such

large engines, and over the very severe route south of Girvan they were not permitted to run. Furthermore only five were built, and in the face of an avowed policy of locomotive standardisation on the LMS they were within a few years marked down for early withdrawal.

3

So far as main-line working was concerned, although the development of new first-line engines hung fire for nearly three years, some very interesting trials were conducted between engines of the constituent companies; Caledonian engines were tested against machines of roughly comparable tractive power of London and North Western, and Midland design, but although Caledonian engines were light on repair and maintenance costs they were relatively heavy on coal, and were not so much masters of the work as were some of their English rivals. The locomotives that emerged from these trials head and shoulders over the rest were the Midland three-cylinder compound 4–4–os; they were not large by the standards of 1923–4, in fact the basic design dated back to 1902, but the boiler was a good one and the engines possessed that priceless attribute where Scottish routes are concerned—an infinite capacity for continuous hard slogging. To those who know the old Midland Railway this may seem a strange statement; for even on the easier sections of its main line, such as between Leicester and St Pancras, in pre-grouping days, the compounds were limited to a maximum tare load of 240 tons.

Many years after these early LMS trials D. W. Sanford, who was in charge of the dynamometer car work, referred most wittily to pre-grouping conditions on the Midland. ' At Derby the nice little engines were made pets of. They were housed in nice clean sheds, and were very lightly loaded. There must have been a Royal Society for the Prevention of Cruelty to Engines in existence.' But when the time came for pitting their strength against the flower of the L & NWR and the Caledonian, the Midland compounds must have astonished their most ardent supporters. The test trains to be hauled between Carlisle and

Leeds over the 1,166-foot altitude of Aisgill summit were at first fixed at 300 tons, but later they were increased to 350 tons; with these loads so greatly in advance of their previous rostered maximum, the compounds did some magnificent work, and as a result the design was chosen as an LMS standard. New engines were wanted all over the system, and while these relatively small 4–4–os could not be regarded as a solution of the entire main-line problem their economical working made them very suitable for intermediate duties.

That was no doubt the official intention, but when numbers of these engines, built new by various contractors, including the North British Locomotive Company, were drafted to the Caledonian and the Glasgow and South Western sections, it soon became apparent that they were cast for a much more prominent role—in Scotland at any rate. The top-link enginemen took to them at once; the feats of weight haulage and hill climbing that the Midland drivers coaxed from them in the heat of competition on the Carlisle-Leeds trials became daily occurrences over both routes between Carlisle and Glasgow. They were included in the same power classification as the great McIntosh 4–6–os of the Caledonian, and the eclipse of those former celebrities was in one way symbolised by the disappearance of the fine old blue livery, the painting of the passenger engines in the Midland colours and the re-emergence of *Cardean's* historic number 903 on one of the new compounds, while *Cardean* herself ran nameless with the unfamiliar number 14752. Twenty-five years later, how-ever, the wheel came full circle, so far as painting was concerned, as the blue of the Caledonian was chosen (but later abandoned) as the national standard for the largest express passenger engines.

4

By the late summer of 1926 the LMS was beginning serious development of the Anglo-Scottish train services, and the prin-ciple was formulated of running 'block' loads wherever possible non-stop over long distances. In the summer service of 1927 non-stop runs were instituted between Glasgow and Carnforth, 165½ miles, and Symington and Carnforth, 136½ miles. The former run was made by certain night expresses, and the latter by the 10 a.m. from Glasgow to London and by the corresponding north-bound train. The purpose of these long runs was to avoid engine-changing at Carlisle and to obtain better utilisation of the engines themselves; and in order to provide an adequate water supply track troughs were laid down for the first time in Scotland, near Carstairs. A further set was installed just south of the border, near Floriston. The 10 o'clock Anglo-Scottish express received the name of *The Royal Scot*, as befitting the premier day express of the Royal Mail Route. This particular train was a heavy one of about 420 tons tare, and the LMS was not fully prepared to undertake its haulage. In consequence it ran double-headed throughout that first summer; north of Carnforth it was worked by two Midland compounds, as were also the heavy night expresses running non-stop from Glasgow to that same engine-changing point.

The introduction of *The Royal Scot* before the LMS had locomotives capable of working it without assistance was one result of the conflicts between the operating department and that of the Chief Mechanical Engineer. The latter had proposed to build some very large compound Pacific engines, but the operating department steadfastly opposed this project, and seemed loth to break away from the Midland small-engine tradition. Opposition or not, plans for the compound Pacifics were passing from mere proposals to a more active stage by the late summer of 1926, though the completion of the first engines of so thoroughly new a design could hardly have been expected in much less than two years. Even then in all probability only one or two engines would have been built for trial, as Sir Nigel Gresley had done with his first Pacifics, and as Stanier did later on the LMS. There was little prospect of new large engines in any numbers being in the hands of the operating department in less than about three or perhaps even four years. It was at this stage that the opposing school of thought, by some means that must still remain a matter

Wreck of the first Tay Bridge: an extraordinary picture showing one of the wrecked girders after salvage, still containing one of the carriages of the ill-fated train

One of the inter-city diesel express trains leaving Waverley Station, Edinburgh, for Glasgow

Macduff terminus: station picturesquely situated on the north coast with typical train of the Great North of Scotland section leaving

Cantilever bridge, Connel Ferry, Argyllshire: this handsome bridge carries both the Ballachulish branch and the main road across the entrance to Loch Etive

for conjecture, persuaded the management to try a totally different line of approach. One of the famous Castle class 4–6–os of the Great Western Railway was borrowed for a month and put through dynamometer car trials between London and Carlisle. These trials showed clearly that a well-designed 4–6–0 of about 30,000 lb nominal tractive effort could do all the LMS required with the new *Royal Scot* train, and having witnessed this demonstration the management embarked dramatically upon one of the most venturesome projects in the history of British locomotive engineering, a project moreover in which Scottish engineers and craftsmen were called upon to play a most vital part.

Instructions were given for a new 4–6–0 express passenger engine to be designed and ready for the summer service of 1927; moreover there was to be no question of prototype—an order for fifty was to be placed at once! Only those who have participated in the design of new machinery on any scale will appreciate fully what this involved in the way of preliminaries before the first engine could be laid down. The only hope of early completion was to put the construction out to contract, and even then specifications had to be prepared from which the prospective builders could make their estimates of cost. But above that there was the matter of design; the LMS had no precedent to work on, and in this crisis the assistance of Mr R. E. L. Maunsell, Chief Mechanical Engineer of the Southern Railway was sought. The proposed new engine was of roughly the same size and power as the *Lord Nelson*, and with the contract awarded to the North British Locomotive Company a complete set of Southern drawings was sent from Eastleigh to Glasgow. The detailed designing was done at top speed in the drawing office at Springburn, under the close supervision of Herbert Chambers, then Chief Locomotive Draughtsman at Derby. Then, to expedite construction as much as possible, the order for 50 engines was divided between Hyde Park and Queen's Park works, and building progressed simultaneously. Although the first engine was not completed until September 1927, two months after the new train began to run, this date represented a remarkable piece of work by all concerned. In such manner were the Royal Scot class engines conceived and built.

But more remarkable than the chain of events leading to the construction of these engines was their well-nigh instant success in one of the most arduous locomotive duties ever essayed in Great Britain. In the winter service of 1927 the *Royal Scot* express was run non-stop between London and Carlisle, 299·1 miles, for many years the longest run in the world made non-stop all the year round. The south-bound *Night Scot* ran non-stop between Glasgow and Crewe, with Caledonian and L & NW men working through on alternate days; and on these long runs the new Royal Scot engines performed with quiet efficiency from the very start. This freedom from teething troubles was a triumph for the North British Locomotive Company, but no less for the men of the LMS who kept all the work under close scrutiny: Chambers in the design stage; and R. C. Bond,[1] as resident inspector during the construction. One hesitates to suggest how far the design was influenced by the Southern Railway *Lord Nelson*; many of the details of the Royal Scots were derived from Midland practice, and that very vital feature, the valve motion, was based upon that of the new LMS 2–6–4 passenger tank engines. As completed the Royal Scots were of roughly the same tractive power as the Great Western Castles and the *Lord Nelson*, though they were fitted with three cylinders against the four of the two English engines. In appearance they were tremendously massive and imposing, and magnificently finished in the Midland livery.

Shortly after construction each of the fifty engines was named, the first twenty-five after regiments of the British Army, and the remainder after historic locomotives. In the first group one found titles like *Royal Scots Grey*, *Seaforth Highlander*, *Grenadier Guardsman*, and in the second group *Novelty*, *Vesta*, *Caledonian* and *Lady of the Lake*. With the regular working of the Royal Scots, Carlisle began to lose something of its old significance as a frontier station; during the summer months the 10 o'clock express between London and Glasgow passed through without

[1] Now Technical Adviser, British Transport Commission

stopping, and stopped to change engines at the locomotive sheds
—Kingmoor on the north-bound run and Upperby Bridge going
south. Then in 1933 the LMS put on the road engines designed
to work through from London to Glasgow without any change.
It was considered that under the old rosters engines spent too
much of their time waiting between turns of duty, and while in
most cases the turn-round time could not be greatly reduced the
percentage utilisation would be higher if the actual time spent on
the road was longer. The Royal Scots ran various duties up to
250 or 300 miles a day, but on the London-Glasgow continuous
trip the daily mileage would be 400. From this the still more
ambitious project was tried of working one engine from London
to Glasgow with a night express, and then after a turn round
time of only four hours making the return trip—a mileage of 800
in 22 hours.

The engines built for this duty were of the Pacific type. They
were designed under the direction of the newly appointed Chief
Mechanical Engineer, W. A. Stanier, late of the Great Western
Railway, and the first two engines were based very largely upon
Swindon practice. At first the two original Pacific engines,
The Princess Royal and *Princess Elizabeth*, were not entirely successful; the boiler was very long and did not always steam well,
although a notable departure from Great Western practice was
made in the use of a wide fire-box with a large grate area. The
men had to master the art of firing this very large grate, with
appropriate variations in technique to suit the differing grades
of coal; and from experience gained with the first two engines
considerable modifications were made to the boilers fitted on ten
subsequent engines of the class. The successful running of the
class as a whole reached its highest point in the wonderful round
trip made on 16 and 17 November 1936 with a special train, on
which engine No. 6201 *Princess Elizabeth* first covered the $401\frac{1}{2}$
miles from London to Glasgow non-stop in 5 hr $53\frac{1}{2}$ min, and
returned next day, also non-stop, in the still more extraordinary
time of 5 hr $44\frac{1}{4}$ min, an average speed of exactly 70 mph.
Although the engine concerned was one of the two original

examples of the class, by the time of this test run a modified boiler had been fitted.

From the Princess Royal class the standard LMS Pacific was developed. The first five of this later class were built in 1937 to work the high-speed *Coronation Scot* service, running from London to Glasgow in 6½ hours with one intermediate stop at Carlisle. They differed from the Princess Royals principally in respect of the boiler, which had a considerably higher steam-raising capacity. Now the Princess Royals were very large and heavy engines, weighing 104½ tons without their tenders; no appreciable increase in weight could be tolerated, but by very skilful design, using high-tensile alloy steels, the total heating surface was increased in the new engines by 22 per cent and yet the completed engine came out at less than one ton heavier than the Princess Royals. Built at a time when streamlining was some-thing of a craze, these engines had a completely faired outer casing, the bizarre effect of which was accentuated by the silver bands meeting in a point on the prow. The five original engines for the *Coronation Scot* train were painted royal blue. From 1938 onwards further engines of this class were built, some with streamlining and some without; the streamlined casing has since been removed from all those engines which were so fitted. Details of some remarkable performances by these engines are included in the Appendix.

During Sir William Stanier's tenure of office as Chief Mechan-ical Engineer of the LMS a policy of thorough standardisation was initiated, one of the most important fruits of which was the pro-duction of the famous Class 5 4-6-0 mixed-traffic engines—the ' Black Staniers ' as they are known in Scotland. These engines are designed to handle passenger trains of an intermediate kind, fast freight traffic and branch-line duties, but have sufficient reserve of power to enable them to deputise for Royal Scots or even for Pacifics in cases of emergency. They are used all over Scotland. On the Highland they work almost all the traffic, passenger and goods alike; on the old Caledonian line they work high-speed turns like the West Coast Postal Special; they work to Stranraer and to Oban, and handle all the fast goods traffic to and from Carlisle. Engines are allocated indiscriminately to passenger or goods train service. The Black Staniers and their ex-LNER counterparts the Thompson B1 4–6–0s surely represent the shape of things to come, when the eventual results of nationalisation will be seen in still further elimination of non-standard types. Stanier's slightly larger Jubilee class, with three cylinders and coupled wheels 6 feet 9 inches diameter against 6 feet in the Class 5s are generally reserved for express passenger working, and operate turns between Carlisle and Aberdeen, and Glasgow and Leeds via the G & SW and Midland route.

The Black Staniers—and with them may certainly be coupled the LNER B1 4–6–0s—are extremely capable general utility engines. Both have well-designed cylinders with large diameter piston valves, generous port openings and short, direct steam passages—all these features contributing towards a free-running engine. The difference between the two lies in the boiler and fire-box. The LNER engines have a straight barrel and round-topped fire-box of typical Gresley design, whereas the Staniers have a coned barrel and Belpaire fire-box derived directly from Great Western practice. In actual performance on the road there seems little to choose between the two types, though it is only since the war that the B1s have operated in Scotland in any numbers. Large numbers of these latter engines have been built in Glasgow by the North British Locomotive Company.

5

Turning now to London and North Eastern practice in the years between the wars, the decision to adopt the Gresley Pacific as the standard heavy passenger engine for the East Coast route brought an order for twenty of these fine engines to the North British Locomotive Company. Appropriately the first of this series, engine 2563, was named *William Whitelaw* after that great and experienced Scottish railwayman who was formerly chairman of both the Highland and the North British Railways, and who was chairman of the LNER between 1923 and 1938. Generally, however, the practice of Sir Nigel Gresley in providing motive power for diverse duties over the various parts of the LNER system was to study the local conditions, and if necessary build special engines for the work. He inherited the old Great Northern distaste for double-heading, in contrast to the LMS policy of building large numbers of standard engines and assisting them in cases of exceptional grading or load, as on the Highland line. Arising from the LNER policy Gresley built two remarkable classes for special duty in Scotland, one for the East Coast Aberdeen route and one for the West Highland.

The need for locomotives of exceptional power on the East Coast route north of Edinburgh may not readily be appreciated; there are no hill ranges of any great height to be crossed; the overall times, between Edinburgh and Dundee for example, do not require higher average speeds than 45 mph at the most, and in general train loads are not greater than those worked southward from Edinburgh to Berwick and Newcastle. But the line north of Edinburgh is like many another that has been built up piecemeal instead of being planned from the outset as a main trunk route. It abounds in sharp curves and gradients which, though not long, are steep while they last. Moreover some of the difficult junctions and curves, where speed limits are 30 mph or less, are placed just at the foot of steep inclines. Any possibility of rushing these inclines is thus entirely ruled out. The powerful Atlantic engines of the old North British Railway were managing very well, but a call for further passenger comforts on the night expresses led to the introduction of third-class sleeping cars; this amenity sent the load of the *Aberdonian* frequently above 500 tons; the Atlantics were overpowered, and even the Gresley Pacifics could not manage such trains single-handed. Third-class sleeping cars were first introduced in the winter of 1928; five years later Sir Nigel Gresley had the answer in his justly celebrated 2–8–2 express engine No. 2001 *Cock o' the North*.

No. 2001 was, however, very much more than a solution of

a difficult local problem. It was the first manifestation of Gresley's acceptance of contemporary French locomotive principles, of his progress towards more efficient front-ends and the elimination of pressure-drop between boiler and steam chests. The passages were internally streamlined in form, and these internal surfaces were given quite a high finish; he fitted poppet instead of piston valves. The nominal tractive effort of the engine was 43,462 lb, still the highest ever to be used in a British passenger engine, but the speedworthiness of No. 2001 due to that magnificent front-end took with some surprise even those most intimately concerned with the design. This capacity for speed was something of an embarrassment on the Aberdeen road, where an engine that needed little encouragement to dash away up to 85 mph was a novelty. In consequence there were many drivers who handled 2001 so gingerly as to make it appear almost as if she was not up to the work. The poppet valves needed rather more attention than the piston valves used on the second engine of the class, No. 2002 *Earl Marischal*, and when further engines were built in 1936 they were fitted with the standard piston valves.

Cock o' the North and *Earl Marischal* paved the way for those amazing engines, the A4 streamlined Pacifics of 1935. They were built originally to run the Silver Jubilee express, and in so doing speeds of over 100 mph in ordinary service, if not necessarily of frequent occurrence, were recorded on a number of occasions. It was not, however, until 1937 that the A4s began regular working in Scotland, in readiness for the *Coronation* express—Edinburgh to London in the even six hours. Just as the earlier Gresley Pacifics had done in working the *Flying Scotsman* non-stop between King's Cross and Waverley, so the A4s took the Scottish end of that wonderful high-speed run in their stride. The one engine ran through, with crews changed at Newcastle, and many a time in the late evening that exquisite blue train having taken the long rising gradients from Berwick to Grantshouse at 65 to 70 mph would come sweeping down Cockburnspath Bank to the sea at nearly 100 mph. Those were great days; but the A4s can still run as of old, and even after

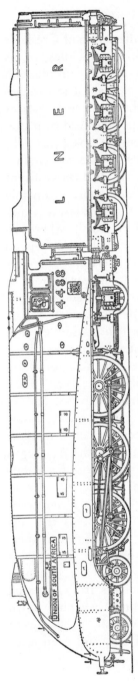

war-time standards of maintenance one of them took the 17-coach *Flying Scotsman* tearing along the Northumberland coast at 84 mph with a load nearly double that of the streamlined *Coronation*.

The later engines of the Cock o' the North class—four of them, grandly named *Lord President*, *Mons Meg*, *Thane of Fife* and *Wolf of Badenoch*—had the same streamlined front as the A4s, and many people, realising how speeds were limited on the Aberdeen route, may have wondered why. Some may even have considered this strange and striking shape as a piece of publicity pure and simple. On the contrary it has a very definite use. On most modern engines, where the chimney is short and the blast from the exhaust very soft, the steam tends to cling to the surface of the boiler and to drift down and obscure the driver's view. *Earl Marischal* was particularly troublesome in this respect in the original form. But when the A4 Pacifics were built the stream-lining at the front end was arranged in the form of a wedge, and this shape proved very effective in deflecting the exhaust steam clear of the front windows of the cab. This same fairing was adopted on the later engines of the Cock o' the North class with equally good results.

At about the same time as the later 2–8–2s were built at Doncaster, the first of the large mixed-traffic engines of the 2–6–2 type was completed, No. 4771 *Green Arrow*. These engines were really a smaller version of the standard non-streamlined

Highland Railway: 4–6–0 heavy passenger locomotive No 55 *Clan Mackinnon* designed by C Cumming and built 1921 by Hawthorn Leslie and Company at Newcastle

Pacifics, but with a pony track instead of a leading bogie. They had smaller coupled wheels—6 ft 2 in against 6 ft 8 in—to render them suitable for heavy freight, fast fish and similar traffic, while north of Dundee they are regularly used in express passenger working. They are extremely useful engines and have a fine turn of speed; they have the wide fire-box of the Pacifics and Cock o' the North class, but despite this I have seen them, like other large LNER locomotives, occasionally fall victims of the really dreadful coal that is sometimes loaded on to their tenders. A fine example of Green Arrow running under such conditions with one of the Aberdeen expresses is included in the Appendix, while a run with one of them on a south-bound express fish train has been described in chapter two.

The Green Arrows were general utility main-line engines available for use anywhere between London and Aberdeen; but they could not be used on many subsidiary routes where engineering restrictions due to curves, clearances, underline bridges or the strength of the road generally are enforced. One such route is the West Highland line from Helensburgh up to Fort William and Mallaig. This exceedingly heavy road was being worked by the ex-North British 4–4–0s of the Glen class and some of Gresley's early 2–6–0s of the K2 series built for the Great Northern Railway. The maximum loads permitted to unassisted engines of these two classes were 180 tons for a Glen and 220 tons for a K2. During the summer tourist season many of the trains were loading to well over their tonnages, and double-heading was frequently necessary. To enable loads of 300 tons to be taken without assistance Sir Nigel Gresley built a new class of Mogul engine with three cylinders, a considerably smaller wheel and a fine steaming boiler. These new engines were designated class K4, and with the exception of the first example No. 3441 *Loch Long* they were named after chieftains of the clans whose ancestral territories are served by the West Highland line. These names were: *Cameron of Lochiel, Mac Cailin Mor, Lord of the Isles* and *MacLeod of MacLeod*. The sixth engine of the class was named *The Great Marquess*—Montrose—the memory of whose lightning campaign is vividly recalled in the region round Fort William.

Sir Nigel Gresley was convinced of the general superiority of three-cylinder propulsion even for locomotives of an inter-mediate character, and he built a class of very handsome 2–6–2 passenger tank engines some of which were allocated to the residential services between Glasgow and Helensburgh. They were ideal for the job, getting smartly away from rest and running up to 60 mph and more between the stops. On the south bank of the Clyde the standard LMS 2–6–4 tanks came to displace the big Caledonian and G & SW pugs, and indeed to take over some of the duties formerly worked by express passenger engines. These LMS tank engines have an astonishing turn of speed; details are set out in the Appendix of a journey on which one of these engines attained a maximum speed of more than 80 mph on level track. They above all engines finally disproved the old theory that to make really fast running one needed to have coupled wheels of 6 ft 6 in or more. These LMS 2–6–4 tanks have wheels only 5 ft 9 in diameter, but in combination with a beautifully designed layout of cylinders and valves the steam flows so freely into and out of the cylinders that speeds up to 85 mph are attained even though the number of revolutions per minute is 415 against the 350 of an officially designated express passenger engine, like the Royal Scots, travelling at the same speed.

6

Mention once again of the Royal Scots leads me, in concluding this chapter, to a later development in Scottish motive power. In the last few years before the outbreak of World War II there was a general seeking after enhanced locomotive power without the necessity of increasing size and weight. The great French engineer André Chapelon had shown what could be done in this direction with the traditional de Glehn four-cylinder compound design as a basis. The boilers were equipped with various aids to steaming, such as thermic syphons in the fire-box to accelerate the circulation of water, and the use of a double blast-pipe and chimney to provide increased draught without the old evil of increased back-pressure. The double chimney had indeed been incorporated by Sir Nigel Gresley on the *Cock o' the North* and subsequent engines of that class. Similar developments were taking place on the LMS at the time war broke out, and already one of the largest Pacifics, the *Duchess of Abercorn*, had given striking evidence of the efficiency of these improvements in a heavy-load trial from Crewe to Glasgow and back. Application of these same principles to the Royal Scots was delayed on account of the war; but the first of the modified engines, No. 6103 *Royal Scots Fusilier*, was completed at Crewe works in the autumn of 1943.

It was very soon apparent that an outstanding success had been achieved, and that excellent though the original engines of 1927 had been, their capacity was altogether exceeded by the modernised engines. I had some experience of them working over the Midland route from Leeds to Glasgow (St Enoch), and in surmounting the long adverse gradients through the Pennines and the more gradual rise through Nithsdale to the windy heights around New Cumnock they displayed a capacity more akin to that of a Pacific than a 4–6–0. It is remarkable too that this modernisation was accompanied not by an increase but by a *reduction* in total engine weight from 85 to 84 tons. It is significant of the esteem in which these engines are now generally held that in the locomotive trials of 1948 these modernised Royal Scots were included with the Pacifics of the London Midland and other regions in the heavy load express passenger trials; and on most of the test routes no reduction of load below the standards agreed upon for the Pacifics and the GWR Kings was granted to the Royal Scots.

7

On the East Coast route an equally striking locomotive conversion has been witnessed, though the reason for it is not so easy to appreciate—none other than the rebuilding of the Cock o' the North class 2–8–2 as Pacifics. On the Aberdeen road, although individual feats of haulage were excellent and work was done with the characteristic thermal efficiency of all Gresley engines, the overall performance as measured in their annual mileage, maintenance costs and casualty records was below LNER standards. During the war, when train loads over the entire East Coast route were so heavy, one might have thought that employment could readily have been found for these very powerful engines between Edinburgh and Newcastle for example, where gradients are heavy in places but on a relatively straight road, which might have gone some way to obviating the heavy maintenance considered to be caused by the constant curvature of the Aberdeen road. Instead, however, the drastic step was taken by Sir Nigel Gresley's successor of rebuilding the engines as 4–6–2s. The adhesion weight was reduced, and they became rather more susceptible to slipping in bad weather. This trait was most graphically demonstrated on a trip I had with the rebuilt *Wolf of Badenoch* in August 1945, when we did magnificently with the down Aberdonian in the earlier stages of the run, in fine weather, regaining a considerable amount of time that had been lost south of Newcastle; but after we ran into heavy rain north of Carnoustie the driver was barely able to hold his own from Arbroath northward. It is true we had a very heavy train of 565 tons, but I could not help feeling that eight-coupled wheels instead of six might have made a lot of difference. Perhaps it was the evergreen memory of *Cock o' the North* and *Earl Marischal* when they were relatively new, and of the superb work put up when I was privileged to ride on their footplates in 1935. It is one thing to put up a first-class show when all the conditions are favourable, and sometimes quite another to maintain a high overall performance year in year out, taking the rough and the smooth equally in one's stride. Certainly the physical characteristics of the Scottish roads are enough to find out the weaknesses in any engine, and since the grouping of the railways it was in many ways Scotland that called the tune where the design of standard locomotives was concerned, both on the LNER and on the LMS.

Since nationalisation of the railways no new steam locomotives have been designed specially for Scotland, and as a major part of the Modernisation Plan the gradual replacement of steam by diesel traction on the main-line services is now in progress. The majority of trains between Perth and Inverness, both passenger and freight, are now diesel hauled, and a similar transition is proceeding rapidly between Edinburgh and Aberdeen. On both these routes the practice is to use locomotives of 'Type 2' capacity—1,150 to 1,250 nominal horsepower—and run them in multiple unit when loads are too great for a single locomotive. On the East Coast main line south of Edinburgh the 2,000 hp 'Type 4' locomotives are in service, and the year 1961 saw the general introduction of the very powerful 'Deltics'.

While modernisation is in full swing it is pleasant to see that the great achievements of the past in Scottish locomotive prowess are not being forgotten, and a number of representative locomotives have been restored to the pre-grouping condition, and used on special trains. In addition to the famous Caledonian 4–2–4 No. 123, referred to in the previous chapter, the Highland 4–6–0 No. 103 has been painted in the gorgeous style of former days, while fine examples of the practice of the North British and Great North of Scotland Railways are now to be seen in their original liveries in the form of the 4–4–0 locomotives, *Glen Douglas* of the NBR and *Gordon Highlander* of the GNSR.

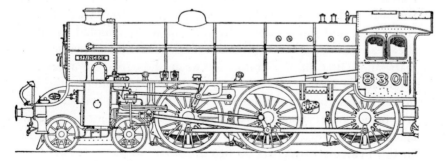

CHAPTER ELEVEN

Scottish Locomotives at Work

I

THE West Coast Postal express sped northward through the night. Penrith had already been passed, and a heavy load of mails discharged at 58 mph into the lineside nets; and now at 70 to 75 mph we were bowling down to Carlisle. The engine, a Pacific of the Princess Royal class, No. 6211 *Queen Maud*, rode easily over the gentle curves in the line; the fireman, after a period of comparative relaxation on the run down from Shap summit, was preparing for the long adverse stretch north of the Solway, dressing the fire, spraying the coal in the tender, occasionally turning the hose on to the footplate itself to keep the dust down. Swiftly he moved in and out of the arc of light from the fire-door, while the driver kept his ceaseless watch on the road ahead, now making an occasional application of the brakes as we neared Carlisle. We had a Crewe engine and men, working over the 245 miles to Glasgow, and on a fine night with some good coal everything had so far gone well. But the Postal is not a heavy train by present standards : north of Carlisle we had 12 vehicles, weighing about 360 tons behind the tender. But no load can be considered light with the Beattock Bank looming ahead. We rolled gently in to a platform stacked high with mails; the Scottish sorters were waiting to take over from their English colleagues, and immediately after arrival we uncoupled and drew ahead so that another engine could pick up the Stranraer van, marshalled first in the train. Fireman Edwards completed his preparations for the second stage of the run by going to the back of the tender to get some coal forward. The later Stanier Pacifics are fitted with steam-operated coal-pushers—a most welcome labour-saving device, especially on a long non-stop run, but not all the Princess Royals are so fitted.

With remarshalling completed, we backed down on to the train ready to take the road into Scotland. In 49¾ miles the line rises to the 1,014-foot altitude of Beattock Summit; no more than 63 minutes are allowed to pass this point, and with the road slightly favourable at first we got away in great style, speed rising to 71 mph at the Solway Firth. The engine was being worked with the controls adjusted to what might be termed the normal running positions: regulator practically full open, and the valves cutting off steam supply to the cylinders after the pistons had travelled 15 per cent of the stroke. Full use was therefore being made of the expansive qualities of the high-pressure steam. No change was necessary to take us up the rising gradients to the first summit point at Castlemilk; the rise here is, however, not steeper than 1 in 200, and with this moderately loaded train the speed at no time fell below 52½ mph. The big engine was taking things very comfortably in her stride. Just beyond Castlemilk automatic signals a temporary speed restriction was in force for permanent-way work, but then we got away for a spell of fast running.

The approach to the hills through Annandale is made through easy country, and while in good conditions the road gives a chance to pile on some speed and make a good time to Beattock station, it is used on less favourable occasions for nursing the boiler in readiness for the great climb into the Lowther Hills. But on this trip, in the dawn of a lovely June day, Driver Walker took No. 6211 along like the wind—in fact he was able to ease the regulator back a little after Lockerbie. We passed Nethercleugh at 72 mph, took the slight rise beyond Dinwoodie at 67½, and then reached no less than 77½ mph at the crossing of the Annan north of Wamphray. But now the great hills were at hand : the gradient changed to 1 in 200 rising; the regulator was pushed hard over; a long blast on our deep-toned Caledonian whistle, and we were through Beattock station and launched in earnest on the bank, getting a glimpse of the postman waiting at the lineside net for the mail bags lowered from the travelling post office vans. We had made excellent time so far, 42 minutes for the 39¾ miles from Carlisle, despite the check near Castlemilk; but 10 miles of gruelling ascent, mostly inclined at 1 in 75, were to prove a testing time for both the capacity of the engine and the skill of the crew.

One can calculate the tractive power of an engine, and assess the steam-raising capacity of the boiler. These values can be related to the tonnage of the train and the inclination of the road, and possible climbing speeds predicted; yet there are many occasions where such calculations can be very wide of the mark. And so, to any theorist, our climb to Beattock Summit that morning might well have been disappointing. With the dawn, mist was rolling down from the hills; the rails were slippery, and with the speed down to about 30 mph the engine showed a tendency to slip. It was no use trying to force the pace uphill; the driver had to find the most she would take, and let the speed look after itself. So we averaged only 25 mph up the last 5 miles of the ascent, with the rough upland country looking very beautiful in the first light of day, our smoke trail hanging almost motionless behind us in the damp air, and the long chain of lights on the sorting carriages still burning. Despite the hindrance of a wet rail we were over Beattock Summit in $61\frac{1}{4}$ minutes from Carlisle, and a brisk run down the Clyde valley brought us into Carstairs, where the train is split up into three sections, for Aberdeen, Glasgow and Edinburgh. I said farewell to Driver Walker and Fireman Edwards, and went back into the train for a wash and a cup of 'TPO Special'—that brand of tea reputed to be so strong that a spoon will stand upright in it !

2

The old Caledonian road from Carlisle is something of a mixture so far as running conditions are concerned; for the most part one can run fast enough, but in the Beattock Bank there is more than a mere hint of what Scotland sets before its locomotives in the way of collar work. As my run with the Postal train showed, a 12-mile bank can take its toll, even with a Pacific of 40,300 lb tractive effort, and even though the incline was charged at 77½ mph. On the Waverley route there is no question of high speed. The curves are too continuous and severe, and the climb from Newcastleton through upper Liddesdale, past bleak Riccarton Junction to Whitrope is as steep, though not quite so long, as the Beattock Bank. And whereas on breasting Beattock Summit Caledonian engines have little save a downhill run right into Glasgow, the Waverley route climbs again steeply up the glen of Gala Water to reach a second high altitude at Falahill, only 17·9 miles short of Edinburgh, and 880 feet above ordnance datum.

On a day of very heavy traffic I joined Driver Ratcliff and Fireman Foster, of Carlisle, on the Gresley A3 Pacific No. 2747 *Coronach* for a run to Edinburgh by the 1.50 p.m. express. This run was made in LNER days, and the engine has since been renumbered 60093. The load was only a moderate one of eight coaches, 275 tons all told; but against this, through congestion of traffic in Carlisle, and our departure just behind a local for Langholm, we were 24 minutes late on leaving Riddings Junction —still in the Border marches and 84·1 miles from Edinburgh. We made the short run to Newcastleton, and from the stop there real business began, starting from rest up the great ascent through Liddesdale. Into the wild moorland country we climbed, with the brisk syncopated beat, characteristic of the Gresley three-cylinder engines, coming sharply from the chimney; regulator full open, cut-off 26 per cent, and the speed held steadily at 31 mph. I sat with my head outside the cab listening to that crisp tattoo that is music in the locomotive man's ears, and watched the road ahead as it snaked its way up and up on that high windswept hillside. The curvature grows increasingly severe as Riccarton Junction is neared, and this increased the resistance to such effect as to bring the speed down to 25 mph. There was no change in the steaming or the gradient; the curves alone were responsible. So we forged our way to the summit point near Whitrope Tunnel, 900 feet above sea-level.

On a different alignment the steep descent into Teviotdale might be taken at 80, if not 90 mph; but the Waverley route was not built that way—the curves are severe enough in places to need check rails, and the 10·9 miles from Whitrope down into Hawick took 14½ minutes. But by the fine hill-climbing from Newcastleton 5 minutes of the lost time had been already regained, and our running through the deep valleys of the Border was really thrilling. Here was none of the exhilaration of long-sustained speeding at 70 or 75 mph, but rather that of a train being lifted away from each intermediate station with the alacrity of an ' electric.' Hawick to St Boswells; St Boswells to Melrose; Melrose to Galashiels—through the Tweedside country beloved of Sir Walter Scott and beneath the stately Eildon Hills we stormed along. The acceleration out of Melrose was typical, with a speed of 55 mph attained in 2 miles from the start, and the 3·7 miles to Galashiels covered in 5½ minutes start to stop. No less smart was the station working, which saved 4 minutes; by the time we left Galashiels the train was only 8½ minutes late.

Up the glen of Gala Water the ascent, although continuous for 15½ miles, is not so steep as through Liddesdale; but the driver used practically the same cut-off position, and on easier gradients the climbing was spectacular, to say the least of it. Round curve after curve, crossing and recrossing Gala Water, *Coronach* blazed away, doing 54 mph for mile after mile. If I had enjoyed our measured progress up the Newcastleton-Whitrope incline, this second ascent was exciting beyond measure. For now there was definite prospect of what, at Newcastleton, I did not think for a moment was possible—a punctual arrival in Edinburgh. And all the time one had to bear in mind that 60 mph was the very maximum we might run down the steep descent from Falahill. While we were tearing into it, uphill, I watched with increasing interest the boiler pressure gauge, for at this speed 27 per cent cut-off with full regulator was fairly hard going. I had no need for apprehension; the gauge needle was stock still, and the water-level in the boiler was well maintained. On the final 2½ miles of the climb the gradient stiffens to 1 in 100, and then becomes 1 in 132 ; but *Coronach* took this final pitch at 47½ mph, and so completed a remarkable ascent of 15·6 miles from

Galashiels in 20½ minutes. Down the bank from Falahill speed at no time exceeded 56 mph, and reductions were made at various points, particularly at Niddrie South Junction and through Portobello. So we came up the final short bank, within sight of Holyrood Palace, through the Calton Tunnel and into Waverley —43¼ minutes for the 33·5 miles from Galashiels, and only one single minute late. In the vigour of the climbing and the notable restraint downhill one could not wish for a finer example of Scottish locomotive working over a heavy road such as the Waverley.

3

Two express trains leave Stranraer Harbour in connection with the evening steamer from Larne: 'The Paddy,' to quote the picturesque and unofficial nickname, a heavy sleeping-car express for London, and the 'Glesca Paddy.' The latter is first away, at 9.30 p.m., and on a rough January night I joined Driver James Stroyan and Fireman Archie McGhee on the footplate of No. 44968, a Black Stanier. A gale was blowing up from the west; we had felt it coming as the *Princess Maud* ploughed her way across the North Channel, and felt it still more on the footplate, as we got away and crossed the open causeway, with a last glimpse of the ship and the harbour lights, and with the wind roaring up the loch. Fifty mph on the slight down grade after Castle Kennedy; a slack to 40 through Dunragit to exchange tablets, then away in tremendous style for the great climb over the Chirmorie. The load was light, only four corridor coaches, totalling 130 tons behind the tender, but on this climb no tonnage can be considered a trifle. Stroyan used 27 per cent cut-off at first in accelerating from Dunragit, but once we were over Challoch Junction and on to the Girvan line he linked up to 15 per cent and this took us up the first stage of broken climbing at an average speed of 48½ mph.

Through New Luce; out over the viaduct, and then on to the dreaded length of 1 in 57 ascent. As we forged our way up over the moorland a brilliant moon shone through the flying clouds. Cut-off advanced to 25 per cent; No. 44968 'barking' in earnest now, and the speed gradually falling till we neared the 'Swan's Neck'—that great reverse curve right on the heaviest part of the grade where many a noble engine has been over-powered by its load, and stalled. But our Black Stanier had things very much in hand, and speed was finely held at 33 to 34 mph till the very last pitch where there was a momentary drop to 32 mph. Over the crest, out on the high open moor an orange light shone in the darkness—Glenwhilly 'distant' on; a long slowing and then finally to a stop in the station. Archie McGhee went to the signal box, and learned that a cattle special from Dunragit to Glasgow was ahead of us, and we had to wait until she cleared the long section to Barrhill. There was no side-tracking her there either, for the 7.35 p.m. milk empties, Glasgow to Stranraer, was waiting in the loop. And so, at the lone, windy little station of Glenwhilly we waited for nearly nine minutes, listening to the alternate soughing and screaming of the wind, with the engine emitting that deep hum that tells of an open blower.

At last we heard the welcome 'ting-ting' of the block-bell in the signal box, and a moment later the signalman came across with the tablet. Under Stroyan's sure touch No. 44968 just 'lifted' that train out of the station, and at 48 to 50 mph, cross-ing and recrossing the brawling Water of Luce, we stormed up the 1 in 100 gradient in bleak and exposed country where the snow fences, glimpsed occasionally in the moonlight, tell their own tale. Then away on the left we saw the light of the shepherd's house of Ardnamoil, a beacon in the all-pervading blackness of the moor. Another hundred yards or so of hard pounding, then steam off. The far light of Ardnamoil disappeared behind a shoulder of the moor, and we were over the Chirmorie Summit, 685 feet above sea-level. Then down between the snow fences, rocketing round the curves, till Barrhill distant was sighted— 'on'! The cattle special was not yet out of our way, and we drew slowly in to wait another 4½ minutes at Barrhill. Then away again, moderately down the steep gradient towards

Pinwherry, and then as we neared this station—signals ' all clear.' The cattle train had been shunted for us. The driver would fain have run really hard here, to charge the 1 in 70 gradient up to Pinmore Tunnel; but the loop had to be negotiated and tablets exchanged and instead of ' charging ' he reduced to 35 mph.

We swung through the station, and with a clang the Barrhill-Pinwherry tablet was delivered; but by one of those occasional misfires of the mechanical exchange apparatus we failed to collect the new one. Brakes on; stop! McGhee, torch in hand, jumped down and ran back. Tablets have been lost in such circumstances, and severe delay caused; but in two minutes he was back in the cab with the pouch and its precious disc, and away we started up the bank. Due to the stops at Glenwhilly and Barrhill, and to this third unforeseen delay we were now ten minutes late; and although with no less than 45 per cent cut-off and the engine roaring all the way, we made good time to Pinmore, the very steep descent into Girvan must needs be taken cautiously, and that night we eased our way down in the teeth of a terrific squall. While we stood, taking water, the wind flung the side doors of the cab open as if they were canvas; the rain lashed the engine and tender as if shot from a hose. Below us in the deserted streets of Girvan the water ran like a river.

' Right away '! Double line now, and every chance of a clear run to Ayr; we were nearly 9 minutes late, and only 21·4 miles to go, but Stroyan and McGhee went for it with a vengeance, and the result was the most exciting 20 minutes I ever remember on the footplate. The road from Girvan to Ayr is a heavily graded switchback, with favourable stretches preceding most of the steep climbs; with a Black Stanier in good form and only four coaches anything might seem possible, but on account of curves and other engineering restrictions the lengths on which speeds of 70 mph can be run are very few. To a good driver bent on regaining lost time there is only one course open, to go hard uphill; and go hard we did! The start from Girvan, in fearful weather, set the standard. Up the Killochan Bank, at 1 in 72, No. 44968 was accelerated to 55 mph on a gradient as steep as

Manson. I rode through to Perth on the leading engine. The climb out of Strathspey to the Inverness-Perth County March in the Pass of Druimuachdar begins in earnest soon after leaving Kingussie, and in the evening of a cloudless day, with the intense blue shadows from the great hills beginning to lengthen across the valley, we set off on the non-stop run of 36·3 miles to Blair Atholl.

We got away smartly, covering the 2·9 miles to Newtonmore in 5½ minutes, but then with the gradient stiffening to 1 in 95 the point of cut-off on No. 45360 was advanced to 35 per cent. The regulator had been absolutely full open from the start, and with 5161 behind us going hard too, we forged our way up the grade to Etteridge crossing loop. Still longer cut-off; 38 per cent for the last mile and a half to the signal box, and speed falling gradually to 31 mph. Clear signals through the loop; valves linked up to 32 per cent, and then much faster climbing of the more broken gradients towards Dalwhinnie. The inclinations here vary between 1 in 100 and 1 in 200, and there are two short lengths of dead-level track; and with the two engines working grandly in harness, we kept going between 35 and 44 mph. Meanwhile the mountains passed in stately procession. There were times when one sensed that isolation in a wild, sparsely populated countryside that I experienced so keenly on that amazing stretch north of Forsinard; but here the main road is never far away, and there is something in the railway itself, with its fine heavily ballasted permanent way, that savours less of the back-of-beyond atmosphere. We swung through Dalwhinnie in great style at 45 mph; even bleak Loch Ericht, shining like a mirror, reflected the brilliance of the evening sky, and then on double-line track we headed up the narrowing ' V ' of Glen Truim.

Gradient 1 in 80 now; cut-off 38 per cent once more, and the exhaust beats of both engines sharpening into a roar. Behind us 5161 was showing the white feather from her safety valves; on 45360 boiler pressure was only just below blowing-off point. The Black Staniers are used so intensively, and run such high mileages between successive visits to plant for heavy repairs, that one often meets engines that are rough, or partly run down. But

45360 was a beauty; her action, even under heaviest pounding, was as sweet as the most finely tuned-up express locomotive, and she was steaming so freely that Maclennan lengthened the cut-off still further to 43 per cent as the speed fell off on the 1 in 80 gradient. Just at the conclusion of this grade we were down to 26 mph; but now the great rounded hills at the head of the pass were coming into the picture, and the speed rose rapidly to 31 mph on a mile of easier grading. Maclennan slightly eased the working of No. 45360, to 40 per cent cut-off, and at 27½ mph we breasted the highest standard-gauge railway summit in Great Britain—the 1,484 feet of Druimuachdar. The 18·6 miles up from Kingussie had been climbed in 33½ minutes.

The line dipped down towards Glen Garry. Regulators were eased, reversers wound back, and the exhausts of our two engines quietened into virtually complete silence. The hills on the west opened out to give a lovely sight of Loch Garry against the strong evening sun, and we rolled through Dalnaspidal at 56 mph. So we went down the long hill towards Blair Atholl, with the engine regulators in the ' drifting ' position, giving just enough steam to provide some cushioning action in the cylinders and to keep the train running steadily without the need for frequent applications of the brake. At 50 to 55 mph we came down from the desolate upper reaches of Glen Garry, through the woods of Struan, and so into Blair, with the striking peak of Ben Vrackie now directly ahead of us: 55¾ minutes for the run from Kingussie.

Away again, along the green level valley where there is not a hint of the supreme thrill to come so soon. But we are work- ing single line again, and the hills are noticeably closing in when we slow down for the next passing loop. Killiecrankie! Through the station the line curves to the left and reveals a single-track tunnel; with tablets exchanged we dive in, but we are no sooner in than we are out again, on a reverse curve, and crossing the high viaduct in the loveliest part of Killiecrankie Pass. It was enthralling to look back momentarily from the cab, to see our long train coming from that narrow tunnel and sweeping round the curve behind us, and to see all around the rays of the setting

British Railways : two former LMS express locomotives in the new standard colours : *City of Edinburgh* in the red chosen for the largest and most powerful types on the west coast, and a Converted Royal Scot *Cameron Highlander* in the dark green of second-line express engines

sun slanting through the exquisite foliage of the trees, ranged from the brawling Garry far below to the slopes of Ben Vrackie above us. We were through the pass all too soon, and then coasting into Pitlochry. A further halt of 3 minutes, and away again for Perth and more placid scenes. Along Strathtay the level going made easy work for two engines, but the Highland line provides a ' tricky ' finish in the last 8½ miles from Dunkeld to its junction with the Caledonian line at Stanley. Here there are gradients as steep as anywhere on the south-bound run from Aviemore, and as we passed through Dunkeld the exhausts of both engines sharpened into a roar as they attacked the 1 in 80 to Kingswood crossing. One's vivid impressions were intensified passing through the short tunnels and the rock cuttings where reverberation was sharp and loud. Cut-off on 45360 advanced to 42 per cent; a momentary but thunderous slip of the driving wheels when passing through the pinewoods, and the summit loop was passed at 35 mph. Then steeply downhill, to exchange tablets for the last time at Murthly, at 53 mph; a short rise at 1 in 108, and then down to the Caledonian, at Stanley, to snake a way through that most curious of junction layouts on to the superb alignment of the Euston-Aberdeen trunk route. Time was well in hand, and we took the last 7·2 miles into Perth quietly to arrive in exactly 42 minutes from Pitlochry, 28·5 miles. In all, the 83·3 miles from Aviemore had occupied 2 hours 18½ minutes, with three stops, and our running average, allowing for the 9½ minutes we were standing, was 39 mph. I climbed down from 45360 at Perth conscious of having seen Highland loco-motive working at its finest—if not necessarily in its more exciting and hazardous aspects amid the winter snows.

5

I never travel to Perth without recalling a run made in the heyday of the Midland compounds, a Saturday of heavy traffic in the late summer of 1934 when I was privileged to ride on the engine working the up *Granite City* express. Throughout from

Aberdeen to Glasgow our engine was No. 1127, with James Grassie at the regulator. Grassie was a great engineman, steeped in the traditions of the Caledonian; for many years the beautiful McIntosh 4–6–0 No. 50 *Sir James Thompson*, illustrated in the colour-plate facing page 4, was his regular engine. We had every need of his enginemanship on that 1934 occasion for the train was made up to eleven coaches, fully 355 tons behind the tender. It was at Perth that the really heavy work began, for we had been assisted by a veteran Dunalastair 4–4–0 from Aberdeen to Forfar. Ahead of us was some stiff climbing—not, it is true, as steep as Beattock, Liddesdale or some parts of the Highland line, but gruelling enough with nothing larger than a 64-ton 4–4–0 engine, as against a 72-ton Black Stanier, or a 96-ton Gresley Pacific. But as their original owners came to learn through the famous Leeds-Carlisle tests of 1924 those compounds just revelled in hard collar work, and the long ascents, first at 1 in 100 to Gleneagles, and then at 1 in 128 up Cumbernauld Glen, provided Grassie with ample scope for a perfect exposition of locomotive capacity.

We began inauspiciously with a dead stand for signals at Hilton Junction, just at the west end of Moncrieff Tunnel; but after a wait of 40 seconds Grassie got No. 1127 away in magnificent style, with regulator full open, and the reverser set 6 notches forward, out of a total of 10. The actual cut-offs were 67 per cent in the high-pressure cylinder, and 55 per cent in the two low-pressure cylinders, equivalent to about 27 per cent in a single-expansion engine. Up the gradual rise through Strathearn we roared, with speed rising to $54\frac{1}{2}$ mph between Forteviot and Dunning, where the grade is 1 in 430 to 1 in 460. With the Ochils looming up ahead we came on to the 1 in 100 grade; Grassie at once put the lever forward to the eighth notch, and the engine fairly pounded her way up the bank. The fireman stoked assiduously; there is an art in firing one of these compounds, and in spite of the heavy working boiler-pressure remained full up. Auchterarder was passed at 32 mph, and the speed was gradually settling to a steady figure; the lowest before steam was shut off for Gleneagles was 28 mph—grand work with such a load.

As we left Gleneagles, still on a gradient of 1 in 100, the haulage capacity of these compound engines was brilliantly displayed. Grassie employed the usual technique, opening the regulator only about a quarter of the way at first, and admitting steam direct to the two low-pressure cylinders. With the lever full forward the exhaust was like gunfire, and into the deep cutting we blasted our way. But once the train was properly on the move the regulator was pushed hard over, and full compound working began, accompanied by a noticeable quietening of the exhaust. Some compound-locomotive designers in their quest for increased efficiency have fitted their engines with a multiplicity of gadgets for varying the methods of control; but there could be nothing simpler than the duplex regulator fitted to the Midland compounds by R. M. Deeley, and this simplicity of control, together with good design and robust construction, made them great engines for the Scottish railways. But there is precious little comfort in their cabs, and their riding can be disconcertingly wild—as I was not long in discovering on No. 1127, to old Grassie's amusement!

The summit is reached in barely half a mile from Gleneagles, and under easier steaming we bowled down towards Kinbuck in good style, with a top speed of 66 mph, though down the steep grade through Dunblane and Bridge of Allan speed was frequently checked by the brakes to keep the train—and the engine!—riding steadily. The timing of 20 minutes for the 17·2 miles from Gleneagles to Stirling certainly left nothing to spare, and we were a little out on arrival. Then came the final run. Dusk was falling; a tiny oil lamp was lighted in the cab to show the water-level in the gauge glasses; the tender was topped up, and then ' right-away.' Grassie set the lever in the seventh notch, cut-offs 72 per cent in the high-pressure cylinder and 62 per cent in the low-pressure, and away we went through Bannockburn to the first summit point at Plean, and then in a swift downhill acceleration to 62 mph at Alloa Junction.

Thrills ! At the moment of writing it is over twenty-five years since I made this trip, but I can remember as vividly as if it had occurred yesterday how in the gathering darkness we bore down upon Larbert; the pale green signal lights standing out clearly, the sharp lurches of the engine, the scream of the whistle as we drew nearer to the station, and then the sudden sharpening of the beat as Grassie put the regulator hard over in readiness for the attack on Cumbernauld Glen. There was something intensely ' alive ' about this 4–4–0 engine; it was not a case of merely travelling in her cab, you had literally to *ride* her—brace yourself against every swing—and once acclimatised to her, she was exhilarating. The log of our exploits, set out on page 228 of the Appendix, gives the technical details of that great climb: 1 in 100 to Greenhill, where speed fell to 40 mph; a quick rise to 50½, then past Castlecary signal box, through the short tunnel and into the glen itself. I read my watches in the brilliant arc of light from the fire; by the same light I watched the gauge needles. Outside, in the intense darkness between the trees, an occasional spark shot from the chimney; but the working of the engine was first-class, and there was no fire-throwing worth mention. So we came to Cumbernauld station, and it was only in the very last mile that speed dropped below 40 mph.

There were no symptoms of flagging after those strenuous nine miles up from Larbert, and on easy gradients the next four miles on to Glenboig were covered in 4¾ minutes. As we passed this junction in only a few seconds over the allotted 28 minutes from Stirling (21·2 miles) the day was all but won, as the concluding stretch into Glasgow permits of some recovery. But on this particular evening an engineers' slack was in operation near Robroyston, and cost us about 2 minutes in running. Despite this we came down the stiff gradient through St Rollox and cautiously into Buchanan Street to stop in less than a minute over our scheduled time from Stirling—41¾ minutes for the run of 30·2 miles. Scottish drivers have given me some great runs with the Midland compounds, and many a time from the train I have listened to the crisp exhaust beat as they fight a heavy gradient, sometimes when the loads were almost of Pacific magnitude. But above all I treasure this experience on the *Granite City* express, and the privilege of seeing how this heavy work was done.

6

The Midland compound design was wholly of English origin; but by adoption, and no less by the excellent use to which the locomotives were put, it became almost as characteristic a feature of Scottish railway working as the Dunalastairs or as James Manson's Pullman engines of the ' Sou' West.' They carried the semaphore head codes of the Caledonian, and the old flair for individual adornments was occasionally seen in such things as bright polished rims to the smoke-box doors. English engines came to the LNER too, and not only the big Pacifics that went to Newcastle and beyond. But out on the West Highland there survived in the full strength of its maximum achievement a 4–4–0 locomotive class, Scottish to the last split-pin. The old NBR had a worthy counterpart to the largest of the Dunalastair family on the Caledonian in the handsome Sir Walter Scott class, and when later engines of this successful class were fitted with super-heaters the performance was enhanced. But it was in the small-wheeled variant of the Scotts, built specially for the West Highland line and named after glens, that the traditional Scottish 4–4–0 locomotive, developed in direct line of succession from the Drummond Waverleys of 1876, seemed to touch its great-est heights of achievement. The design remained unchanged over nearly forty years. *Glen Aladale*, *Glen Gloy*, *Glen Beasdale*, *Glen Mōidart* and the rest, have borne the colours of the North British Railway, the apple-green of the LNER, and the black adopted in the lean years following 1931; after the war some of them reappeared in apple-green, but with Gill Sans lettering, and now as they pass through the shops they are taking the ' lined-black ' of British Railways. But throughout this period their true NBR lineaments have been preserved. No-one has tried to fit 'flower-pot' chimneys or flat-topped dome covers; their silhouette is the same as in 1913.

On a rough day in the late summer of 1937 I was travelling south from Fort William; the train was the noon service from Mallaig connecting with steamers from Portree and from the Outer Isles. I was down at the running sheds in the morning and learnt that the load was to be a heavy one, worked by two Glens. From past experience I had found that two Glens together made a most formidable combination, and when the load of the train was wired as 320 tons tare, I looked forward to an interesting trip, as this tonnage, 160 apiece, was not far short of the maximum of 180 tons permitted to the class over the West Highland line. The engines turned out to be 9406 *Glen Croe*, leading, and 9494 *Glen Loy*, and as we backed down towards the station, away across the water could be seen the steam of the Mallaig train as she approached Corpach. Then the bright sunshine was followed by a squall of rain; loch, distant station, train and the mountains behind them disappeared as behind a curtain.

I rode through to Crianlarich on the leading engine, and through storm and sunshine those two Glens exceeded my expectations. There was no precise setting of the reverser; no delicate adjustment of the cut-off to one or two per cent at a time that one sees on modern engines; the wheel was turned till the blast was full-throated and clear, till to the driver's experienced ear the engine showed no sign of choking herself at the front end—neither too much steam nor too little. Then we blazed away. Twenty-nine mph up the first stretch of 1 in 59 ascent; brief stops at Spean Bridge and Roy Bridge, and then a crashing orchestration of exhausts as we threaded our way through the superb Monessie Gorge, where one looked from the cab almost vertically down to the swirling brown waters of the Spean while the engines fought their way at 26 mph up the 1 in 64 gradient. Tulloch—skies clearing—and then again the dual cannonade from *Glen Croe* and *Glen Loy* as we passed the dam at the foot of Loch Treig and mounted high above the water towards the summit point at Corrour.

There was something supremely competent and reliable about these two relatively small engines; easy and comfortable to fire, steaming with the greatest freedom, and yet for all their 1913 vintage doing heavy work. Up the long 1 in 67 gradient overlooking Loch Treig speed varied between 26 and 28 mph, and at length we drew into Corrour in 35 seconds over the hour from Fort William, including three stops totalling 3 minutes standing time. The distance is 28·0 miles, and in those miles the train, weighing 345 tons with passengers and luggage, had been lifted from the pier-side at Fort William to an altitude of 1,347 feet above sea-level. Heavy working was now over for a while, and with regulators in the drifting position we bowled across Rannoch Moor making as fast a time as the over-all speed limit of 40 mph permits, while the brilliant sunshine turned the brown peat bogs of the moor to wave upon wave of glistening gold. Down the steeper gradients towards Bridge of Orchy, past the ancient pines of Crannach Woods, the train was beautifully controlled, with that same smoothness of running that marked the run from Dalnaspidal down to Blair Atholl on the Highland Mail. Then came the climb from Bridge of Orchy, round the Horseshoe Bend and up the 1 in 55 gradient to the Perth-Argyll County March. In certain conditions this might have been an anxious time, but with these two engines, so masters of their work, it was a delight. In mist and rain once more we rounded the Horseshoe at 40 mph; over those slender viaducts, with cab glasses streaming, and belching clouds of smoke from the two engines rolling up the flanks of Beinn Odhar; on the 1 in 55 gradient to the County March speed fell away only to 26½ mph.

We were running non-stop over the 28·1 miles from Rannoch to Crianlarich, and came cautiously down the steep grade from this intermediate summit to exchange tablets at Tyndrum. Rounding the curve there the whole expanse of Strathfillan was spread out below; once more the mountain tops were clear, and broad patches of sunshine were sweeping the farther hillsides. Down that curving track we wound our way, keeping mostly between 35 and 40 mph, and so to the final bend, across the strath and into Crianlarich, just 46 minutes from Rannoch. I was staying a while in that pleasant Highland village, and later that day I saw the LMS mail from Oban approach from the head of Glen Lochy, and then the Fort William-King's Cross sleeper snake its way down the hill from Tyndrum as we had done, showing up in the dusk as a chain of lighted windows.

There is certainly thrill and romance in everyday locomotive working in Scotland, even in these austere times; but in recalling some recent exploits, when speed restrictions were faithfully observed and interest arose from the development of high-power output on a straight or level road, the imagination turns inevitably to earlier occasions when under the stimulus of intense competition, restraint, if not necessarily thrown to the winds, was certainly stowed away in the locker on the tender! The stage is indeed now set for ringing up the final curtain, on a chapter of reminiscence, anecdotes and Scottish railway lore. In this the amazing August of 1895 takes first place.

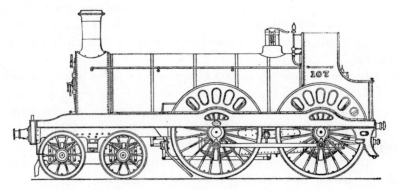

CHAPTER TWELVE

A Scottish Miscellany

I

On 14 August 1895 Patrick Stirling, Locomotive Superintendent of the Great Northern Railway, wrote thus to his District Superintendent at Peterborough:

'The L & NW Co. have expressed their intention to reach Aberdeen before us. This of course we cannot permit, and arrangements are being made by this company and the NE and NB Railways to accelerate the speed of the above train [the 8.0 p.m. King's Cross to Aberdeen] commencing on Monday next.

'We must reach York at 11.15 p.m. The load will not exceed 6 whenever possible to keep it to that number and 7 will be the maximum in every case. The NE Company have undertaken to run their share of the distance at high speed, over 60½ miles per hour York to Newcastle, and the NB also.

'Please put your men on their mettle!'

In such emphatic terms was ushered in the most exciting week in the history of the British railways. It was the culmination of two months' time-cutting, in which time-tables came to be scrapped fortnightly until the West Coast companies conceived the astonishing idea of ignoring booked time altogether and running the famous 8 p.m. 'Tourist' express from Euston just as fast as their engines could take it. It was publicly advertised to arrive in Aberdeen at 7 a.m., but more often than not rolled in around 5 a.m.! It was exploits of this kind that finally stung the East Coast into very thrilling action; but on Monday 19th August the train was handicapped by the last lingerings of orthodox operating. A new schedule had been planned, which it was hoped would be adequate for dealing with the West Coast; but while all concerned on the Great Northern and on the North Eastern understood that this timing was merely laid down as a guide, and that actually the train was to be worked through as quickly as possible, the Scots did not, and the racing train was delayed at both Edinburgh and Dundee waiting for time.

The dramatic interest of the race was heightened by the convergence of the two routes at Kinnaber Junction, just north of Montrose. Now Kinnaber was a Caledonian signal box, and partisans questioned what might happen if both racing trains were offered simultaneously, the one from Montrose and the other from Dubton. Excited crowds gathered at King's Cross and Euston, and the rival trains went off amid cheers. The delay to the East Coast train on the first night naturally brought strong representations from King's Cross and York, and the North British Railway certainly made no mistakes afterwards. The night of 20th August was the closest of all, when the West Coast train passed Kinnaber less than a minute ahead of her rival; but on the 21st the East Coast won a resounding victory. Edinburgh was reached in 6 hours 19 minutes from London, including stops to change engines at Grantham, York and Newcastle—an inclusive average of 62 mph. Only those who are fully acquainted with the running difficulties of the line north of Edinburgh will appreciate the magnificent contribution of the North British Railway in running the 59·2 miles from Waverley to Dundee in exactly 59 minutes, and the remaining 71·3 miles on to Aberdeen in 78 minutes. The result of this energy was to effect an arrival in Aberdeen at 4.40 a.m.—14½ minutes ahead of the West Coast.

The following is an abridged log of the run:

Miles		Minutes
0·0	Edinburgh	0
9·5	Dalmeny	11
25·9	Kirkcaldy	27
30·7	Thornton	32
50·9	Leuchars Jc	51
59·2	Dundee	59
0·0		0
17·0	Arbroath	20
33·3	Kinnaber Jc	39½
55·2	Stonehaven	61
71·3	Aberdeen	78

A modest 2 minutes was taken to change engines at Dundee.

The contest was not made on altogether equal terms. While the East Coast carried the heavier load the West Coast had the harder route and 16½ miles farther to go. Thus after their experience on the night of 21st August the L & NWR and the Caledonian made a supreme final effort. The train was divided, and a first portion of only three coaches was worked through over the 540 miles from Euston to Aberdeen in the absolute record time of 512 minutes. The final stretch from Perth to Aberdeen was run at the high average speed of 66 mph. The times made in the closing stages of the 1895 race were indeed very much faster than those in the earlier race of 1888; this was partly due to the improved locomotives, but more so I think to the increasing use of harder steel for tyres and rails. It was not only in the Aberdeen race that speeds ruled generally higher than in former years.

But the bald results of the race give little idea of the incredibly exciting journeys involved, nor yet of the risks that undoubtedly were taken. One story comes from the racy pen of Norman D. Macdonald: 'The last night of the "Race" was nearly the death of a group of famous and infamous folk, i.e. the Rev. W. J. Scott, Sir William Acworth, C. Rous-Marten, Percy Caldicott, W. M. Gilbert (the chief of the staff of *The Scotsman*) and myself. It fell on this-wise. My East Coast friends (NER, NBR and GNR) always put on a sleeper for my party when any new spurt effort came to the birth. Till I got the NER to build the first transverse-berthed sleeper these were made up of cabins of two beds placed longitudinally, entered from a passage across the car.

' At Portobello (Edinburgh) there then was a very bad S-curve with our usual half-hearted British elevation, ending on a high bridge above a wide road.

' At Inveresk Rous-Marten, with his four split watches (one in each hand and one in each trouser pocket), called " 82 mph." I said " If these two big Worsdells don't slack off we will be thrown through the windows, even if we stay on the rails, at the Portobello S." I quickly got the six into the cross-passage, where we jammed our legs and arms against the walls, myself at one window and Rous-Marten at the other. Just before the curves he called " 8 1½," and I yelled " Look out !" as we struck it. The whole of them were thrown on to me, and we collapsed, as does a Rugby maul, and in the next second we were hurled up again and on to the top of C. R-M. In his dry Dutch way he was heard to say, "We would have made bonnie raspberry jam in that Duddingston Road!" When we emerged into Waverley out of the Calton Tunnel (after a mile of 1 in 78 up) we were doing about 64 mph and Acworth remarked, "Thank goodness we are working Westinghouse and not vacuum, and that Waverley is very long!" '

2

Macdonald was a famous Scots lawyer; but so far as railways were concerned, he describes himself with characteristic humour in a letter to *The Railway Gazette* in 1937: ' Nigh 50 years ago General Managers looked on me as a pestiferous fellow who troubled their waters in the press, and also in private—pressing for progress.' Sir George Gibb of the North Eastern once remarked, ' When Macdonald providentially dies you will find big red letters of blood branded deep into his back:

BIGGER BOILERS
BETTER BRAKES '

And Macdonald troubled their waters on points of detail no less than with matters of high policy. There was the episode of the roofboards. Construction of rolling stock for the East Coast joint services was shared between the companies, but to the annoyance of all good Scots the English works had a way of coining strange abbreviations when it came to painting the legends on the roofboards; one might see, for example, ' King's Cross and Edinbro',' ' King's Cross and Edinboro',' and ' King's Cross and Edinburgh' all on the same train! Eventually things got too much for Macdonald to stand. Letters had no effect; mild remonstrances with senior officers still less, so one day he set about an Anglo-Scottish express standing in Waverley Station and stripped it of its roof boards. Shortly afterwards one set, including Edinbro', Edinboro' and Edinburgh was found adorning the book-cases in Sir George Gibb's library, while another set somehow found its way on to the seats of the first-class compartment in which the Great Northern Superintendent of the Line was to return to London after a visit of inspection to Doncaster!

There was a time when Scotland might have become an all-Westinghouse country: the Highland Railway alone stood apart, until the middle eighties of last century, when the close associa-tion of the Glasgow and South Western with the Midland led to a change at Kilmarnock. Although the Midland was one of the earliest British companies to use the air brake, there was a strong feeling among certain influential persons on that line that it was not wholly desirable for an English railway to be dependent upon an outside firm, and particularly one of American origin, for so vital a matter as brakes. Certain other forms of brake were being tried on the Midland at the time; one in particular was being actively developed, to the annoyance of the Westinghouse Brake Company; annoyance led to strained relations and eventu-ally to a complete breach, by which time the automatic vacuum brake had been developed to the stage that use of the air brake could be discontinued. Having made this decision the Midland persuaded the Glasgow and South Western to do the same. The North British, however, stood firm, and their immediate partner on the East Coast route, the North Eastern, remained a Westing-house line. The joint rolling stock running in the Anglo-Scottish expresses had to be fitted with both brakes, as the Great Northern adopted the vacuum. It was the same on the West Coast, with the L & NWR and the Highland using the vacuum and the Cale-donian using the Westinghouse.

Until the Great Western introduced their direct admission valves some 45 years ago, the Westinghouse was unquestionably the quicker-acting of the two forms of continuous brake. This was a well-known phenomenon in the days when some railways used one brake and some the other; thus the remark of Sir

William Acworth on that somewhat hectic approach to Edinburgh. On their numerous fast runs the Caledonian used to save time by very rapid approaches to the stations, a practice born of the confidence drivers had in the air brake, though on certain parts of the former North British the tradition has remained long after the vacuum brake was adopted as standard for Great Britain after the grouping. When travelling on the footplate over the West Highland line, and particularly on the Mallaig extension, I noticed how drivers made very rapid approaches to the stations, even when those approaches were round blind curves, and came in to stop smoothly and dead on the mark. The change to vacuum on the G & SWR no doubt met the wholehearted approval of one old driver, who, on a memorable occasion roundly declared that he ' did not like thae *Washin' hoose* brakes'!

3

The change of brakes on the G & SWR might well have been made out of pure cussedness, since the Caledonian adhered to the Westinghouse. For with enmity between the two companies at the pitch it was, anything the Caley did was a thing to be studiously avoided by the ' Sou' West.' This rivalry was not a thing confined to the management, lingering from the old controversy over the Nithsdale and Annandale routes from Carlisle to Glasgow; it extended to the humblest members of the rank and file on both sides. David L. Smith quotes the poem made up by a young fireman at Dumfries while working on a Stirling 0–4–2 engine No. 259:

'We left St Enoch station, our time was eight-sixteen,
The electric light was shining; her beauty there was seen.
We ran our miles so speedily and reached Dumfries to time,
And we beat the Caledonian with the Two-five-nine!'

' Beat the Caledonian'—that was the spirit; Smith relates the stories told by older men of the ' Sou' West ' about the head-on collision at Dalbeattie in 1874, on the line from Dumfries to

Stranraer—'how the "Sou' West" man on the ballast train, when he saw the Caley goods coming head-on to him on the single-line, seized the staff which was his authority to occupy the section and swung it on to his shoulder, and how, as he lay insensible in the wreckage, Caley men were found *trying to take the staff from him.*' As Smith remarks, this may or may not have been true, but G & SW men of those days were ready to believe anything of the Caley, even to such a trick as faking the evidence in a collision.

4

Dalbeattie was, of course, a relatively minor incident. Under the stress of war conditions, in 1915, the Caledonian was unfortunate enough to sustain the most terrible accident in British railway history. It occurred at the extreme south end of the line, only just on Scottish soil, at the intermediate signal box of Quintinshill, halfway between Gretna and Kirkpatrick. The first factor in a tragic chain of events was the late running of the midnight express from Euston to Glasgow on the Saturday before Whitsun 1915. This train should have left Carlisle at 6.5 a.m., but the 6.17 a.m. local was dispatched ahead of it, and arrangements were made to shunt this local for the express at Quintinshill. Adjacent to this signal box there are lengthy sidings on both up and down sides of the line, but on this particular morning both sidings were occupied by freight trains. The only available procedure was to propel the local train backwards through the crossover road on to the up main line. This is a normal movement, but its use entails the taking of certain important precautions, one of which is to send what is termed the 'blocking-back' signal to the box next on the line, to warn the signalman that the line is blocked, and another is to put a collar on the lever of the main-line signal concerned as a physical reminder of the obstruction.

Now the signalmen normally change shift at 6 a.m. The men at Quintinshill that morning had a private and quite unauthorised arrangement enabling the relief man to travel to his work by the 6.17 a.m. train from Carlisle. So that the authorities should not be aware of this arrangement the night signalman kept a copy of train movements since 6 a.m.—which should have been recorded at once in the train register—on a separate sheet of paper, for the relief man to copy into the book when he came on duty. The local train duly arrived, and was shunted on to the up main line; the relief signalman went to the box, took over and began at once to copy into the register the train record made since 6 a.m. The night man, having completely failed in his duty by neither 'blocking back' to Kirkpatrick nor placing a collar on the up home signal lever, handed over. One would have thought that the day man, having travelled in the Carlisle local, would have made sure it was properly protected, standing as it was temporarily on the up line; but he seems to have been so preoccupied with the register that when Kirkpatrick box, unaware of the obstruction, asked for 'line clear' for a south-bound troop train he gave it at once and lowered all his up-line signals. Similarly the down-line signals were cleared for the midnight express from Euston. The results of this negligence were appalling. The troop train approached, running fast on a down gradient, and collided so violently with the standing local train that the great 4–6–0 engine of the latter was smashed beyond repair, and the wooden-framed coaches of the troop train were shattered upon the steel mass of the two engines. The down express was too near to be stopped, and less than a minute after this first fearful crash the 'midnight,' drawn by two engines, was ploughing its way through the wreckage. Fire broke out among the shattered wooden coaches of the troop train, and the combined effects of the collision and fire were such that the casualty list included more than 80 officers and men whom the Military Authorities could only classify as 'missing,' no recognisable traces having been found. Including this number, no fewer than 227 persons were killed and 250 injured. All but 12 of the killed were officers and men of the 7th Battalion The Royal Scots.

Nearby, at the Solway Firth in 1881, there was an accident that might have been a catastrophe as great as that to the Tay Bridge. The Solway Junction Railway, running between

Kirtlebridge on the Caledonian main line and Brayton in Cumberland, on the Maryport and Carlisle Railway, crossed the Firth on a viaduct 1,940 yards long; it consisted of no less than 192 spans, each 30 feet long and carried on cast-iron columnar piers. The winter of 1881 included some severe weather, and after one particularly hard spell of frost large masses of ice floated down the channel on the swift-flowing ebb tide and damaged the viaduct to such an extent that 45 spans collapsed. Fortunately there was no loss of life. The viaduct was rebuilt and opened to traffic once again in the spring of 1884, but business never grew to any appreciable extent and in 1921 the line was closed. The viaduct itself was dismantled in 1934–5.

A curious accident occurred in Glasgow in 1928 in the tunnel outside Queen Street (High Level) Station. The one-time Edinburgh and Glasgow Railway was carried out of the terminus on a very steep incline—1 in 51 at the entrance to the tunnel, steepening to 1 in 43, and finally to 1 in 41; here the loading regulations are very severe, and most trains are provided with two engines. But on this particular evening the first part of the 9.45 p.m. express to Edinburgh had only five coaches—a one-engine load. On entering the tunnel the engine began slipping, so badly indeed as not merely to stall but to permit the train to run backwards down the incline. The tunnel was so full of smoke that the driver did not realise his train was running back, and, unfortunately, a train of empty stock had been permitted to shunt into the tunnel after the departure of the express, in violation of the working rules at Queen Street. The two trains collided inside the tunnel and three passengers were killed. Such a gradient calls for most careful working at the best of times, and for many years trains were assisted up the incline to Cowlairs by a cable attached to a stationary winding engine at the summit. This method was used from the opening of the railway in 1842 until 1909, when the North British Railway adopted the practice of providing rear-end banking engines. The illustration facing page 30 shows splicing of the endless steel rope in progress. In this arduous service the average life of a cable was only 12 months. In the background of this picture can be seen some of the braking trucks that were used for controlling trains on the descent of the gradient ; in this direction of running the locomotive was detached at Cowlairs. It is strange to see that on these special wagons brake is spelt 'break.'

5

Passing now to the opposite end of the Edinburgh and Glasgow Railway the present locomotive running sheds at Haymarket are worthy of particular notice, not so much on account of track layout or servicing facilities, but for the method of allocating engines and men, which is a revival of earlier practice that was general in Great Britain. At one time engines were allotted for lengthy periods to one or, at the most, two drivers. Some companies, including the Great Northern, carried this practice to the extent of exclusive use so that if, for example, a main-line express engine had to be nursed back into full commission following some mechanical failure, the express driver had to go through the process with the engine, working light duties, stopping trains and so on until the condition was fit for resumption of normal work. One reads also of drivers becoming so intensely possessive as to fit padlocks to the regulators so that ' their engine ' could not be moved unless they were present ! But regulations concerning the hours of daily duty, combined with the need to obtain the most use out of engines, broke down the old 'one man one engine ' tradition, and generally it was found possible to operate a system of double-manning.

The stringent economic condition of the early thirties led to a further breakaway. Modern design of working parts and mechanised aids to servicing at the running sheds suggested that still more extensive use could be obtained from locomotives, and thus the traffic might be operated with fewer engines. A system of common-user was introduced, first on the LMS and later on the LNER, in which locomotives had no regular crews, and might indeed be handled by four or more sets of men in the course of a single round of duty. While this certainly achieved its object in obtaining a greater weekly mileage than hitherto out of individual engines, there is no doubt that the general condition of engines deteriorated not only in outward appearance but in mechanical condition. It is hardly to be expected that a crew taking over a locomotive that in all probability they had never worked before would take the same interest and care as they would in a regular engine. Those small jobs that make all the difference between ordinary and first-class performance would not be done—indeed there would be no opportunity with the engine passing into the hands of a further crew after, say, 100 to 150 miles of running. The question requires the closest economic study. The factors to be balanced, as I see them, are the additional mileage obtained against the higher coal and oil consumption resulting from poorer mechanical condition, while the psychological effect upon the enginemen is a further point that cannot be disregarded.

At Haymarket shed the practice of double-manning has been revived, and in this connection I must tell the story of *Hyperion*, one of the Gresley non-streamlined Pacifics. She was one of the black sheep of the class, wouldn't steam, wouldn't run, rode badly, full of alarming knocks—in fact was a thorough dud. She had been a common-user engine, nobody's baby, and when she came back from Doncaster Works newly overhauled she was no better. Now it happened that the regular engine of a certain top-link driver was due for plant at this time, and he was given *Hyperion* as his regular engine for the time. Being an extremely keen and capable man he set out to find what was the matter, and in the columns of the *Locomotive Express*, writing under the pen name of Toram Beg, he told his experiences:

' Both of us spent a miserable first week together, but we could do nothing in the dark, with little time between return trips.

' The following week was ideal, a run to Perth, with Glenfarg to climb—dour as a Highland bull, but a place to tell engines and men where the troubles lay. Broad daylight, and a reasonable margin of time for investigations and testing between trips, and believe it or not, *Hyperion* told me all I wanted to know. She indicated, one by one, just where those knocks were coming from, and one by one the driving-box wedges were adjusted until she was running like a sewing-machine—that is for sound.

'Her speed on the level was still of the forced variety, however, but here again she told me something was amiss by the way she dipped into every junction crossing—and seemed to be putting more effort into a sideways motion than going straight ahead. A readjustment of weight on the springs, and incidentally a tightening of the intermediate drawbar—and wallah! you could almost hear her sighs of relief. So that was that, but she was still anaemic, weak as water, and she was doing her best to tell me what was wrong as I flogged her up the cruel 1 in 74 of Glenfarg. There was a blind spot somewhere in the steam distribution, and for four days I watched those crank pins revolving slowly up Glenfarg, and listened to the exhaust hitting the rocks on either side. It took me four days to decide that more steam was needed on the back port of the centre cylinder.

'Next day *Hyperion* slipped out of Edinburgh like a ghost, didn't seem to touch the rails at all on the level and kicked the mountains beneath her with contemptuous ease. Later she was decked out in all her finery for the Royal Train. . . .'

So much for a chronic dud! As Toram Beg concludes : ' The regular men can follow up and get things remedied. They generally have the complete co-operation of the maintenance staff. I personally can vouch for the interest and will to get at the root of troubles by every fitter and foreman I have contacted.' One of *Hyperion's* subsequent exploits in the hands of one of her regular drivers may be studied from the log on page 214 of the Appendix.

A personal experience with these keen enginemen from Haymarket shed may be added. During the period following the great floods of August 1948, the engine workings were so dislocated that regular rosters were impossible, and the Haymarket Pacifics were used by all and sundry. I made a trip on the *Flying Scotsman* during that time, via Galashiels and Kelso, and by more of a coincidence than anything else the Haymarket driver and fireman who ran the train as far as Tweedmouth did have the streamliner that was their regular engine before the emergency. She was beautifully turned out, it was true, but I could see the old Scots driver was uneasy during the long spell of heavy going up to Falahill; when we stopped at Galashiels to take water, he said he thought she was heating on the right-hand side. Sure enough the driving-axle box was a good deal warmer than it should have been; but no substitute engine was available, and with the agreement of a senior locomotive officer who was present, they decided to make a run for Tweedmouth, particularly as under the emergency working no hard steaming was possible east of St Boswells. After 79 minutes we rode into Tweedmouth Junction with flames coming from that axle box, but nevertheless on time. The driver took the failure of the engine very much to heart. It hurt his pride to think that ' his engine ' had become a casualty. As I climbed down from the cab he added with some vehemence, ' This would never have happened if we'd had regular charge of her.' And so I could well believe.

6

Mention of the Royal Train, in connection with *Hyperion's* exploits, leads me to special workings on the Deeside line. In later Victorian days, and throughout the reign of King Edward VII a large number of specials was run during the period each year when the Court was at Balmoral. During King Edward's short reign no less than 31 Royal trains for the King and Queen were run over the Deeside line. The Great North of Scotland Railway had its own Royal Train, while the famous London and North Western train was well known on Deeside. But from the historic point of view the ' Messenger Trains ' are perhaps of greater interest than the Royal specials. They were introduced in October 1865, to carry the Queen's dispatches; the down train left Aberdeen at 4 a.m. and ran to Aboyne, then the terminus of the line, with only one stop, at Banchory. Hitherto the dispatches had been brought by rail to Perth and conveyed thence by road to Balmoral via Blairgowrie, the Cairnwell Pass and Braemar. In addition to the Queen's Messenger's carriage, a limited amount of first-class accommodation was provided for ordinary passengers, and of third-class for the servants of first-class passengers. A corresponding train for the south-bound Messenger ran in the early afternoon, at first leaving Aboyne at 2.15 p.m. When the line was eventually extended to its present terminus at Ballater, the Messenger trains continued thence. By the end of the nineteenth century the one-time exclusiveness of the trains ended and accommodation was provided for ordinary third-class passengers.

When the Queen's Messenger trains commenced running, the Deeside line was still an independent concern with its own locomotives, painted dark blue and lined in black. One of the old tank engines, however, was specially allocated to work the Queen's Messenger trains, and was at one time painted in the Royal Stuart tartan! The Deeside line was amalgamated with the Great North of Scotland in 1876, and after that the Royal train engines were decked in the bright emerald green that lasted until a change was made to black during the first world war. It was William Pickersgill, later of the Caledonian, who introduced the very attractive style of carriage-painting on the Great North —purple lake bodies, with cream upper panels. This was yet another variant of the two-colour idea, used on the Caledonian, the London and North Western, the Great Central and by the Railway Executive since nationalisation. The 'plum and spilt milk' tried out in 1948 was very similar to the old L & NWR style, while the new British Railways standard is not unlike the old GN of S or the Caledonian, save that there is rather more yellow in the 'cream' of the modern colour-scheme than in the older ones. The Highland, in earlier days, painted their coaches with white panels and olive-green bodies, while further English variations were the royal blue and white of the Furness, and vandyke-brown and white of the Brighton. But by the time nationalisation came only one, the historic chocolate and cream of the Great Western, remained. The attractiveness of a two-colour scheme is, however, undisputed, and one is glad to record the standardisation of a livery that recalls some of the pleasantest carriages of former days. After grouping, the LMS proposed to paint the old L & NWR Royal Train in Midland colours; but King George V expressed a wish that it should remain in the sepia and white of the North Western, and so it remained until the special armoured Royal Train was built for use during the second world war.

7

The colour schemes of locomotives and carriages form a fascinating subject about which one might go on gossiping for page after page. In no country were more striking liveries to be found than in Scotland, especially if one takes the pre-grouping companies at the height of their gaiety: the Highland in the bright apple-green days, when the louvred chimneys were brass-capped, the underframes were crimson and most ornate lining in red, black and white adorned the boiler cleading sheets, the cab sides and the tenders; or the Caledonian, in the magnificence of its ' blue,' with the purple-lake underframes, and the unique semaphore head codes signifying the route of the train, carried either on the buffer beam or on the lamp-iron just in front of the chimney. After grouping, the series of semaphore route indications was extended to cover the G & SW lines; Scottish engines from Polmadie, working the English expresses, carried the well-known Glasgow-Carlisle head code as far south as Crewe on the Royal Scot locomotives, and when the Stanier Pacifics came upon the scene the famous 6201 *Princess Elizabeth* carried it right through to Euston.

From quite early days all Caledonian engines down to the humblest goods and shunters carried the coat of arms; and what a coat of arms it was! Enough it surely was in the first place for this line to adopt the all-embracing name of Caledonian Railway; but to follow this by taking the Royal Arms of Scotland surpassed all—or nearly all—for its English ally modestly took

Britannia and the British Lion for its arms. It must be conceded, however, that this latter beast did at least *look* like a lion! The other Scottish companies used their coats of arms only to a limited extent on rolling stock. The North British crest was carried only on the Atlantics, among passenger engines, and that of the Highland on the Clan 4–6–os and the later Castles. But these crests, and no less those of the LMS and of the LNER, were all works of art, embodying in the dignity of their design and the richness of their colouring something of those bygone days that produced railways like the North British and the Caledonian; that inspired men like Joseph Locke, Mitchell and Hope Johnstone. The traditions of the former five railways are now gathered into the new Scottish Region. In these austere and difficult days the task of administration and running calls for hard work, inspiration and genius no less than when Mitchell took the Highland line over Druimuachdar, when Benjamin Baker set out to design the Forth Bridge while the ruins of the first Tay Bridge still lay in the firth, or when Charles Forman's constructional parties were leading their pack-horses up the steep slopes to Corrour to ' float ' the West Highland line over the peat bogs of Rannoch. All who have railways at heart will wish Scottish Region god-speed in their great task.

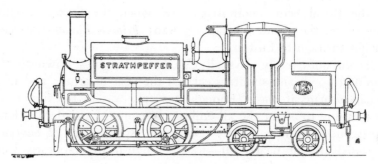

APPENDICES

Scottish Locomotive Performances

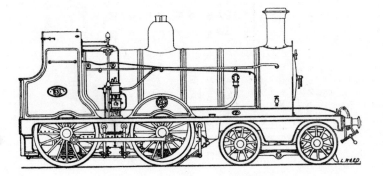

WEST COAST ROUTE—CARLISLE–CARSTAIRS

Run No.		1	2	3	4	5	6	7	8	9	10
Engine No.		123	—	903	1140	4794	6108	46241	5636	6201	6234
Engine Name		—	—	Cardean	—	—	Seaforth Highlander	City of Edinburgh	Uganda	Princess Elizabeth	Duchess of Abercorn
Engine (Class)		4-2-2	(Dunalastair I)	—	(Mid. Comp.)	Class 5 4-6-0	(Royal Scot)	(Duchess)	(5XP 4-6-0)	(Prin. Royal)	(Duchess)
Load tons		90	170	360	345	330	430	405	245	230	610
Mls		m s	m s	m s	m s	m s	m s	m s	m s	m s	m s
0·0	CARLISLE	0 00**	0 00	0 00	0 00	0 00	0 00	0 00	0 00**	0 00‡	0 00
8·6	Gretna Jc	9 38	—	11 00	11 15	10 36	10 40	9 40	9 31	8 04	10 40
13·0	Kirkpatrick	14 00	13 29	16 20	16 25	15 04	15 15	13 38	13 34	12 15	—
25·8	LOCKERBIE	26 46	25 50	31 05	30 35	27 10	p w slack 29 25	24 27	24 39	22 16	28 10
34·5	Wamphray	34 38	—	39 25	38 45	39 22	36 35	31 47	31 40	28 34	—
39·7	BEATTOCK arr	38 37†	37 41†	45 35*	45 05*	sig 46 29	41 00†	35 56†	36 10†	32 11	39 40
	dep	—	—	47 00	46 25	0 00	—	—	—	—	—
45·3	Greskine Box	44 49	—	57 40	57 55	p w s 11 59	50 40	42 01	42 50	36 06	—
49·7	Summit	52 31	52 48	65 40	66 00	sigs 22 07	61 15	48 50	50 08	41 42	56 10
63·2	Lamington	—	63 59	78 20	78 35	many delays	73 42	60 55	61 38	54 01	—
66·9	Symington	—	—	82 05	82 10	—	76 45	—	64 35	57 49	—
73·2	Strawfrank Jc	74 44†	—	88 35	88 50	—	—	sigs 73 03	—	—	74 00
73·5	CARSTAIRS	—	72 01†	—	—	57 55	83 50	74 13	70 33†	64 06†	—

NOTES
† Passing times
* Stop for bank engine
‡ Non-stop run Euston to Glasgow
** Non-stop run Carlisle to Edinburgh

The runs tabulated opposite range from the record trip of the famous single-wheeler No. 123 in the London–Edinburgh race of 1888 to the special runs with the Stanier Pacifics in 1936 and 1939. But in many ways the runs on ordinary service trains, when locomotives were being driven little faster than bare time-table requirements, are still more remarkable. The work of the Dunalastair engine on the Tourist express of 1896 reveals a most exacting schedule. The road from Carlisle to Beattock is generally adverse, with a total of 16 miles rising at 1 in 200, and the remaining distance only slightly favourable ; then comes the 10-mile bank leading to the 1,014-foot altitude of Beattock Summit at 49·7 miles from Carlisle. Yet it will be seen that the single-wheeler and the Dunalastair passed Beattock station in less than level time, and the single-wheeler climbed the 10 miles from Beattock to Summit in the remarkable time of 13 minutes 54 seconds, an average of 43·2 mph. But the Dunalastair on the Tourist express, with nearly double the load, put up a truly wonderful performance—albeit very little faster than the time-table of 1896 required. Columns 3 and 4 show typical work of the great Caledonian 4–6–0 *Cardean* and of a Midland compound, while No. 5 run, on the Perth section of the present-day *Royal Scot*, sets out an exceptionally rapid start from Carlisle by a Stanier Class 5 mixed-traffic engine, no heavier than *Cardean*, but a very efficient engine. In this run a speed of 86½ mph was attained near Wamphray.

The Royal Scot No. 6108 *Seaforth Highlander* did some fine work with a heavy train, though the load took its toll on the main climb to Beattock. In column 7 are shown details of an extremely fine run with a Duchess class engine, on which the racing times of 1888 and 1895 were substantially beaten, yet with a load of 405 tons. Again, as shown in column 8 the 5 X P 4–6–0 engine *Uganda* handsomely beat the 1888 racing record of the Caledonian 4–2–2 No. 123, but with a load of 245 tons against no more than 90. Note should be taken on *Uganda's* run of the average speed of 72·5 mph from Lockerbie to Beattock, and of the average of 43 mph up the bank. The *Princess Elizabeth* on a special test run with a light train averaged more than 60 mph up the bank, following upon a run from Gretna to Beattock at an average of 77·4 mph ; though perhaps even more impressive was the work of the Duchess class engine No. 6234 *Duchess of Abercorn*, in working a 20-coach train of 610 tons from Gretna to Beattock at an average of 64·3 mph, and of taking the full 10 miles of Beattock Bank in 16½ minutes —36·4 mph. This table does indeed summarise a few of the great runs of the past and present, and it still leaves us marvelling at the day-to-day work of the Dunalastairs in 1896 in making such times as 37 minutes 41 seconds to Beattock and 52 minutes 48 seconds to Summit with loads of 170 tons.

209

SCOTTISH REGION—DOWN MIDDAY SCOT

Load : 8 vehicles, 264 tons tare, 280 tons full

	Engine No. (Duchess class)		46236			46234		
	Engine Name		*City of Bradford*			*Duchess of Abercorn*		
	Engine Driver (Polmadie Shed)		Crawley			Herries		

Mls		Sch	m	s	mph	m	s	mph
0·0	**CARLISLE**	0	0	00		0	00	
	No 3 Box					sigs		30
2·0	*Kingmoor Box*		4	00	55	4	01	53
4·1	*Rockcliffe Box*		5	58	70	6	03	55
6·1	*Floriston Box*		7	38	80	7	50	74
8·6	Gretna Jc	10	9	33	76	9	53	70
13·0	Kirkpatrick		13	05	73/72	13	45	67/65
16·7	Kirtlebridge		16	01	82/85	16	53	78
20·0	Ecclefechan		18	31	78	19	32	76
22·7	*Castlemilk*		20	30	77	21	38	72
25·8	**LOCKERBIE**	24	22	45	85	24	08	84
28·7	Nethercleugh		24	48	88	26	11	88
31·7	Dinwoodie		26	52	83	28	17	86
34·5	Wamphray		28	58	85	30	18	85
39·7	**BEATTOCK**	36	32	52	78	34	10	76
45·4	*Greskine*		38	31	49	39	33	53
49·7	*Summit*	51	44	55	38	45	20	45
52·6	Elvanfoot		47	40	75	47	50	83
55·3	Crawford		50	25	*pws*	49	52	79
57·8	Abington		53	00	68	51	53	76
60·4	*Wandelmill*		55	04	78	53	42	87
63·2	Lamington		57	12	83	55	44	82
66·9	SYMINGTON		60	04	71	58	34	74
68·5	Thankerton		61	23	79	59	53	75
70·0	*Leggatfoot*		62	39	68/74	61	09	72/75
73·5	CARSTAIRS	73	65	45	53	64	30	47
76·3	Cleghorn	76	68	48	60	67	30	60
78·5	*Craigenhill*		71	01	60	69	40	61
80·9	Carluke		74	08	76	72	49	72
84·0	Law Jc	84	75	57	50	74	40	60/50
86·4	Wishaw South		78	36	65	77	05	71
89·4	MOTHERWELL	92	81	30	*pws*	79	46	61/75
93·9	Uddingston	95	88	37	*sigs*	83	23	74
95·7	Newton	97	92	00	*pws*	85	52	*pws*
98·3	*Rutherglen Jc*	100	95	28	65	89	31	
101·3	Eglinton St	103	99	27		93	30	
102·3	**GLASGOW CENTRAL**	107	102	30		95	53	

Net times	96 min		94 min
Departure	3 min late		10 min late
Arrival	1½ min early		1 min early

210

The limitation of load on the day Anglo-Scottish expresses over the West Coast route and the use of the Duchess class Pacific locomotives has enabled a reasonably fast overall schedule to be maintained between Glasgow and London despite the considerable easing out of running times south of Weaver Junction. Here the engineering works in connection with electrification are very heavy, and much slow running is involved. To permit of a good overall average very fast running is now required over the northern section of the line, and the non-stop run of 102·3 miles from Carlisle to Glasgow, including the ascent of the Beattock bank, had to be made in 107 minutes. Even with locomotives of such proved capacity as the ex-LMSR Duchess class it might seem there would not be a great deal of margin for recovery. I am, however, indebted to Mr W Robertson for details of the two remarkable runs opposite, clocked in December 1959 and May 1960, on one of which schedule time was cut by a clear 11 minutes, and on the other a late start of 3 minutes was changed to an arrival 1½ minutes early, despite delays to the total of 6½ minutes *en route*.

On the first of the two runs, with the *City of Bradford*, speed was worked up to 80 mph at the Solway Firth, and the average speed over the gradually rising 33·6 miles from Floriston to Beattock station was exactly *eighty miles per hour*. The long stretches of 1 in 200 gradient included in this stretch were climbed without speed falling at any time below 72 mph, and a maximum of 88 mph was attained on the slightly falling stretch north of Lockerbie. The second run, with the *Duchess of Abercorn*, was not quite so fast in the early stages, but from Lockerbie there was little to choose, and this second run included by far the more vigorous ascent of the Beattock bank. Whereas the *City of Bradford* climbed this 10 miles of exceedingly severe gradient in 12 minutes 3 seconds, falling to 38 mph at the summit, the *Duchess of Abercorn* took no more than 11 minutes 10 seconds with a high minimum speed of 45 mph. The former engine was passing Beattock on time, and her driver was able subsequently to get sufficient in hand to offset the effect of the permanent-way checks to come, whereas the *Duchess of Abercorn* was still over 4 minutes late on passing Beattock summit. With a clear road and some splendid concluding running the arrival in Glasgow was 2 minutes early— a magnificent performance. The Midday Scot is no longer a limited load train, and the schedule has been eased a little.

211

Engine 5XP 4–6–0 No. 5565 *Victoria*
Load 13 cars 364 tons tare 410 tons full
Driver S Walker, Fireman A Hudson (Leeds Holbeck shed)

Mls		Sch	m	s	mph	Reg'r	Cut-off	Remarks
0·0	KILMARNOCK	0	0	00		Full	15	B.P. at 205–220
1·7	Hurlford		4	06	—	Full	30	from Kilmarnock
2·7	*Milepost 36½*		5	33	38½	Full	45	to Polquhap
3·7	*Milepost 37½*		7	11	35	Full	45	
4·2	*Milepost 38*		8	05	33½	Full	50	
5·2	*Milepost 39*		9	53	34½	Full	40	
6·2	*Milepost 40*		11	48	31	Full	47	
7·2	*Milepost 41*		13	46	30	Full	25	Water 3 in. down
8·2	*Milepost 42*		15	18	43	½	15	
9·4	MAUCHLINE	14	16	38	53			
11·2	*Brackenhill Jc Box*		19	01	45	Full‡	27	‡Regulator opened
13·8	Auchinleck		22	31	43	Full	23	wide at
15·8	Old Cumnock		25	15	48	Full	27	Ballochmyle
18·6	*Polquhap Box*		29	11	42	Full	15	Viaduct
				p w s	30			
21·1	New Cumnock	28	32	48				
24·7	*Upper Cairn Box*		36	35	—	1st valve	45	
28·6	Kirkconnel		40	30	67	1st valve	45	
31·9	SANQUHAR	39	43	26	68	1st valve	45	
34·2	*Mennock Box*		45	25	61	1st valve	27	
36·7	*Ardoch Box*		47	43	eased	Full	15	
40·5	Carronbridge		52	08	50	1st valve	45	
43·8	Thornhill	52	55	16	74	—		†Opened at foot
46·6	Closeburn		57	32	75/70½	—	—	of 1 in 200
50·4	Auldgirth		60	46	72½	—	—	
54·6	Holywood		64	14	72	Full†	15	
56·3	*Cairn Valley Jc Box*		65	40	—	—	—	Net time
			sigs					66 minutes
58·0 / 0·0 }	DUMFRIES	{ 68 / 0	68 / 0	02 / 00		½	75	
0·6	*Milepost 92¼*		1	55	—	Full	30	B.P. 225
0·9	*Milepost 92½*		2	29	—	Full	45	throughout
1·4	*Milepost 93*		3	23	—	Full	30	
3·4	*Milepost 95*		5	52	—	Full	27	
3·9	Racks		6	39	58½	Full	30	
5·4	*Milepost 97*		8	09	61½	Full	30	
7·4	*Milepost 99*		10	25	50½	Full	30	
8·5	Ruthwell		11	44	56	1st valve	45	
12·0	Cummertrees		14	57	71	1st valve	45	
					easy	—	—	
15·5 / 0·0 }	ANNAN	{ 19 / 0	18 / 0	39 / 00		½	45	
0·6	*Milepost 108*		2	09	—	Full	35	
2·9	Eastriggs		5	04	54½	Full	25	
4·8	Rigg		7	04	60	Full	17	
7·9	Gretna Green		10	12	—	Closed	—	
8·9	Gretna Jc	11	11	17	53	Full	15	
11·4	Floriston		13	37	66½	Full	15	Steam off only for
					distant on	Closed	—	a few seconds
13·4	Rockcliffe		15	32	62½	Full	15	
15·5	*Kingmoor*		17	31	64	Full	15	
16·8	*Carlisle No. 3*	20	18	55	—	—	—	
17·5	CARLISLE	22	21	14				

Piloted by 4–4–0 No. 617 St Enoch to Kilmarnock

It is more than fifty years since the morning express to London by this route conveyed Pullman cars, but the old name for the train lingers. This was an exceptionally fine run made in 1945 on a day when the usual Royal Scot was not available, and one of the 5XP Jubilee class was substituted. The capacity of these engines for high speed is shown in Mr Nelson's timing of engine No. 45580 *Burma* on the up Postal Express (see page 222); this run of mine, with *Victoria*, is complementary, as displaying their capacity for heavy working on adverse gradients or in accelerating rapidly from rest. Over the very steep banks of the Barrhead Joint Line we had been double-headed, as the load was 39 tons over the maximum permitted to an unassisted 5X engine. From Kilmarnock up the 1 in 100 grade that extends from Hurlford to Milepost 41 the driver fairly flailed the engine in an attempt to keep the very severe uphill timing of 14 minutes to Mauchline; at one time he was using no less than 50 per cent cut-off. The boiler steamed magnificently, but the water-level could not be maintained, and the working had to be eased somewhat, from 50 to 40 per cent, with a consequent falling off in the speed. Very fine work was performed in the restarts from Dumfries and from Annan, in both cases on roughly level road; the acceleration was rapid, and the sharply booked timing between the stops was closely maintained.

This engine was in charge of Leeds men working home, and the continuation on the English part of the journey was equally good—in fact the boiler stood up to heavy pounding better than ever on the long climb to the 1,166-foot altitude of Aisgill Summit, showing how well these locomotives are fitted to continuous hard duty of four or five hours at a stretch. In Scotland they work through over the 240 miles from Carlisle to Aberdeen, often with very heavy trains.

1.25 P.M. WAVERLEY–NEWCASTLE

Engine A3 class 4–6–2 No. 60037 *Hyperion*
Load 13 cars 415 tons tare 440 tons full
Driver N McKillop, Fireman G Brown (Haymarket shed)
Inspector J Cunningham (Waverley) also on footplate

Mls		Sch	m	s	mph	BP	SCP	Reg'r	Cut-off
0·0	WAVERLEY	0	0	00		190	75	$\frac{1}{4}$	65
						190	80	$\frac{1}{4}$	15
0·9	*Abbeyhill Jc*		2	31	34½	195	80	$\frac{1}{4}$	15
1·8	*Piershill Jc*		3	54	39	200	155	$\frac{3}{4}$	12
3·0	Portobello	6	5	32	49½	195	72	$\frac{1}{4}$	12
4·7	Newhailes		8	11	—	195	72	$\frac{1}{4}$	12
			p w s		20*	195	187	Full	25
						205	195	Full	22
6·1	*Monktonhall Jc*	12	10	42	48	210	195	Full	19
6·5	Inveresk		11	13	49½	210	195	Full	15
						210	195	Full	17
9·5	Prestonpans		15	01	49	205	190	Full	17
						205	190	Full	12
13·2	Longniddry Jc	20	19	23	63½	205	187	Full	14
14·8	*Aberlady Jc*		21	06	57	205	187	Full	12
17·8	DREM JC	25	24	13	65	205	190	Full	12
					71½	210	195	Full	15
20·8	East Fortune		27	04	61½	205	190	Full	15
					63	205	190	Full	15
23·4	East Linton		29	36	61	200	185	Full	12
27·0	*Beltonford Siding*		32	58	66½	205	155	$\frac{5}{8}$	12
					68½	205	155		12
29·2	DUNBAR	36	35	02	60 slack	210	195	Full	15
31·3	*Oxwellmains*		37	26	51½	210	195	Full	15
33·8	Innerwick		40	12	63	205	190	Full	18
						210	197	Full	20
36·5	Cockburnspath		43	11	50½	210	200	Full	23
						205	140	$\frac{1}{2}$	30
			p w s		20*	210	175	$\frac{1}{8}$	33
					29½	198	177	$\frac{7}{8}$	33
41·3	Grantshouse	56	54	13	—	185	10	$\frac{1}{10}$	25
				temporary bridge slacks					
56·4	*Marshall Meadows*	95	91	09	—	195	30	$\frac{1}{8}$	15
57·5 ⎱	BERWICK	⎰98	93	29					
0·0 ⎰		⎱0	0	00		205	160	$\frac{3}{4}$	65
1·2	Tweedmouth		2	33	42	205	185	Full	23
3·4	Scremerston		5	33	55	200	180	Full	16
6·1	Goswick		8	08	72½	210	190	Full	16
8·3	Beal		10	04	68	205	187	Full	19
12·0	Smeafield		13	26	62	210	190	Full	24
15·3	BELFORD	18	16	55	56½	207	190	Full	18
17·7	Lucker		19	23	67	205	185	Full	18
			p w s		20*	202	30	$\frac{1}{8}$	28
19·8	Newham		22	37	25½	202	187	Full	28
20·9	Chathill		24	22	46½	205	192	Full	25
23·9	Christon Bank		28	03	58 max	210	195	Full	25
					50/55½	210	195	Full	25
27·5	Little Mill		32	14	53	200	185	Full	15
29·4	Longhoughton		34	18	69/74	195	155	$\frac{5}{8}$	12
32·1	ALNMOUTH	35	36	46	60 slack	200	185	Full	25
35·0	Warkworth		39	48	55½ min	210	195	Full	18
38·4	Acklington		43	05	69½	215	200	Full	18
41·3	Chevington		45	47	66	210	195	Full	18
43·7	Widdrington		48	06	62½	205	190	Full	15
46·7	Longhirst		50	53	71	210	200	Full	15
50·3	MORPETH	54	54	39	40 slack	195	175	Full	30
			easy running ; 4 min recovery time allowed						
65·2	Heaton		73	27	—	—	—	—	—
			sigs						
66·9	NEWCASTLE	80	78	11					

214

This run was a particularly fine example of a Gresley A3 Pacific at work. It was made at the time when the slacks due to the flood damage between Cockburnspath and Berwick were at their worst, and extra time was allowed for them; but normally fast running was made out to Cockburnspath, and again south of Berwick. That portion of the log between Newhailes and Cockburnspath is worthy of close study, for there the handling of the engine was most artistic in the way the driver worked his reverser, varying the cut-off to maintain a relatively even speed over this undulating road. Many drivers are content to set the reverser in one position, say 15 per cent, and allow the engine to make its own pace, but McKillop made frequent variations, down to a minimum of 12 per cent cut-off, and was using the steam to the very best advantage. The speeds along the Lothian Coast were very good with this fairly heavy train; but in general harder running was needed south of Berwick, owing to the faster timing and recovery from the permanent-way slack near Newham.

The first of the special slacks—aftermath of the floods—came right on the Cockburnspath Bank, 1 in 96; from it, with the use of 33 per cent cut-off, recovery was made to 29½ mph while still on the grade. Another fine recovery was made from the slack at Newham, where speed was worked up from 20 to 58 mph in 3½ miles of roughly level road, and the Christon Bank of 2½ miles graded at 1 in 150 taken at a minimum speed of 50 mph. With this, and fast running along the undulating stretch from Warkworth to Longhirst the train was practically on time through Morpeth, and the four minutes of recovery time provided between Morpeth and Newcastle were not needed. This run is of particular interest in that the engine in question had, not many weeks before this run, a thoroughly bad reputation. The story of how her failings were diagnosed and put right is told in Chapter Twelve.

THE THAMES–FORTH EXPRESS—WAVERLEY–HAWICK

Engine A3 class 4-6-2 No. 60067 *Ladas*
Load 9 cars 296 tons tare 315 tons full
Driver A Charters, Fireman P Walker (Hawick shed)
Chief Inspector J Bartholomew (Waverley) also on footplate

Mls		Sch	m	s	mph	BP	Reg'r	Cut-off
0·0	**WAVERLEY**	0	0	00		190	$\frac{1}{2}$	65
						190	$\frac{1}{2}$	25
0·9	*Abbeyhill Jc*		2	09	36½	190	$\frac{1}{2}$	20
1·8	*Piershill Jc*		3	36	37	200	$\frac{1}{2}$	20
3·0	Portobello	6	5	29	47½	200	Full	25
						200	Full	30
4·5	*Niddrie South Jc*	8	7	48	35½	200	Full	25
6·0	Millerhill		9	54	49	215	Full	15
					38*	220	Full	20
8·0	Eskbank		12	33	45½	220	Full	20
8·2	*Hardengreen Jc*	14	12	49	47	220	Full	25
9·7	Newtongrange		14	55	38½	210	Full	30
			sigs		2*	210	Shut	30
12·0	Gorebridge	20	47		—	210	$\frac{3}{4}$	55
						215	Full	40
						220	Full	30
12·7	Fushiebridge		23	26	18½	220	Full	30
					25½	200	Full	27
			p w s		15*	200	Full	20
14·4	*Borthwick Bank*		25	59	—	205	Full	20
						205	Full	30
16·0	Tynehead		32	44	22¾†	195	Full	35
—	*Top of 1 in 70*		—	—	27½	195	Full	30
17·9	*Falahill*	38	37	50	29	195	Full	25
						195	Full	15
						195	$\frac{1}{2}$	15
19·1	Heriot		39	49	51½	180	$\frac{1}{4}$	15
					60	190	$\frac{1}{10}$	15
22·6	Fountainhall		43	44	—	190	$\frac{1}{10}$	15
26·7	Stow		48	07	60	210	$\frac{1}{10}$	15
29·8	Bowland		51	38	50*	220	$\frac{1}{10}$	15
32·5	*Kilnknowe Jc*		54	34	—	205	Shut	25
33·5 }	**GALASHIELS**	{ 57	56	44				
0·0 }		{ 0	0	00		215	$\frac{1}{2}$	65
						215	Full	30
1·0	*Selkirk Jc*		1	54	47½	215	Full	25
2·6	*Darnick Siding*		3	56	58	220	Full	25
3·7 }	**MELROSE**	{ 6	5	32				
0·0 }		{ 0	0	00		205	$\frac{3}{4}$	65
						205	Full	35
						200	Full	25
1·9	*Ravenswood Jc*		3	37	48½	200	Full	25
					53	200	Shut	25
3·4 }	**ST BOSWELLS**	{ 6	6	03				
0·0 }		{ 0	0	00		220	$\frac{3}{4}$	65
						220	Full	35
1·2	*Milepost 41¾*		2	21	45½	220	Full	25
					54	220	Full	15
3·1	*Greenend Siding*		4	41	55½	220	Full	15
					61	220	Full	25
4·6	Belses		6	23	54	215	Full	25
6·1	*Standhill Siding*		8	06	51½	200	Full	15
7·9	Hassendean		10	12	68‡	205	Full	15
					73½	215	Shut	25
12·2	**HAWICK**	15	14	54				

† at Milepost 16½ ‡ at Milepost 50
Slow stop at St Boswells water column ; this avoided similar slow stop at Hawick

THE THAMES–FORTH EXPRESS—HAWICK–CARLISLE

Engine A3 class 4-6-2 No. 60067 *Ladas*
Load 9 cars 296 tons tare 315 tons full
Driver J Leitch, Fireman T Scott (Canal shed)
Chief Inspector J Bartholomew (Waverley) also on footplate

Mls		Sch	m	s	mph	BP	Reg'r	Cut-off
0·0	HAWICK	0	0	00		220	½	65
						220	Full	30
1·0	*Milepost 53¾*		3	16	19½	220	Full	30
2·0	*Milepost 54¾*		5	43	28½	220	Full	30
3·2	*Stobs Camp*		8	12	26½	220	Full	35
3·9	Stobs		9	53	25¼	220	Full	40
5·0	*Milepost 57¾*		12	15	33	210	Full	40
7·0	Shankend		15	51	38½	210	Full	40
9·9	*Whitrope Tunnel N end*		21	04	30½	210	Full	30
10·9	*Whitrope Siding*	26	23	01	31	210	½	25
			p w s		15*	200	Shut	25
13·1	RICCARTON JC	29	27	05	20*	190	½	25
						190	1/10	25
16·6	Steele Road		32	11	51½	190	1/10	25
21·2	NEWCASTLETON	39	37	29	53	220	½	25
24·3	Kershope Foot		41	06	52	220	⅝	25
					44½	220	⅜	25
28·8	Penton		46	58	53	220	1/10	25
31·3	Riddings Jc		49	51	53½	210	1/10	25
33·5	Scotch Dyke		52	13	62	210	½	25
35·8	LONGTOWN JC	56	54	27	63	205	⅝	25
38·8	Lyneside		57	13	67½	205	⅝	25
41·0	Harker		59	22	58	200	⅝	25
			sig stop			220	Shut	25
			63	08		215	¾	65
			63	24		—	—	—
						215	¾	40
43·9	*Canal Jc*	66	65	00	—	215	½	40
						215	⅝	25
						215	Shut	25
45·4	CARLISLE	70	68	54				

Banking assistance from Hawick out of platform only

THE UP *THAMES-FORTH* EXPRESS

Locomotive working over the Waverley route provides a fascinating study of continuous hard steaming on heavy gradients. The line ascends practically from sea-level at Portobello to an altitude of 880 feet above ordnance datum at Falahill, with 9 miles continuously at 1 in 70 save for a break of one half-mile at 1 in 111; and then after the descent to Galashiels and some sharp gradients through the valleys of the Tweed and the Teviot, there comes another hard climb to Whitrope in the Cheviots. On this latter climb, so powerful an engine as a Gresley A3 Pacific needed 40 per cent cut-off, with full regulator, to make the speed, even though the load was no more than 9 coaches. On this latter climb, although the inclination is nowhere quite so steep as that between Hardengreen Junction and Tynehead, the curvature is constant and severe, and this appreciably increases the tractive resistance.

EAST COAST ROUTE—DUNDEE–ABERDEEN

	Engine No.	9509				60920			
	Engine Name	*Duke of Rothesay*				—			
	Engine Class	ex-NBR Atlantic				ex-LNER 'V2' 2-6-2			
	Load tons empty/full	359/380				462/490			
	Driver	J Moodie (Dundee)				F Chapman (Ferryhill)			
Mls		Sch	m	s	mph	Sch	m	s	mph
0·0	DUNDEE	0	0	00		0	0	00	
0·7	*Camperdown Jc*		2	30	—		2	56	—
2·6	Stannergate		5	33	—		6	35	43
4·0	Broughty Ferry		7	30	50		8	20	51
6·4	Monifieth		10	08	55½		11	05	57
9·3	Barry Links		13	04	62		14	06	63½
10·9	Carnoustie		14	34	65		15	39	64
12·7	East Haven		16	14	67		17	24	64½
—			—		—		sigs		54*
15·6	Elliot Jc		18	50	67		20	39	61½
—			sig stop		—		sigs		—
17·0	ARBROATH	22	22	20		23	23	00	
0·0		0	0	00		0	0	00	
0·6	*St Vigeans Jc*		1	56	—		2	07	—
2·5	*Milepost* 19½		—		27		5	51	31½
3·0	Letham Grange		7	00	—		6	40	—
6·2	Inverkeilor		10	37	71½		10	25	68
8·8	Lunan Bay		13	22	46		13	16	48½
9·7	*Milepost* 26¾		14	38	40½		14	27	41½
11·6	*Usan Box*		16	51	—		17	05	—
13·7	MONTROSE	21	19	43		22	20	18	
0·0		0	0	00		0	0	00	
1·3	*Milepost* 32		3	07	33½		3	32	34
2·3	*Milepost* 33		4	57	30		5	31	30
2·6	*Kinnaber Jc*	6	5	42	15*	6	5	57	31
4·7	Craigo		9	28	56		9	18	53½
6·8	Marykirk		12	02	46½		11	47	44½
8·8	*Milepost* 209¼		15	05	37½		14	42	39
10·0	LAURENCEKIRK	17	16	46	48	17	16	34	47½
—			—		---		sigs		38*
13·3	Fordoun		20	17	66		21	09	49
17·3	Drumlithie		25	21	39½		26	34	42½
19·0	Carmont		27	45	49½		29	03	46½
—			—		—		sigs		45*
21·9	*Dunnottar Box*		30	40	71 max		32	45	64 max
24·5	STONEHAVEN	34	33	27		34	36	08	
0·0		0	0	00		0	0	00	
1·6	*Milepost* 226½		3	23	33		3	43	31½
2·6	*Milepost* 227½		5	14	32½		5	36	33
4·5	Muchalls		7	46	64		8	07	63½
5·7	Newtonhill		8	58	57½/50		9	18	63½/52½
7·9	Portlethen		11	30	54½		11	41	60½
9·1	*Milepost* 234		12	45	50½		12	48	57
11·3	Cove Bay		15	02	63½		15	02	64½
14·4	*Craiginches South*		17	58	66		17	58	70/59*
15·5	*Ferryhill Jc*		19	34	—	22	19	44	—
16·1	ABERDEEN	22	21	07		24	21	17	

The two runs tabulated opposite provide an interesting contrast between the work of one of the old North British Atlantics, now scrapped, and a Gresley 2–6–2 of the Green Arrow class. Both engines were most ably driven and the correspondence between the times achieved was very close. I recorded the Atlantic run from the footplate in the early spring of 1935; whereas the run with the Green Arrow was recorded by Mr Ronald I Nelson in 1948, on an occasion when he was travelling as a passenger. The Atlantic was steamed hard for most of the journey, and it was an impressive and often exciting experience on the footplate. The lever reversing gear of these engines involved lengthening or shortening the cut-off by 10 per cent at a time, and when the driver gave the engine 'another notch,' increasing for example from 34 to 44 per cent, the exhaust would suddenly sharpen into a roar. For one of these engines 380 tons was a heavy load over the stiff gradients from Arbroath northward, and the climbing is reflected in the speeds of 27 mph approaching Letham Grange on 1 in 103½, 30 near Kinnaber Junction on 1 in 88, 37½ before Laurencekirk on 1 in 106 and 32½ ascending from Stonehaven on 1 in 118. The Green Arrow with 110 tons additional load did equally well, making due allowance for the relative weight and tractive power of the two locomotives. Note should be taken too of the swift down-hill accelerations after the steep gradients were surmounted, particularly from Letham Grange to Inverkeilor and from Milepost 227½ down to Muchalls. On the level stretch of line from Camperdown Junction, Dundee, to Arbroath the honours rest with the Atlantic, though by modern standards the engine was being worked rather hard, with the reverser in 34 per cent cut-off and the regulator wide, though not quite full open.

SCOTTISH REGION—EAST COAST ROUTE

9.46 A.M. ABERDEEN–EDINBURGH

Engines Type 2 1,160 hp diesel-electrics Nos D5340 and D5345
Load 10 cars 340 tons tare 360 tons full
Drivers : A McRobb (Tay Bridge) to Dundee ; A Hyde (Haymarket) from Dundee

Mls		Sch	m	s	mph
0·0	ABERDEEN	0	0	00	
0·6	*Ferryhill Jc*		1	55	26¾/46
4·8	Cove Bay		7	54	41¼/45
7·0	*Milepost* 234		10	39	52¼
11·6	Muchalls		14	37	75
13·5	*Milepost* 227½		16	18	67¾/72¾
16·1	STONEHAVEN	22	19	17	—
2·6	*Dunnottar*		4	46	44¾/51½
4·7	*Milepost* 220¼		7	19	47¾/57
			sig stop		
7·2	Drumlithie		11	44	—
			pws		73/25*
14·5	LAURENCEKIRK	15	20	08	62½
17·7	Marykirk		22	53	76½
21·9	*Kinnaber Jc*	23	27	25	15*/63¼
24·5	MONTROSE	27	30	48	—
1·7	*Milepost* 29		3	31	38¾
2·1	*Usan Box*	6	4	20	25*
4·0	*Milepost* 26¾		7	20	45¼
4·9	Lunan Bay		8	19	59½
			pws		73¼/57*
10·7	Letham Grange		13	53	64¾/62¼
13·1	*St Vigeans Jc*	19	16	12	64 max
13·7	ARBROATH	20	17	47	—
1·4	Elliot Jc		2	48	27/57¼
6·1	Carnoustie		7	07	71
10·6	Monifieth		10	46	73¾
			pws		60*
12·5	*Broughty Jc*	14	12	24	—
14·4	Stannergate		14	13	68½/69¼
16·3	*Camperdown Jc*	18	16	52	15*
17·0	DUNDEE	21	19	33	—
0·8	Esplanade		1	58	24¼/34½
2·7	*Tay Bridge South*	8	5	24	27*
4·6	St Fort		7	54	59½/63¾
8·3	LEUCHARS JC	15	12	23	—
3·3	Dairsie		4	50	59½/60¾
6·3	CUPAR	8	8	31	—
5·5	Ladybank Jc	8	7	29	55/47*
6·4	Kingskettle		8	27	57¾
9·7	*Lochmuir*		12	14	48½
			pws		30*
13·9	THORNTON JC	19	18	22	28*
15·0	*Randolph Siding*		20	22	35¼
			pws-sigs		30*
18·7	KIRKCALDY	28	26	44	—
3·2	Kinghorn		4	37	51½/30*
5·8	Burntisland	8	8	41	49¾/25*
			pws		10*
8·5	Aberdour		13	05	49/42¾
9·9	*Dalgetty*		14	51	46¼/53
12·6	*Inverkeithing Central Jc*	20	18	36	25*
14·7	*Forth Bridge North*	25	22	07	38¼/36¾
16·4	Dalmeny	28	24	48	41¾/59
			pws		20*
22·6	*Saughton Jc*		33	13	41
24·7	HAYMARKET	37	36	08	35*
25·9	WAVERLEY	40	39	01	—

* Speed restriction

The log detailed opposite relates to a particularly fine piece of modern running with a pair of 1,160 horsepower diesel-electric locomotives running in multiple unit. The two locomotives are electrically coupled and as such can be operated by a single engineman. It is important to appreciate, however, that though the combined output of the diesel engines is approximately 2,300, the horsepower available for traction at the drawbar of the second locomotive would not exceed about 1,600 as a maximum. Even so such power is available to the driver for the mere turning of the controller handle, without the necessity of a careful build-up of the fire, the judicious regulation of the water supply to the boiler, and always the close teamwork of driver and fireman which is essential to success on a steam locomotive.

Again, while it is extremely rare to see a steam locomotive worked at absolutely full capacity, on modern non-steam locomotives, both electric and diesel, it is a common and indeed normal occurrence. This results in some spectacular hill-climbing, as on this run, and it is interesting to compare the performance up the banks from Aberdeen and Stonehaven with that of the up Postal express, as detailed on pages 222 and 224. Although starting from rest at Stonehaven speed rose to no less than $51\frac{1}{2}$ mph on the Dunnottar bank, and did not fall below $47\frac{3}{4}$ mph on the final length inclined at 1 in 102. The start out of Montrose was also extremely good, on the continuous ascent of 1 in 88 to the Usan box. Here the two locomotives in harness had attained so high a speed that a reduction had to be made passing through the loop to exchange the single-line tablet. South of Dundee, after a change of drivers, excellent work continued. Particularly impressive was the ascent to the Forth Bridge, after passing through Inverkeithing at the prescribed limit of 25 mph. On the continuous 1 in 70 gradient to the Forth Bridge speed rose to no less than 38 mph.

3.30 P.M. ' UP SPECIAL ' TPO

	Engine No.			44704			45580	
	Engine Name			—			*Burma*	
	Engine Class 4-6-0			Class 5 mixed traffic			Class 5X 3 cyl	
	Load tons empty/full			271/285			299/315	
	Driver (Ferryhill shed)			W Nicol			A Robertson	

Mls		Sch	m	s	mph	m	s	mph
0·0	ABERDEEN	0	0	00		0	00	
							sigs	10*
0·6	*Ferryhill Jc*	2	2	54	12½/24	2	51	14/24½
1·7	*Craiginches South*		5	19	34/35½	5	01	36/38½
4·8	Cove Bay		10	47	33½/37½	9	54	37½/40
7·0	*Milepost 234*		14	34	33/39½	13	27	35½/42
8·2	Portlethen		15	54	57	14	43	61½
10·4	Newtonhill		18	13	71 max	16	52	74
11·6	Muchalls		19	24	—	17	46	83
				pws	40*			
13·5	*Milepost 227½*		22	23	38	19	34	65
							pws	15*
16·1	STONEHAVEN	23	25	14	63	22	47	39
18·3	*Milepost 222¾*		27	50	46½	26	18	36½
18·7	*Dunnottar Box*		28	26	45/47½	26	58	39/44
20·8	*Milepost 220¼*		31	21	42½	30	02	37½
21·6	Carmont		32	21	49	31	05	49
23·3	Drumlithie		34	29	58	33	12	61
27·3	Fordoun		38	03	73	36	26	84
30·6	LAURENCEKIRK	40	41	02	64½	39	04	73½/68
31·8	*Milepost 209¼*		42	17	60	40	15	—
							pws	35*
33·8	Marykirk		44	04	70	42	29	63
35·9	Craigo		45	54	74½/69	44	19	74/70½
37·3	*Milepost 203¾*		47	14	65	45	39	68 min
				pws	25*		pws	35*
38·0	*Kinnaber Jc*	48	48	15	—	46	37	—
39·2	Dubton		49	46	60½	48	12	58½
41·9	Bridge of Dun		52	18	67	50	42	67½
							pws	30*
45·0	Farnell Road		55	16	58½	54	55	43
47·8	*Milepost 193¼*		58	41	46½	59	07	39½
48·3	Glasterlaw		59	14	54	59	42	50
50·3	GUTHRIE	60	61	18	60½	61	50	58½
52·3	Auldbar Road		63	13	66	63	51	62
							sigs	69/58*
54·9	Clocksbriggs		65	37	67	66	21	—
57·3 ⎱	FORFAR	⎰ 68	68	23		69	24	
0·0 ⎰		⎱ 0	0	00		0	00	
0·7	*Forfar South Jc*		2	19	—	2	05	—
2·9	*Kirriemuir Jc*	4	4	57	60½/65	4	35	63/66½
5·7	Glamis		7	33	62/75	7	09	64/77
7·9	Eassie		9	22	74½	8	59	73½
12·0	ALYTH JC	12	12	43	72½	12	21	71
14·2	Ardler		14	34	74	14	13	76½
16·7	COUPAR ANGUS	16	16	33	77½	16	09	80½
18·9	Burrelton		18	23	76½	17	57	76½
21·2	Cargill		20	18	73/78	19	51	73/77
23·1	*Ballathie Box*		21	44	85/78½	21	13	88½/84
							pws	30*
25·3	STANLEY JC	24	23	33	72	24	33	44½
27·4	Strathord		25	13	78	26	43	72
28·3	Luncarty		25	56	79	27	30	74½
30·9	*Almond Valley Jc*	30	27	58	82 max	29	44	81 max
32·5	PERTH	34	30	49		32	29	

Between Aberdeen and Perth this train can be regarded as one of the fastest in Scotland, or indeed at the present in the whole of Great Britain. The booked average speed of 50½ mph over the heavily graded route from Aberdeen to Forfar involves hard climbing and swift acceleration from each summit point. There is a hard grind for the first 7 miles out of Aberdeen, on gradients varying between 1 in 102 and 1 in 164, and another stiff pull up the glen of Carron Water from the crossing of Stonehaven Viaduct. Next, following a fine downhill run from a summit point near Drumlithie, there is another stiff rise from the level road alongside the Montrose Basin almost to Glasterlaw—4 miles mostly at about 1 in 100. The table opposite compares the running of a Black Stanier, No. 44704, with that of a 3-cylinder Jubilee class express 4-6-0. With only two slacks in prospect, the former engine climbed out of Aberdeen in a style that might almost be called leisurely for this train; but the going was good from Stonehaven to Carmont. After this, time was practically maintained to Forfar, in spite of the second permanent-way slack. But the 5X engine was delayed by no fewer than four slacks for permanent way work. To offset the effect of these slacks Driver Robertson steamed the engine hard, and some high speeds were run on the downhill stretches, including 83 mph at Muchalls and 84 mph at Fordoun.

The second stage extends over a course that is virtually level for the first 25 miles. The undulations are only slight except at the dip to the Tay Viaduct beyond Cargill. It is here that the maximum speed of this part of the run is usually attained, as on the more pronounced descent from Stanley engines are steamed easily in the approach to Perth. The Class 5 engine ran magnificently here, and despite driving wheels of no more than 6 feet diameter averaged 77 mph over the 23·6 miles from Glamis to Luncarty, with a top speed of 85 mph at the Tay Viaduct. But with the heavier train Driver Robertson got some no less extraordinary work out of the 5X engine *Burma*, averaging 73·3 mph on the level stretch from Glamis to Cargill and attaining no less than 88½ mph at the Tay Viaduct. This is one of the fastest runs I have ever seen with a 5X; it is fully up to the standard of performance displayed by engine No. 5660 *Rooke* in the special dynamometer car trials between Bristol and Glasgow in 1937, when many LMS records were broken.

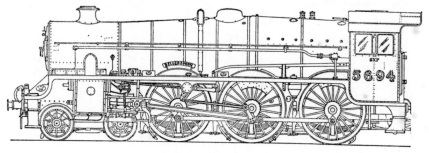

Engine class 5 4–6–0 No. 44727
Load 11 cars 321 tons tare 345 tons full
Driver J Christie, Fireman Soutar (Ferryhill shed)

Mls		Sch	m	s	mph	BP	Reg'r	Cut-off
0·0	ABERDEEN	0	0	00		220	½ main	75
						220	½ main	50
0·6	*Ferryhill Jc*	2	2	33	—	215	½ main	50
						215	⅝ main	40
1·7	*Craiginches South*		4	39	—	210	⅝ main	30
						210	⅝ main	35
3·0	*Milepost 238*		6	46	39	205	⅝ main	30
4·0	*Milepost 237*		8	15	41	205	⅝ main	35
4·8	Cove Bay		9	26	—	200	⅝ main	35
5·5	*Milepost 235½*		10	32	37½	200	⅝ main	30
7·0	*Milepost 234*		12	40	44	195	1st valve	25
					61½	195	1st valve	25
8·2	Portlethen		13	48	—	195	1st valve	25
					58	200	1st valve	25
10·4	Newtonhill		15	55	71½	200	1st valve	25
11·6	Muchalls		16	53	75½	200	1st valve	25
13·5	*Milepost 227½*		18	37	64	200	Shut	50
					68	200	Shut	50
			p w s		41*	205	⅝ main	35
16·1	STONEHAVEN	23	21	25	42½	205	⅝ main	35
17·0	*Milepost 224*		22	47	40½	200	Full	35
18·0	*Milepost 223*		24	27	—	200	Full	35
18·3	*Milepost 222¾*		24	53	34½	200	Full	35
18·7	*Dunnottar*		25	33	37	195	Full	30
					42	200	Full	35
20·8	*Milepost 220¼*		28	43	38	200	Full	30
21·6	Carmont		29	42	—	195	Full	25
						195	¾ main	25
22·5	*Milepost 218½*		30	50	50	190	½ main	25
23·3	Drumlithie		31	44	62	185	1st valve	25
27·3	Fordoun		35	01	77	180	1st valve	25
30·6	LAURENCEKIRK	40	37	49	—	185	1st valve	25
31·8	*Milepost 209¼*		39	01	62	185	1st valve	25
33·8	Marykirk		40	53	70½	190	1st valve	25
					76	195	¾ main	25
35·9	Craigo		42	42	68	195	¾ main	25
						200	Shut	50
37·3	*Milepost 203¾*		44	31	—	200	Shut	50
			p w s		40*	205	Shut	50
38·0	*Kinnaber Jc*	48	45	36	—	205	½ main	30
						205	⅝ main	25
39·2	Dubton		47	05	—	210	⅝ main	25
					67½	210	Shut	50
41·9	Bridge of Dun		49	38	—	210	Shut	50
			p w s		47*	205	⅝ main	45
43·8	*Milepost 197¼*		52	05	50	190	¾ main	45
						195	⅝ main	35
45·0	Farnell Road		53	32	—	200	⅝ main	35
46·8	*Milepost 194¼*		56	09	41	215	⅝ main	35
47·8	*Milepost 193¼*		57	38	40	220	⅝ main	25
48·3	Glasterlaw		58	12	—	215	⅝ main	25
						205	1st valve	25
50·3	GUTHRIE	60	60	23	58	205	1st valve	25
52·3	Auldbar Road		62	18	63½	200	1st valve	25
54·9	Clocksbriggs		64	42	65	195	1st valve	25
			sigs		45*	195	Shut	50
57·3	FORFAR	68	68	13				

The run tabulated opposite was recorded jointly by Mr Nelson and myself. It is worthy of close study as providing a fully detailed example of the working of the LMS Class 5 4–6–0s on a fast and heavy duty; the load, on a busy Saturday afternoon, was indeed one coach over the normal maximum for the train. The joint efforts of two observers—Mr Nelson on the footplate and myself in the train—enabled the engine working and the times and the speeds to be recorded in greater detail than usual; otherwise on a route and on a service where speed fluctuation is at times quite rapid, some of the finer details might have been missed. The hill-climbing of the Black Stanier, particularly in view of the additional load, was first-class ; but as the record of boiler pressure shows, this hard steaming was comfortably within the capacity of the boiler, and the driver allowed his engine to accelerate very rapidly after passing the summit points at Milepost 234 and at Drumlithie. If reference to the other Postal runs, on page 222, is made it will be seen that No. 44727 was nearly 2 minutes faster to Milepost 234 than No. 44704, though with 345 tons against 285 tons. The climb from Stonehaven Viaduct to Carmont was seriously hampered by the permanent-way slack near the viaduct itself. The effect upon the subsequent speeds can be seen by comparison with the run of engine No. 44704 on page 222 of the Appendix when speed through Stonehaven was 63 mph, against $42\frac{1}{2}$ mph with engine No. 44727. On the faster stretches the engine was worked in the manner most usual with this class, with a relatively long cut-off of about 25 per cent and quite a narrow regulator opening. In general the Class 5 engines show a tendency to ' kick ' if the reverser is wound back much below 25 per cent; though both Mr Nelson and I have been on the footplate when 15 per cent cut-off was used on these engines with complete success.

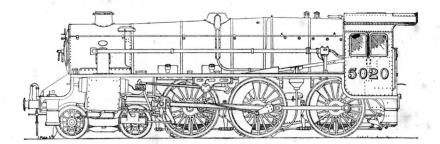

The Stanier 2–6–4 tank engines

6.56 p.m. **FALKIRK–EDINBURGH**

Engine 2–6–4T No.	42199	42198
Load tons empty/full	151/160	150/160
Driver (Stirling shed)	Stevenson	P Meikle, Fireman J Leyden

Mls		Sch	m	s	mph	Sch	m	s	mph	BP	Reg'r	Cut-off
0·0	FALKIRK	0	0	00		0	0	00		195	½ main	45
										195	½ main	25
					48				49½	195	Shut	45
							sigs		20*	200	Shut	45
3·2	POLMONT		5	38	—	6	5	39	—	200	Shut	45
							sigs		5*	200	½ main	20
										200	½ main	15
5·7	Manuel		8	14	66½		10	12	58½	200	½ main	10
			p w s		10*				67	200	Shut	45
7·9	LINLITHGOW	pass	12	31	45½	12	12	51				
0·0						0	0	00		195	½ main	45
										190	½ main	20
										185	½ main	15
										180	½ main	10
3·1	Philipstoun		15	52	64		4	34	57½	180	½ main	10
										180	Shut	45
							p w s		15*	185	Shut	45
5·0	*Winchburgh Jc*	18	17	38	72	7	7	20	—	185	Shut	45
5·6	Winchburgh		18	04	76½		8	32	28½	180	⅝ main	15
										180	⅝ main	10
									57	180	Shut	45
6·8	*Broxburn Jc*				—		9	58	—	185	Shut	45
			p w s		52		p w s		30*	190	½ main	15
					—					195	½ main	10
9·4	Ratho		21	32	68		14	46	52½	200	½ main	10
12·1	Gogar		23	46	76		17	42	63	200	½ main	10
					81½				71½	195	Shut	45
14·1	*Saughton Jc*		25	24	—		19	31	—	195	Shut	45
			sigs		5*							
15·3	*Haymarket W Jc*	31	27	29	31/42½	20	20	53	28*	190	½ main	25
									37½	195	Shut	45
16·3	Dalry Road	35	29	18		23	22	47				
0·0			0	00		0	0	00		200	½ main	45
										200	½ main	20
0·7	PRINCES ST	3	2	18		3	2	41				

NOTE—Run with engine 42199 made in July 1949, before the insertion of a stop at Linlithgow

The LMS Standard 2–6–4 Tanks

The capacity of the fast passenger tank engines designed for the LMS by Sir William Stanier could scarcely be displayed better than in the two runs opposite. The original LMS 2–6–4 tank engines designed under the direction of Sir Henry Fowler were regularly run with very short cut-offs; I had ample experience of these on the Euston and Watford suburban service, and now the later engines are being worked in the same tradition. But whereas the Fowler locomotives used to attain speeds of over 80 mph running down the 1 in 339 gradient from Hatch End to Wembley, the Scottish 2–6–4s from Stirling shed attained over 80 mph on no steeper gradient than 1 in 960. But it is not all easy running on the journey from Larbert to Edinburgh. From the start at Falkirk (Grahamston) the line climbs steeply at 1 in 100 to join the old LNER main line at Polmont; here, on both the runs tabulated, speed was worked up in fine style, and on the second of the two runs this uphill acceleration needed no more than 25 per cent cut-off, with the main valve of the regulator about half open. On a third journey, not tabulated, an even faster climb was made with engine No. 42198, with speed worked up to $52\frac{1}{2}$ mph on the 1 in 100 gradient; but subsequent running was not so fast as on the two trips detailed opposite. For the fast running east of Linlithgow engine No. 42198 was worked with the reverser in 10 per cent cut-off, and this produced a rapid acceleration to $71\frac{1}{2}$ mph before steam was shut off in the approach to Edinburgh. On the 1948 run engine No. 42199 attained $76\frac{1}{2}$ mph at Winchburgh, and $81\frac{1}{2}$ mph at Saughton Junction. Frequent delays from engineering slacks have for long been a feature of operating on this route, and this explains why despite the very fine locomotive work faster end-to-end times cannot be scheduled. These 2–6–4 tank engines are extensively used on the Clyde coast services, and put up consistently good and economical work.

LMSR 'THE GRANITE CITY' EXPRESS
FORFAR–GLASGOW

Engine Midland 3-cylinder compound No. 1127
Load 11 cars 332 tons tare 355 tons full
Driver J Grassie, Fireman T Hollywood (Balornock shed)

Mls		Sch	m	s	mph	Reg'r	Cut-off hp	Cut-off lp
0·0	FORFAR	0	0	00		¼	79	71
0·7	*Forfar South Jc*		2	15	—	Full	72	62
2·9	*Kirriemuir Jc*	4	5	01	53	Full	67	55
5·7	Glamis		7	56	60	Full	67	55
7·9	Eassie		10	01	64½	Full	67	55
12·0	ALYTH JC	13	13	52	63½	Full	67	55
14·2	Ardler		15	56	65	Full	67	55
16·7	COUPAR ANGUS	17	18	14	65	Full	67	55
18·9	Burrelton		20	21	62½	Full	67	55
21·2	Cargill		22	32	71	Full	67	55
23·1	*Ballathie*		24	10	64	Full	67	55
25·3	STANLEY JC	25	26	16	62½	½	67	55
28·3	Luncarty		29	01	69	½	67	55
30·9	*Almond Valley Jc*	31	31	39	—	Shut	—	—
			sig	stop	—	—	—	—
32·5	PERTH	35	41	17				
0·0		0	0	00				
			sig	stop	—	—	—	—
2·0	Hilton Jc	4	5	50				
			6	30		Full	75	67
3·9	Forgandenny		10	10	48½	Full	67	55
6·8	Forteviot		13	29	53	Full	67	55
9·6	Dunning		16	36	54½	Full	75	67
11·3	*Milepost* 140		18	52	41½	Full	75	67
13·7	Auchterarder		22	43	32	Full	75	67
15·3	*Milepost* 136		26	05	28	Full	75	67
15·8	GLENEAGLES	26	27	10				
0·0		0	0	00		Full	75	67
2·2	Blackford	4	5	15	48	Full	67	55
4·3	*Carsebreck*		7	25	63½	Full	67	55
6·4	Greenloaning		9	27	65	Full	67	55
9·6	Kinbuck		12	20	66	⅗	84	77
12·3	DUNBLANE	14	14	55	—	almost shut	84	77
14·3	Bridge of Allan		17	04	51/62	Shut	84	77
17·2	STIRLING	20	20	43				
0·0		0	0	00		Full		
2·4	Bannockburn		4	43	42	Full	72	62
4·1	Plean		7	33	35½	Full	72	62
5·9	*Alloa Jc*	8	9	36	62	⅘	72	62
8·1	LARBERT		11	58	55	⅗	72	62
9·3	*Carmuirs West Jc*	12	13	14	60	Full	72	62
11·7	Greenhill	16	16	32	40	Full	72	62
12·3	*Milepost* 106		17	26	43	Full	72	62
13·5	*Castlecary Box*		18	57	50½	Full	72	62
15·1	*Milepost* 103¼		20	59	44½	Full	72	62
17·1	Cumbernauld		23	54	39	Full	72	62
18·8	*Madgescroft Box*		26	08	62	Full	72	62
21·2	GLENBOIG	28	28	36	56	⅗	72	62
23·0	Gartcosh	30	30	28	60	⅗	72	62
24·2	Garnkirk		31	40	60	Shut	72	62
			p w s		—	⅗	72	62
26·8	Robroyston		35	52	—	Shut	72	62
29·2	St Rollox	36	38	43	—	—	—	—
30·2	BUCHANAN ST	41	41	48				

INDEX

INDEX

Printed in Great Britain by
Thomas Nelson and Sons Ltd, Edinburgh